The "and" in the title of this book is significant for it sounds the keynote of this whole remarkable appraisal of the Church and the 19th Century in their relations to each other.

In a very brief way, Father Corrigan has done a monumental work. Swiftly, deftly, completely he has portrayed the whole dramatic picture of the place of the Church in the Century. He has caught all the seething undercurrents of 19th-Century revolutions and isms from which have emerged many of our present-day ills. He has given a vivid picture of the life of the Church, and of her friends and of her foes. And he has painted fine and sympathetic portraits of the successive Pontiffs whose lives illumined those times with their sufferings, their heroism, or their learning—Pius VII, Pius IX, Leo XIII, and Pius X, men whose works endure and of whose toils, and pains, and struggles, we, ourselves, are the inheritors.

With this book, Father Corrigan offers the key to many of the questions which puzzle the reader of recent Church History.

THE CHURCH
AND THE NINETEENTH CENTURY

THE CHURCH
AND THE
NINETEENTH
CENTURY

Raymond Corrigan, S.J., Ph.D.
Director of the Department of History
St. Louis University

THE BRUCE PUBLISHING COMPANY
MILWAUKEE

Imprimi potest: P. A. Brooks, S.J., Praep. Prov.,
Provinciae Missourianae
Nihil obstat: H. B. Ries, Censor librorum
Imprimatur: ✠ Samuel A. Stritch, Archiepiscopus Milwaukiensis
July 1, 1938

Christo Regi eterno
Ecclesiaeque Capiti
adversus quem gentes
fremuerunt et populi
meditati sunt inania

PREFACE BY THE GENERAL EDITOR

TO TELL THE COMPLETE STORY OF THE CHURCH IN THE nineteenth century would of necessity call for many volumes. And yet it is not impossible to give within the limits of a less pretentious work a correct impression of the entire period here under question, so far at least as its relations with the Church are concerned. From the reader's point of view it is highly desirable that this be done. To understand properly the age in which we live it is necessary to understand the spirit of the nineteenth century.

There is an old seaman's phrase, found in one of the early English ballads, which here comes to mind. It represents the new moon appearing in the sky, with the old moon in her arms. Curiously enough this sufficiently familiar phenomenon, expressed in so poetical a way, is regarded as the inevitable sign of squalls and shipwrecks. The new twentieth century, seen in its early decades, its first quarter, can similarly be described as rounded out by the wraith of the nineteenth century enclosed in its embrace. And it is precisely that inseparable connection with what had gone before which betokens the upheavals and monstrous developments that were to follow, beginning with the World War and ending with Bolshevism and Nazism. The specter seen in the arms of the twentieth century was above all else the materialistic Liberalism of the nineteenth century, from which in particular these evils flowed.

Many of them had, in fact, sprung up already in the preceding century and now merely reached their maturity and wrought their full havoc. They were the legitimate offspring of the false philosophies which dominated education, politics, and business in those years. The ghost of the past was achieving its work in the present.

The nineteenth century can most characteristically be studied in its relation to the world-wide Catholic Church with which it came into conflict almost everywhere. For that reason, too, this book is not entitled the Church *in* the nineteenth century, but the Church *and* the nineteenth century. It is equally a study of both in their relations to each other. Nowhere is the spirit and inner soul itself of that century more completely revealed than in the attitude of so many of its dominant men of learning and influence, of its governments and rulers, of its political cliques and secret societies, toward that one and only institution which boldly confronted them, at every turn, in the name of God and of eternal Truth. "Destroy the outcast!" was their watchword. But though the Church might be lowered to the dust or lifted up in obloquy, like Christ on the Cross, yet she could never be destroyed and she would never capitulate. She might be attacked, and actually was, with every weapon forged in the armory of Satan. She might be doomed to death, and so she was a million times. And yet she must survive her foes, for she was destined not to die. There is the theme of an Epic.

If we behold the almost complete disappearance for a time of the Church's prestige, we are only made the more indisputably aware of that divine power which kept alive the undying glow beneath the ashes of her humiliations until the flame leaped up once more and scintillated beneath the breath of God.

It is quite in place to recall here a poem of Victor Hugo where the proud Napoleon is made to exclaim in a frenzy of exaltation at the birth of an heir: "The future: it is mine!" "No," replies the poet. "The future: it is God's alone!" It is He who overrules all history.

What greatly simplifies the historic treatment of the overwhelmingly vast and important subject dealt with here is the fact that the drama of the Church's life of action and suffering in the nineteenth century can be viewed as worked out mainly along that world's highway which we may regard as extending from Rome to the British Isles, provided only it is sufficiently widened midway to include both France and Germany. In this restricted area, then, can be found nearly all that could influence the attitude of the Church toward the century and of the century toward the Church.

This explains, too, why a country as mighty and ultramodern as the United States is given comparatively little attention here. The obvious reason is that it was still to a large degree influenced by foreign traditions and continued to reflect at this period the ideas and sentiments, the movements and institutions that had originally arisen in Europe. Without discussing other similar nationalistic objections it need only be said that to have broadened the scene of action geographically, to have multiplied details and brought ever new actors on the central stage, to have explored in all directions the ramifications of events, would have been a comparatively easy matter, but could have ended only in the production of a library instead of a volume.

As it is, a vivid picture of the Church is given us here, of her friends and of her foes. Before us, as we read, pass on in review the successive Pontiffs whose lives illumined those times with their sufferings, their heroism, or their learning. Notable among them are Pius VII, Pius IX, Leo XIII, and Pius X. These men are more than mere shadows of great names. Their works endure and we ourselves are the inheritors of their toils, their pains, and their struggles.

In particular has the writer sought to portray the living Church in her relations — here, too, mostly of trial and conflict — with the dominant Bourgeoisie and the steadily rising masses. Socialism and Communism, as well as an unregenerated Capitalism, have their roots sunk deep into the fertile subsoil of the nineteenth century. It is the century of attacks on the Papacy, the century of concordats, the century of Liberalism, blind materialism, and greedy *laissez faire*. Well may we speak of "The Nineteenth Century and After."

As a final paragraph it will be appropriate here to say a few words on what I might call the author's credentials. While the background of his education had been secured at American universities, his more advanced studies were pursued in the Collegio Maximo at Saria, Spain; in the Ignatiuskolleg at Valkenburg, Holland; and at the universities of Bonn and Munich. In addition he continued his historical researches at

Rome, Paris, and London. A teaching experience of some years in Central America still more broadened his horizon and widened his sympathies. Since 1927 he has held the position of Director of the Department of History successively at the University of Detroit and St. Louis University. The subject developed in this volume has long been with him a favorite topic of class discussion.

JOSEPH HUSSLEIN, S.J., PH.D.,
General Editor, Science and Culture Series

St. Louis University,
June 13, 1938

CONTENTS

xiii

ILLUSTRATIONS

INTRODUCTION

I

INTRODUCTION:

A SURVEY OF THE CENTURY

1. THE NINETEENTH CENTURY WAS AN AGE OF UN-precedented expansion. The population of Europe increased enormously from roughly 180,000,000 to almost 400,000,000. Significantly, the Latin countries lagged behind both the Teutons and the Slavs. England nearly trebled her population, while Ireland's was cut in half. The mounting millions swarmed into the growing towns; they also spread over the earth carrying European civilization with them. Transplanted to America, they aided in making the two continents virtually an extension of Europe, raising the total population to 200,-000,000. They Europeanized the ancient cultures of the Orient, and began the exploitation of the backward natives of Africa. Greed and idealism, imperial ambitions, business enterprise and missionary zeal transformed the world. Science applied to industry augmented the means of livelihood by producing abundant food and clothing; science, too, by the conquest of death and disease, prolonged human life. There were reasons for the optimism which pervaded the nineteenth century.

In any chronological table of the century a few dates stand out: 1815 marked the fall of Napoleon, and the conservative reaction under Metternich; 1830, with its resurgence of Revolutionary Liberalism, brought with it Catholic Emancipation, the overthrow of the Bourbons, the independence of Belgium, and Parliamentary Reform in England; 1848, another year of revolution, became notable as the period when Liberalism and Nationalism stirred the peoples of Europe only to prove the latter was in reality the more powerful sentiment; 1870, finally, saw the triumph of Italian and German Unification and the collapse of the Second Empire in France. But there were economic and social changes as well as changes in the political scene. The year 1815 found industrial and financial England ready to assume world leadership; 1830 may be taken, though somewhat arbitrarily perhaps, as the turning point toward Bourgeois predominance on the Continent; 1848 might be called the birth year of the "Scientific Socialism" based on the *Communist Manifesto;* while 1870, a crucial year in the life of the Church, inaugurated the "Era of the Benevolent Bourgeoisie," and set the train of the events that led to the World War. The relative importance of the great men of the century will be gauged according to different standards, but the biographies of Napoleon and Metternich, of Cavour, Napoleon III, and Bismarck, not to overlook Queen Victoria and her great ministers, supply us with the material for a fairly complete survey of political history insofar as this bears relation to the Church.

The nineteenth century may in truth be termed a "Century of Revolution." It was a child both of the French Revolution and of the Industrial Revolution. This age of phenomenal expansion and progress, with its mounting wealth and increased material well-being, was emphatically an age of emancipation. Its spirit is revealed in characteristic "isms." Nationalism, Liberalism, Materialism, Individualism, Rationalism, Naturalism, Indifferentism, Relativism, Subjectivism, Agnosticism, Atheism, Anticlericalism, Positivism, Pragmatism, Skepticism, Secularism, Utilitarianism, Darwinism, Socialism, Communism, Anarchism, Pantheism, Modernism. Some of these philosophies, these deviations from right thinking, are hangovers from earlier centuries; all are the progeny of the long period of social disintegration covered by the Renaissance, Reformation, and French Revolution. Into this century funneled the Baconian, Cartesian, Rousseauvian systems. The makers of its "Modern Mind" were Calvin, Luther, Descartes, Rousseau, Kant, Marx, and, in a lesser degree, Bacon, Adam Smith, Hegel, Spencer, Darwin, Comte, Renan. "The Mind of Europe," writes Peter Wust, "was *secularized,* the world stripped of its sacred meaning, the Church ruled out of public affairs, God dethroned in the soul of man." This condition was partly due to the absorption of the vital energies of the century in non-religious pursuits and a consequent lack of interest in things of the spirit. But there was also a deliberate attempt to establish social atheism. In the new century the old Church was to find a hostile milieu.

2. THE CHURCH is the Kingdom of God on earth, the *Ekklesia Kyriake,* the visible Society founded by Jesus Christ, the God-Man, to continue His mission. The Church has a divine and human element (body and soul). In Scriptural language, she is the Bride of Christ, the Body of Christ, the Fullness of Christ, Christ living on in His members. She is an Organism vivified by the Holy Ghost. She is also an Organization, monarchical, hierarchical, visible; a "perfect society," independent of the State, possessing infallible authority to teach, divine power to rule, efficient means to sanctify her fallible, fickle, failing human members. She has the promise of immortality. She must survive in spite of scandals within, and attacks, violent or insidious, from without. This may be taken as a mere working hypothesis. For the Church herself it is revealed truth, and it is the verdict of history down to the present time. "They who do not consider the supernatural and divine virtue inherent in the Church," says Donoso Cortes, "will never understand her influence, nor her victories, nor her tribulations, nor . . . that which is spiritual, essential, and profound in European civilization."

3. THE HISTORY OF THE CHURCH is the story of a super-human *vitality, stability, fecundity.* Again and again, she has been pronounced dead or dying; she has always renewed her youth. She was born for "eternal resurrections." She points to history as the proof of her divine mission. The bold words of the Vatican Council are a challenge to critics:

> The Church, moreover, of her very nature, by reason of her marvelous growth, her eminent holiness, and her inexhaustible fruitfulness in good works of every kind; by reason of her unity and catholicity, and her unshakable stability, is a great and enduring motive of credibility and an unimpeachable witness of her own divine mission.

This statement must be true of the nineteenth century as well as of the Age of the Apostles, the Martyrs, the Fathers, or of the Ages of Faith, when the Church was the soul of civilization.

4. THE CHURCH IN THE NINETEENTH CENTURY. The living Church should show evidence of vitality and fecundity, of energy attributable to a Vital Principle within, of the indwelling of the Holy Ghost. Her recovery, growth, and adaptation to a changing world should not be explainable by purely natural causes. In reality the life of the Church during this period appears in the survival and eventual triumph of the Papacy; in the close-knit organization and functioning of the hierarchy; in the energy of outstanding bishops and priests; in the spontaneous activity and loyalty to the faith of great Catholic laymen; in the renewed vigor of Religious Congregations; in foreign-mission work; in Catholic thought; in the saints, canonized and canonizable.

Religious activity, Catholic and near Catholic, is further evident in the Romantic Revival, the Oxford Movement, French Catholic Liberalism, the Cologne affair, the School of Munich, and in French, English, and German social work under such outstanding Catholic leaders as Ketteler, Manning, DeMun.

In maintaining her stand against the rising pretensions of the Nationalist State the Church still more abundantly displays her marvelous stability. Her will to live and the soundness of her constitution are conspicuously patent in her reaction to the poisoned "modern mind." The problems and dangers created by a society estranged from God and by the individual asserting his autonomy in the face of heaven, only serve to render more striking the steadfast loyalty of the Church to her mission.

Thus through the course of the nineteenth century we behold her as she steadily recovers her strength, reorganizes her forces, combats false systems, boldly champions religion, morality, and truth. She tries to work in harmony with governments (thirty concordats); gradually turns toward Public Opinion (pulpit and press); finally disentangles herself from the State and the Modern Mind (Syllabus, Vatican Council, Encyclicals of Leo XIII, condemnation of Modernism). So the yeoman work was done and the preparation was made that the twentieth century might usher in the Catholic Revival with its

THE VATICAN AT THE END OF THE NINETEENTH CENTURY

great leading interests: the Eucharist, the Sacred Heart, Philosophy, Theology, Scriptural studies, History, Mission zeal, the Liturgical Movement, the exaltation of the Papacy, the Social Reign of Christ, and Catholic Action.

In the United States the Church kept pace with the development of American culture and civilization, which in turn were an extension of European conditions. Up to the year 1908, when the American Church ceased to be under the Congregation de Propaganda Fide, it was technically a mission Church. Its clergy had been recruited largely from Catholic centers in Europe, from Ireland, France, Germany, Belgium, Holland, and Italy. Its Religious Orders and Congregations were likewise largely European in origin. Even the laity who made up the great body of the faithful were in very considerable numbers immigrants and the children of immigrants. Add to this the financial assistance received by it, which made possible the building of churches and the truly remarkable growth of educational and charitable institutions, and the Church in the United States appears for what it was, a favored child of the Church in Europe. When we arrive at the close of the century, we find that Church in America grown to full maturity. Bound closely to the Holy See, it no longer needed nor wanted the tutelage of the older churches in the various nations of Europe. Like the American nation, it, too, had grown in numbers, and like that nation was prepared to make its presence and its power felt in world affairs. Conscious of its vitality, its numerical strength, its spiritual sinews that had been toughened by a century of struggle and expansion, it now partook of the aggressive attitude of American society. Too frequently, perhaps, with the pardonable frankness of youth, it was prone to express something rather akin to contempt for the centuries-old ways of Catholics of other lands.

The rise of the United States to world influence is among the most significant historical facts in the nineteenth century. The same may be said of the Church in the United States. But this observation belongs to the twentieth century. The most patriotic American can afford to admit that in the history of civilization during the nineteenth century the nations of Europe played the leading roles.

THE CHARACTER OF THE CENTURY

II

THE BOURGEOIS CENTURY

THE STORY OF THE NINETEENTH CENTURY HAS BEEN rewritten, and the college student may read it with some assurance that he is getting nearer to the objective truth than did the student of earlier days. Not only has distance provided a better perspective, but the lapse of time has permitted bitter fruits to mature. The roseate optimism which pervaded the speech and writing of a generation ago has been badly shattered by the Great War and its aftermath. But thoughtful men[1] who are terrified by international anarchy and who are painfully aware of the moral degeneracy about them, will look beyond the War for the poisoned sources of present disorders. Clearly the nineteenth century has been calling for re-interpretation.

A New Appraisal

In this new appraisal of the near past lies a new opportunity for the historian of the Church. A humbled humanity is now more likely to be interested in the struggle of religion against discouraging odds than were fair-weather worshipers of material progress. Church history is no longer *merely* Church history. Religion is recognized to be more than a by-product of human activity, a weakness to be tolerated or treated with contempt. It is seen to belong to the very essence of society as God intended it to be. Though its absence may seem to be a negative thing, in reality it has positive effects. The exclusion of religion from society is analogous to the absence of health in the human body.

---

[1] There is a mounting mass of historico-philosophical writing, often caustic and iconoclastic, on the historical origins of present-day social ills. Among the best known Catholic and near-Catholic writers on this subject are: Hilaire Belloc, Nicholas Berdyaev, Martin D'Arcy, Christopher Dawson, Ross Hoffman, Jacques Maritain, Peter Wust, and Waldemar Gurian. A dozen other names will occur to the reader of reviews devoted to Agrarianism, Guild Socialism, Co-operatives, Catholic Action, or the Liturgy.

11

"Man without God," writes Berdyaev, "is no longer man." At best he is a diseased, distorted creature. He is dehumanized. Leaders of a few decades ago may have felt, though with what sincerity it is hard to judge, that they could ignore religion and the Church. But the historian who reviews their work can now sense how the exclusion of a vital element from wide fields of human activity created a void, while the stream of life was vitiated. What the Church did in the nineteenth century is a marvelous story. What she was prevented from doing may belong to the realm of things that might have been, but it has all the interest of a huge abnormality for the student who wishes to learn what actually happened.

If, then, from our point of vantage we can look out in judgment upon the past, it is well to remember that the man in the midst of the whirl and rush of events was not so fortunate, and that his view of life was a historical fact which influenced and conditioned his amazing output of energy. It was only in the present decade that Carlton Hayes, for instance, could completely rewrite a volume which earlier critics had pronounced eminently satisfactory and which has been most widely used as a text on European History. The key to his revision is found in the brilliant concluding chapter, with its constantly recurring refrain: disillusionment. A striking feature of the book is the author's inclusion of innumerable terms, several thousand of them at least, in quotation marks. Giving things their proper names is a long step toward clear thinking. Or rather, the right use of words supposes clear thinking. In any case, the use or misuse of language is symptomatic of a more fundamental disorder. And it helps us to understand the historical process. The man of the nineteenth century may or may not have been convinced that "God was in His heaven" — far away — but he had no doubt that all was right with his world.

Typical of his convictions and of his general attitude is a panegyrical history published at the end of the century, and written, oddly enough, by a scientist. The author, Alfred Russell Wallace, called his book *The Wonderful Century*. He saw, truly, that phenomenal progress had been made. He would have been shocked, in fact, had anyone questioned the claim

Disillusion-
ment

The
Wonderful
Century

of his century to greatness. It was not merely great, not merely even the greatest of centuries; it was more than all that. "Not any previous century or group of centuries," he triumphantly proclaimed, "but rather the whole preceding epoch of human history" must be set in the balance against the nineteenth in order to get any adequate estimate of its comparative excellence. This contrast he makes the more graphic by drawing up parallel lists of achievements in the way of new inventions and discoveries. Needless to say, his count is in favor of the "wonderful century" by a margin of twenty-five over fifteen against all past ages. This sort of reckoning, of course, reveals a type of mind and a philosophy of life that was quite generally prevalent before the World War. The existence of this mentality is a historical fact of some significance which found its apparent justification in the expanding dominion of man over nature.

The absurd self-confidence of the modern man was but slightly ruffled by a brilliant, if somewhat overdrawn picture from the pen of Doctor James J. Walsh. If the thirteenth could be called the greatest of centuries, it was for reasons that had little appeal to admirers of the age of the machine. The men who fought the Crusades or built the Cathedrals, the genius who created the *Divina Comedia,* or the saint who gave the world its most complete system of thought in the *Summa Theologica* were mere pygmies alongside the industrial magnates, the engineers, the scientists, who were daily adding to the "comforts, the enjoyments, and the refinements of life," who had conquered the secrets of the universe and its complex forces, who were abolishing pain and lengthening the span of human existence in an earthly paradise. If these moderns admitted any comparison whatever with the nineteenth century, it must be sought somewhere in the still brighter future which an advancing humanity had before it.

But the onward march of the race was rudely halted in 1914. Out of the orgy of death and destruction emerged a sobered and disillusioned world. Old autocracies had been swept away, but new dictatorships were arising, Democracy was dead or dying. Pale liberals were fondly dreaming of better days gone by, while they despaired of the future. The old battle cry of

Optimism Checked

Progress had a hollow ring. Peace still had its vociferous champions, but a deluded world had little enthusiasm for a hopeless cause. Education had palpably failed to do its impossible task, though educationists still found it profitable to keep up the old pretense. Even Science was wavering; it confessed its limitations and turned to the revision of some of its dogmas. No wonder the optimism of the pre-War period had given way in many quarters to a pessimism and a sense of futility.

We shall understand the nineteenth century better if we know what went into its making as well as what came out of it. It was the immediate offspring of the French Revolution and the Industrial Revolution. It not merely bore the unmistakable features of its parents, but, to a pronounced degree also those of its more remote ancestors. From the era, "diabolic or divine" — of Liberty, Equality, Fraternity — it inherited its Democracy and Nationalism; from the still continuing era of mechanical inventions and their application to industry came its materialistic love of comfort, its monopolist Capitalism, and its alarming social problems. Far behind these great revolutions lay the Renaissance, the beginning in both its good and bad aspects of the modern world. In it Europe had experienced a tremendous release of energy which was displayed in art and literature, in commercial enterprise and in oversea expansion. But the forward surge tore up roots that were struck deep in medieval soil, and a whole section of life was exposed to the danger of atrophy from lack of nourishment. Ascetic restraint and a lofty vision fixed upon eternity and infinity gave way to the more appealing lure of the warmth and beauty of earthly satisfaction. The supernatural outlook was not rejected, at least theoretically, but in practical life it was threatened with something very like suffocation. Moreover, the Humanists of the time, by their revival of paganism, became the source of a widespread infection. The period has been regarded as a rebirth, an awakening. For the prince, for the aggressive individual it was such. Self-assertion and self-indulgence quickened the tempo of life, but did so by setting humanity on the downward slope, with its gaze averted from Christian ideals and hopes. At closer range and as a natural and logical

The
Making
of Modern
Man

consequence of the Renaissance, we have the "Enlightenment." Whether regarded in the form of English Rationalism or French *Philosophie* or the German *Aufklärung,* it is essentially a deistic stage on the road to out-and-out atheism. As such it aided mightily toward dissolving the old order and disinheriting the modern man.

It is, of course, difficult to determine the relative importance of various interdependent factors, or to apportion credit or blame for what was humanly good or bad in the long unbroken movement. Machiavelli still has his disciples, at least in practical politics; so has Voltaire, though the influence of either is vague and elusive. Locke has admirers who do not suspect his errors and are incapable of detecting them. John Calvin has been accorded the sorry distinction of having invented a Bourgeois church. The eye wanders back over the devious course of history to discover other makers of the modern mind. Luther, besides breaking the unity of Christendom, bequeathed his subjectivism, or if you will, his individualism in religion. Descartes, without intending to do so, divorced man from the supernatural. Rousseau left a legacy of false dogmas, including a denial of original sin and an artificial, omnipotent state. Francis Bacon, for good or for evil, turned the attention of his readers to the harnessing of nature. And Adam Smith unleashed primitive greed when he attacked government regulation of business. By exaggerating half truths and partly by way of reaction against earlier exaggerations and abuses these and other "emancipators" of the human spirit generated the twisted mentality of the nineteenth century. And their heirs have been grateful to them not only for the fragments of truth which their teachings had to possess in order to survive, but even for a bad philosophy which ran counter to reason and revelation.

His Ancestry

It is often possible in a given set of circumstances to discuss the relative importance or unimportance of thought and action, of words, written or spoken, and of deeds. In the present instance it may appear that undue prominence has been given to leaders who have led the world astray, and that undue emphasis has been laid upon the unsound elements in their doctrines to the virtual exclusion of their more wholesome thinking. But we are concerned primarily with what affected the Church. And since the relations of the Church with the world in which she works have to do for the most part with the maintaining of orthodox doctrine and the defense of the moral law, we naturally direct our attention to those writers whose perverse originality, limping logic, and fervid eloquence have created new problems for the Church to meet.

From another viewpoint the outstanding feature of the "Enlightenment" was the advance of the natural sciences. Each new study of the period which preceded the Industrial Revolution seems to give more and more space to the men who, by uncovering the secrets of the physical universe, prepared for the age of mechanical invention. Roger Bacon and Francis Bacon, Copernicus, Galileo, and Newton are supremely significant figures that stand out above the crowd. They and a host of others including, for example, da Vinci, Descartes, and Leibnitz were the architects of the earthly paradise of which modern man has been so proud. Not only have they formulated the laws that govern the hidden forces of nature; they have produced by their tireless experimentation, classification, and happy discoveries a new mentality. Their success in the practical things of everyday existence has made the star gazing of the medieval theologian look foolish! In place of the old sterile speculations of the Scholastics they have introduced fruitful concentration on real facts! For the aimless groping in the dark that failed even to scrape the surface of an enigmatic nature they have substituted a scientific method that gets results infallibly! Where formerly a chance discovery might occur once in a century or a millenium, the scientist, or a collaborating group of scientists, by deliberate, systematic processes burrow into the hidden corners of the material creation and force it to yield up its secrets.

Experiment, painstakingly pursued, has worked marvels. And the scientist knows he can continue his task. With the new certainties have come an increased confidence in the future and an increased contempt for the benighted people who were dependent upon authority for their knowledge of the physical universe, and whose knowledge never got beyond helpless wonderment and puerile superstition! Man, insofar as his

The Age
of Science

animal life is closely linked to material things, must gratefully acknowledge the benefactions of Science. But by a
strange lapse of logic he has assumed that the things that loom
so large in day-to-day experience are the whole of life. He has
allowed the teachers who have lightened his labor and improved his food, clothing, and housing to prescribe for his soul
and to pontificate about his origin and eternal destiny. And the
scientist has not been slow to usurp the chair of the theologian
and the philosopher.

The forerunners of modern technology were optimists. But
it is safe to say that the achievements of the nineteenth century fulfilled, when they did not surpass, their fondest hopes
and their wildest guesses. Werner Sombart, writing a generation ago, turns from a futile attempt to enumerate the
encyclopedic array of recent inventions to a search for the principle which underlies them all.[2] This he discovers in the "transformation of empirical experience into rational knowledge," in
the "complete replacement of quality by quantity," in "practical emancipation from the limitations of the organic." Technique, he observes, has become "surer, more easily controllable,
more exact." Through the machine man manipulates the forces
of nature to suit his every purpose. But he also observes that
"in nature . . . there is no longer room for an artisan-God,

> Heedless even of her Maker's honor,
> Like the dead beat of the pendulum,
> A slave, the chains of Gravity upon her
> Moves Nature, Godless, dumb. . . ."

In a word, "the Creator has been separated from His work."
Man has triumphed over space and time. He has weighed the
sun, counted electrons, and measured the wave of light. He has
made his myriad fingers of steel labor with a delicacy of touch
that the human hand could not imitate. He has indeed
harnessed powers of nature to a degree beyond the dreams of

[2] Cf. Werner Sombart, *Die deutsche Volkswirtschaft im neunzehnten
Jahrhundert* (Berlin, 1913). Quotations in this paragraph are taken from
the excellent translation by Jonathan F. Scott and Alexander Baltzly,
Readings in European History since 1914 (F. S. Crofts & Co., New York,
1931), pp. 113–124.

the seventeenth-century sage. But has he not missed the larger meaning of it all? He has seen great secrets through the microscope and the telescope. He has pushed his analysis of matter until he discovered only dust. He has probed beyond the atom and the electron; his mind has soared beyond the outmost visible star, but he seems to have forgotten that some One must have made the things he studies as well as the mind with which he studies them. Where imagination well might totter he has allowed reason and judgment to lose their balance. For him "Science" (with a capital letter and in quotation marks) has by a strange contradiction become divine. He has no time and no need for religion. With the first commandment of the Decalogue thus flouted, the Church was faced with a seemingly hopeless task. She could not get a hearing for His message.

The nineteenth century was essentially a Bourgeois century. The rise of the great Middle Class has been called the "central theme of modern history." Its long march down through the centuries, from its insignificant beginnings in the feudal age, is an interesting study and an important one. The story of business and banking, of expanding trade and mounting industry, reads like an epic. The French Revolution and Industrial Revolution and the, in some respects more influential, English Revolutions mark the term of a steady upward development. But before we turn more specifically to origins we must insist upon the essentially earth-bound character of the Bourgeois mind. Whatever inadequate distinctions one may make between the perverted mentality of the Liberal and of the Capitalist, or for that matter between the philosophies of life behind extreme Democracy and its inevitable outcome, Dictatorship, he uncovers the ubiquitous dominant note of materialism. It may be seen at a glance, therefore, that where the Church maintains that the Bourgeois also has a soul she is bound to meet with disheartening opposition in any effort to convince the contented slave of money and of power of the primacy of the spiritual.

In the "era of the benevolent Bourgeoisie," which fell in the final quarter of the nineteenth century, it seemed quite natural that those who owned the world should also rule it, that the

Rise of
the Middle
Class

laws should be framed to protect their interests, and that
government should act as an agency under their orders. They
possessed the aggressiveness, the energy, the resources of a
ruling class. "Divine right" had no place in their vocabulary,
but they held, by whatever title, a position analogous to that
of royalty in a former age. And yet their dreams of unlimited
security of tenure should have been toned down by a reflection
on the lowly origins from which they had sprung.

Not so long since, the middle classes had been a rather in-
considerable element in European society. Their ancestors had
been known as the Third Estate at the dawn of the modern
period. Nor was it due to a usurpation of power, to tyrannical oppression, or to an artificial system that they had been
virtually excluded from active participation in affairs of
State. So far from being capable of ruling the State, they had
in fact been quite incapable of self-government, as they were
incapable also of self-defense. They had once looked to the
now superannuated nobility for protection and guidance. They
had looked to the clergy as the only source of light in the darkness of their abysmal ignorance. The dominant Bourgeois of
the late Victorian era might logically conclude that the strange
dialectic of human history, which had lifted their class above
the privileged classes of an earlier time, would in turn call
forth a new class to supplant them. The same process which
set the Third Estate above the First and the Second would in
time set the once despised Fourth Estate above the Third.
There is something absurd in the picture, like the standing of
a pyramid on its apex. But whatever consolation the Bourgeoisie might draw from the unworkableness of this unstable
condition could not obscure the fact that their own order
would be nonetheless effectually supplanted. The only justification for their own pre-eminence had been reducible to the
argument that might makes right. And the day was not far
distant when might would rest with numbers and strong arms
as opposed to economic wealth and legality. If the masses
could not rule, they could at least overthrow those who stood
in their way. Then out of the chaos would arise a new hierarchy with a single strong man, it might be, at its head. In
any case, the Bourgeois as a ruling class belong in a peculiar

way to the nineteenth century. Before this time they had little power outside of England. At its end they could read the handwriting on the wall. But throughout the century they were decidedly in the ascendant, and they impressed their view of life upon its institutions. And this did not lighten the task of the Church whose preaching of Christ and His supernatural religion was out of harmony with what they held to be the business of life.

III

CAPITALISM, LIBERALISM, NATIONALISM, SECULARISM

WITHIN THE PAST FEW DECADES MUCH HAS BEEN written about Calvinism and Capitalism or, more specifically, about the debt of Capitalism to Calvinism. And the admirer of Calvin did not resent the doubtful compliment. Even those who disowned the "protagonist of human depravity" were smugly grateful for the wealth amassed as capital; they were proud of the capitalist who had climbed to power by the display of qualities of mind and will that looked like virtues; they accepted and applauded, unwittingly it may be, the capitalist spirit. But of late we have become more critical. Sobered by the debacle of Big Business and taught by the devastating attack of the anti-Capitalist on our self-satisfied Bourgeois civilization, we have come to a reconsideration of values. We still admit the close connection between the so-called "economic virtues" of thrift and industry, which the "Elect" were urged to practice, and success in business, which was deemed a mark of Heaven's favor. We have seen how an acquisitive concentration on the single objective of enriching the individual led to the great fortunes which rewarded the strong and the fit in the struggle for a comfortable existence. But since the misery of millions has been the inevitable concomitant of the abundance of the few the historian has turned to a more accurate analysis of the origins of modern social thinking.

With less sympathy and less emotional bias in favor of mere success we can discuss the essence and the instruments of

Calvinism and Capitalism

---

[1] According to Christopher Dawson, "no book deals so adequately with the whole subject" here discussed as Amintore Fanfani's *Catholicism, Protestantism and Capitalism* (Sheed & Ward, New York, 1935).

Capitalism, its rise and its capture of the modern State, and finally, its relation to Catholic and Protestant culture.[1] Maximum individual economic profit has been the goal to be attained by intensity in the use of all legal means. Efficient methods have been aided by political influence and the elimination of restrictions, even such as are associated with the recognition of moral criteria.

A cardinal fact to be kept in mind is that the growth of the Capitalist Spirit preceded, accompanied, and followed a weakening of faith. An important distinction is that drawn between the money-minded individual and our money-minded society. Individual greed is as old as human nature; social approval of mere financial success is a modern phenomenon. In the more healthy period of the Middle Ages theology and religion dictated to mere politics, while purely economic considerations, though necessarily present, were not allowed to parade in public. The Reformation mothered the absolutist Monarchy, and politics usurped the place of religion, but still maintained its control of economic forces in the interests of national power. The nineteenth century saw the culmination of an evolution that made the State the obedient servant of the Capitalist and reduced the Church, in the minds of the new rulers of the world, to a merely tolerated relic of the past. In the order of values economics took precedence; politics gave a blind, but effective support; religion veiled her eyes and vainly protested or mutely acquiesced. A Bourgeois oligarchy could count on the applause of Bourgeois-minded "Democracy."

The Protestant who disclaims responsibility for the new order can point to the existence of medieval capitalists in the person of Jacques Coeur, twin spirit of Henry Ford or Pierpont Morgan, five hundred years ago, and to Italian bankers, who lacked nothing of the drive and resourcefulness of a later day. But the medieval capitalist was a man born before his time. His pursuit of gain as the highest purpose of human endeavor was out of harmony with the moral atmosphere in which he found it hard to breathe. His virtues, if he had any, were, like the "economic virtues of Calvinism," good old Catholic virtues turned to vices by undue exaggeration. The new thing that was born of religious upheaval was a distorted perspective and a

Ancient Greed

Social Approval

progressive this-worldly materialism. The social climate was altered, and both Protestants and their Catholic imitators found it quite comfortable in an era in which the unmorality of politics had given way to the unmorality of economics.

"The Canonization of Capitalism" is something more than a clever bit of alliteration. The phrase was coined to label a process similar to that by which the saints of God are raised above the common crowd, set upon a pedestal and crowned with a halo of glory. We need not cling too closely to the parallel. A nonreligious age had to have its strange gods. And it created them to its own image and likeness. Self-interest was declared to be God's Providence. "Natural Laws" were evoked out of airy nothingness by the fancy of philosophers and pseudo-philosophers to sanctify a system of "jungle ethics." Wealth and the untrammeled pursuit of wealth put on a sacred character. Economic Individualism, which in the concrete is nearly synonymous with Capitalism, had its Bible, its Gospel, its dogmatic teaching, its moral code, and something akin to a ritual of worship. The pious hypocrisy of its devotees ranged in degree and culpability from naïve ignorance almost to the extreme of blasphemy. They appealed to "Natural Rights" against any power that might interfere with the amassing of riches. They appealed to "Natural Laws" against the dictates of a conscience that might condemn the ruthless exploiting of the weak.

The Bible of the Classical Economists had been published in the historic year, 1776. Mercantilism, or government regulation of industry and trade in the interests of national wealth, had become unwieldy and was encumbered with artificial restrictions to the point of decrepitude. Its tyranny was oppressive. Then came Adam Smith's Declaration of Independence for Business. The work was not altogether original, but it did contain some excellent common sense. Had the author been able to foresee the misuse to which his ideas would be strained, he might have been more cautious. But even where he actually did introduce a saving clause or two, these were overlooked or glossed away. Like the devil quoting Holy Writ for purposes of his own, a new generation carried over the gospel of "enlightened selfishness" and adapted it to a new

Enlightened
Selfishness

situation in ways never intended by its author. New dogmas were evolved and defined by the Classical School. Adam Smith had been an optimist who believed and hoped that his individualist doctrines would lead to the general welfare and to prosperity for all classes of society. But practical men seemed to have learned only his lesson in selfishness, and to have neglected utterly his "enlightenment," while the theorizers built up an unsightly structure of "laws" and "principles," which reduced the poor to inevitable and unending misery, and completely exonerated the holder of economic power. There would never be enough wealth to go around; the fund available for wages would always be limited. There was an "iron law of wages"; wages would never rise above, at least never remain above, the "subsistence level." This was, indeed, pessimistic economics. And the worst feature of the doctrine was that it prevented or postponed a remedy by discouraging all human effort against the holy "laws" of nature.

On the other hand, the capitalist was reassured by a whole litany of maxims. He would help others by helping himself; his private interests were identified with the public weal; competition was the life of industry; the right of property was a sacred right. The champions of *laissez faire* long clung to two principles "free competition" and "freedom of contract." Throughout the greater part of the nineteenth century Liberals as a group held to these specious, and to themselves quite obvious, expressions of "natural right." With these shibboleths they attempted to silence all demand for government regulation of business. But noninterference was too palpably to the advantage of the strong man. However "natural" it might appear for the lion to be allowed to eat the lamb, it was certainly to the interests of the State and of human society to put some check on practices of the jungle. The capitalist might claim the "right" to crush his smaller rivals; he might insist upon the "right" of his dependent employees to accept starvation wages or to starve without the wages. But the world was bound to awaken eventually to the absurdity of it all. The reaction in a mild form came from labor unions and from economic nationalists who refused to be impressed by the arguments of the economic individualist. It came in a more terrible

Laissez
Faire

form in a movement that now threatens to sweep away the whole capitalist system. And the Church finds herself in the uncomfortable position of being unable to agree with either of the two world forces. She has to flee the embrace of the Bourgeois Capitalist, and she must fight atheistic Communism with all her strength. An infusion of natural ethics into Capitalism or into Communism would have enabled the Church to live in harmony with either of them. It was not so much their opposition to Christianity as their contempt for the moral law that made the task of the Church difficult.

The Communists have written their own version of nineteenth-century history. It is a story written for a purpose. It is a distortion of actual facts in which events and movements are made to fit into a prearranged framework. But it is a version of history we cannot ignore. Its materialist conception of the universe and its economic determinism may be demonstrably false. But for the Marxian who is predisposed to accept these dogmas there is enough of the appearance of truth in them to make Marxian history plausible. There is certainly no lack of conviction in the writers who apply this pseudo-philosophy to the past. And in one sense, at least, they have made a contribution to historiography, not so much because they have in some instances probed below the surface of events to deeper lying causes, but because they have, like all heresy makers, forced defenders of the truth to investigate more critically in order to refute them.

Marxist History

The central theme of all history according to the Marxian is the Class Struggle. The textbooks of Soviet Russia are full of it, and study clubs for adult workingmen have the idea drummed into them. It requires, of course, considerable literary gymnastics to draw the whole past into this simple scheme. But when by a process of elimination and clever manipulation of evidence the story is thus presented to a mind that has been prepared for it, the effect is easy to imagine. The workingman understands, or thinks he understands, the problems that have baffled scholars.

Class Struggle

And Marxian historians find in the nineteenth century a field where their theories can be applied with happy results. Society is divided along economic lines. By its wealth acquired in trade, industry, and finance the Bourgeoisie muscled their way into power. And with them rose, or sank, the Proletariat. The possession or privation of property was the determining factor in the division. The stage had been set in England by the Middle-Class revolutions of the seventeenth century, and in France by the great upheaval at the end of the eighteenth century. As late as Sieyès it was still good tactics to lump ninety-nine parts of the population under the battle standard of the Third Estate. But as the Industrial Revolution got under way a new aristocracy of merchants and manufacturers took over the place vacated by the nobility. The propertyless proletariat were beaten down, and a new Feudalism began to develop. Marx was wrong when he applied his "dialectic" to conditions as he observed them in England and in the industrialized sections of the Continent. But to many a Marxian class cleavage and mounting class consciousness seemed to be following the lines indicated by the Father of Scientific Socialism. The Capitalist system must inevitably, by some inner necessity, call forth its Nemesis. The exploiters must go on amassing unwieldy wealth until conditions would become intolerable and the oppressed masses rise up to "expropriate the expropriators."

In the light of later developments it is now clear that Karl Marx should have been taken more seriously. He was a fanatic, but he had analyzed up to a point the most dynamic forces of the time. Still, when his *Communist Manifesto* appeared in 1848, Scientific Socialism was a puny creature. Even when in 1864 he organized his First International or when three years later the ponderous first volume of *Das Kapital* appeared, few men would have believed that the infant he fathered would grow into the colossus that now threatens Christian civilization. The "Utopians" who preceded him had been mere philanthropists, whose projects for social reform had scarcely stirred the surface of society. Marx, himself, was a Utopian. His system was, and still is, so contrary to human nature that it could never be realized. But under the impact of Rationalism, Liberalism, Materialism, and a dozen other diseased "isms" man had so far been dehumanized and the powers of resistance had been so lowered in society that the most de-

Strength of
Marxism

structive revolution in history was not only possible, but under a leader like Lenin all but inevitable. For our present purpose the growth of Marxian Communism affords an insight into the nineteenth century and the conditions in which the Church had to function. God, the supernatural, the soul, and the moral law were meaningless terms to too many people in the Bourgeois century. The crass Materialism and the irrational Atheism which are essential elements in the Marxian Gospel were not invented by the Communist leaders. They found them ready to hand and sufficiently familiar to be acceptable in wide circles.

The transition from Communism to a discussion of Liberalism and Communism — and Fascism, too, for that matter — apart. But the opposition is more apparent than real. Liberalism and Communism — and Fascism too for that matter — have fundamentally very much in common. They are, in fact, all tarred with the same materialistic stick. And a recognition of this essential likeness is more important in the present discussion than is the tabulation of surface features in which they disagree. There are those who would accuse the two dominant contemporary perversions of having killed Liberalism, as there are those who still look to what they call Liberalism for salvation from the excesses of dictatorship. But the Liberalism of a hundred years ago is dead and buried, except, perhaps, insofar as it lingers on in a metamorphosed form. The name is still with us. And the Liberals of today, at least in non-Latin countries, are not unlikable people. In fact they stand for some of the best American ideals. But their harmless mouthing of old shibboleths only obscures an understanding of what integral Liberalism really was. The same may be said of the most exhaustive study of the subject now in print. Guido Ruggiero, in his comprehensive *European Liberalism*, discusses the topic from every angle, but after nearly four hundred pages he leaves his reader, at least the uninitiated reader, wondering what it is all about. And yet in the history of the Church in the past century, Liberalism played a major, if not the leading role.

Liberalism, we are told, is not a creed, a doctrine, a system; it is a way of life, a spirit, a habit of mind, a *Weltanschauung*,[2] a kind of religion, "a belief in the natural dignity of man, in his high destiny, in his ability to perfect himself through natural reason and self-determination, in the ultimate triumph of truth, justice and freedom." It is "the consciousness which the free man has of his rights and of his duties as well. . . . It stands for loftiness of views, for generosity of sentiment; it is based on the idea that Humanity . . . can be enlightened by discussion and improved by the very experience of its errors." Here we have a definition of Liberalism at its best, a definition in which the unwary may not detect anything wrong.

A briefer, more succinct definition has been given by Sarda y Salvani. Sarda y Salvani was a Spaniard. He wrote in the land where the name was first used, in a land where the lines between Liberalism and Christianity were most clearly drawn, in a land in which the most radical French thought was boiled down to its most un-Christian and anti-Christian essence. Sarda y Salvani wrote a book to which he gave the title: *El Liberalismo es pecado*. In the quite literal French version the title was translated: *Le Liberalisme c'est le péché*. The English translator, Conde Pallen, was more delicate. He called his book: *What is Liberalism?* But his answer had the augmented strength of Anglo-Saxon terseness: Liberalism is sin. And his arguments, or rather Sarda y Salvani's, are convincing. For Liberalism is, if anything, a repudiation of Revelation and of Reason. It is, in its essence, as old as human pride and the first human sin.

Here, of course, there is question of integral Liberalism, not of its partial manifestations. The relatively innocuous political liberal, whose program, besides constitutional, representative forms in government, calls for a minimum of authority in the sovereign, and who would have the state perform the functions of the corner policeman by preserving order and protecting property, need not detain us here. Nor need the economic liberal, otherwise known as the economic individualist, who would have the government keep out of business altogether and

What Is Liberalism?

Integral Liberalism

---

[2] Enthusiastic volumes have been written on Liberalism. For a very satisfying brief analysis of the subject see John Messner's article, "Liberalismus," in *Staatslexikon* (Herder, 1929), III, pp. 968–989.

who would abolish tariff-barriers and trade unions. Only when these Liberals, practical men for the most part, reject ethical restrictions in business do they become a problem for the Church. Quite different is the case of the intellectual liberal who "advocates absolute freedom of thought, religion, conscience, speech, the press and politics, thus denying any authority derived from God." Newman has defined this species with his usual clarity:

> Now by Liberalism, he writes, I mean false liberty of thought, or the exercise of thought upon matters, in which, from the constitution of the human mind, thought cannot be brought to any successful issue, and therefore is out of place. Among such matters are first principles of whatever kind; and of these the most sacred and momentous are especially to be reckoned the truths of Revelation. Liberalism then is the mistake of subjecting to human judgment those revealed doctrines which are in their nature beyond and independent of it, and of claiming to determine on intrinsic grounds the truth and value of propositions which rest for their reception on the external authority of the Divine Word.[3]

Newman regarded his fight against this aberration of the century as his lifework. Toward the end of his long life he could boast: "For thirty, forty, fifty years I have resisted to the best of my power the spirit of Liberalism in religion."

Liberty is a beautiful word in any language. But its meaning and the sentiments woven about it change with changing circumstances. It may be a synonym for anarchy. It may stand for that freedom of action which can exist only in an ordered society. There is the physical liberty of the savage or the dumb brute; there are the civil liberties of the citizen; there is a freedom of the saints of God. Leo XIII began his encyclical condemning Liberalism by declaring that "Liberty is God's most precious gift to man." But the nineteenth century had little time for defining terms, and its unconscious distinctions were based on feeling and individual interests. "Liberty," like "Equality," "Fraternity," "Reason," "Natural Law," and a few

A Misused
Term

---

[3] *Apologia pro Vita sua,* Appendix A (page 493 in Oxford edition, 1913). This masterly excursus on Liberalism was originally printed as a "footnote" in the edition of 1865.

other terms carried over from the "Enlightenment," could be misused, and crimes could be committed in its name. We may be clarifying the obvious if we insist that this essentially negative term receives its specific meaning from the thing, evil or good, from which one would be free. Liberalism means a throwing off of restraint, a cutting loose from what "oppresses" the individual. Historically, it has stood for resistance to absolute, arbitrary government, to undue interference with industry, trade, and business. It has also stood for rejection of authority in Church and State; for a repudiation of tradition, custom, and convention. Its history is that of a long series of emancipations by which modern man has without discrimination cast off whatever restrictions cramped his expanding energy. From the individualism of the pagan Renaissance, down through the religious upheaval of the sixteenth century, to the revolutions, political, economic, and intellectual of the seventeenth and eighteenth centuries, there was a steady evolving of the "autonomous" man. In the nineteenth century this contradiction in terms was further molded by a line of great "emancipators." This creature, this abstraction rather, which never did nor could exist, was given a touch of nobility by Emmanuel Kant. It was inflated by writers whose mastery of words made men think they were gods. Finally, at the close of the century, it found in Friederick Nietsche's demented drivelling a symbol of the "superhuman," and a warning against excessive Liberalism.

Integral Liberalism makes man the master and measure of things, and asserts his independence of God and divine law. With this absurdity the Church had to wage continuous war. The Liberal might be saved by a lack of logic. But his principles led to destruction. The Church had to insist that the only liberty worthy of a man is the liberty to do the things he ought to do, not the liberty to do the things he naturally likes to do. She had to protect, in her often too hampered way, man's freedom to climb without restriction; she had to raise her voice against the almost universal demand for freedom to crawl. But neither the Church nor the Pope, nor any other institution or individual on earth ever possessed an unlimited liberty.

Liberty
Limited

POPE PIUS IX

"Il Papa Liberale" (Pope 1846–1878)

POPE LEO XIII

"The Peacemaker" (Pope 1878–1903)

Political Liberalism has something in common with Democracy. But the two are by no means identical. What Democracy demands for all the people, Liberalism would, by a characteristic contradiction, restrict to its own "People." Where Democracy was radical or, if you will, logical, the Liberal was, for his own practical purposes, a conservative. Typically Liberal measures were the Parliamentary Reform of 1832 and the Victorian Compromise, by which the landlords and the industrial magnates agreed to divide between themselves the "representation" of the people of England. Democratic in the sense of giving all the people a share in the government was the abortive Chartist Movement. Democracy could repudiate the liberal spirit and find itself on the brink of an inverted Caesarism; Liberalism could ignore the people, and become an aristocracy or an oligarchy. Democracy was a leveling system; Liberalism tended to build up a caste. Democracy stood for equality, and curbed the liberty of the strong; Liberalism gave a free hand to the strong man, and called it equality of opportunity. Liberalism was reformatory and demanded capacity in its constitutional governments; Democracy was revolutionary, and was often satisfied with mediocrity in the elected agents of its imaginary popular sovereignty. Under either system the State could, in spite of accidental forms and more or less complex machinery, become absolute. The Church, on the other hand, was forced to oppose absolutism, whether theoretical or practical. She could bless, as she did, government by popular consent; but she must condemn any Machiavellian pretense at a sovereignty that disregarded the moral law, Divine revelation, and the rights of God.

Nationalism and Liberalism could be close allies; they could also be in conflict one with the other. The same may be said of Nationalism and Democracy, or of Democracy and Liberalism. What Liberalism was to the individual, that Nationalism was, up to a point, for the group. The Liberal demanded self-determination, and rejected all constraint from without; the Nationalist declared for national autonomy and grew furious at the thought of foreign interference within the frontiers of his country. Nationalism, again, was a kind of self-assertion

Democracy

Liberalism and Nationalism

on the part of the Nation as distinguished from those who presided over its government; Democracy tended to identify the people, or the whole nation with its government, and make them conscious that they possessed common interests to defend and common dangers to ward off. The Liberals, finally, had enlisted the support of the common people in their fight for power, and the common people somehow felt that they were more closely connected with the Liberal, who was after all, a commoner, than they were with the old privileged classes. But the Liberals found it convenient to kick down the ladder on which they had climbed to the top, and during three decades or so of the Victorian Compromise they effectually guarded the power they had gained. Nationalism, likewise, when Liberalism (one might substitute Democracy) threatened to be a source of weakness, was able to flout the claims of the Liberals, as was done in the building of Bismarck's Empire and in the struggle for German ascendancy within the Dual Monarchy. But allies or enemies, Nationalism, Liberalism, and a rationalistic Democracy were a potential menace to inalienable rights, to the claims of religion, to order, and consequently to the Church. Nurtured by the same French Revolution, and influenced in their growth by the Industrial Revolution, they had the dominant traits of a revolutionary age. They were, in fact, the French Revolution living on through the century, in its most vicious as well as in its beneficent character. At the same time the economic, political, intellectual, and other changes brought about by increased wealth, individual and national, by the concentration of population in the growing cities, by improved means of communication and transportation had a decided effect on the development of all three. Quite naturally, then, the Church, which had been enslaved, robbed, and all but killed by the French orgy, and which was completely out of harmony with the earthly aims of the Bourgeois businessman, not to mention the radical Jacobin spirit of agitators for Revolutionary Democracy or Republicans, could not hope to fare well wherever and whenever the heirs of either revolution were active.

Origins of
Modern
Nationalism

Nationalism, we are told, was born in 1792, at the Cannonading of Valmy. This thesis would seem to call for an explanation of terms. Certainly, there had been national monarchs in Europe with decidedly national policies, at least since the days of Philip the Fair. Something like national antipathies had been a factor in the failure of the Crusades. And no one would question the presence of a growing national consciousness in the Hundred Years War. But the thing we call Nationalism dates from the French Revolution. The Tricolor, the Marseillaise, the Fête de la Fédération, the populace around the altar of *la Patrie,* these were new things in France and in Europe. Fighting for France, conquering or dying for France, filled the minds and fired the feelings of enthusiastic thousands. The army became a "nation in arms," which swept foreign foes before it. The guillotine destroyed the enemies of *la Patrie* at home. The "People" had risen against kings and aristocrats, who had once made their own laws and ruled the land as they might rule a private estate. The men of 1789 had made the law a mandate of the sovereign people and the king their dependent functionary. Then, when the king refused to be a mere servant of the popular will, they killed him. Meantime, France became conscious of a mission. The Nation would not only defend the Revolution; it would bring to other lands the blessings of Liberty, Equality, Fraternity. There was a spontaneous upsurge of patriotic fervor, but a wild idealism was rapidly perverted into Jacobin frenzy. A common indignation, a common sense of wrong, had awakened the Nation to a consciousness of solidarity. Common dangers, fears, and hopes strengthened the new spirit. Success, a taste of victory, and lust for conquest destroyed the nobler strains in the Revolution, and Fraternity degenerated into bitterness, in which there was a large element of hatred. And the Nationalism, which was to be a mighty force, more satanic than divine, in the nineteenth century, had reached its full stature.

Nationalism in the Nineteenth Century

For a decade or more the genius of Napoleon at the head of the soldiers of the Revolution fed the national passion with the inebriating glory of conquest. But other nations were learning, by imitation partly, but more effectively by the experience of common wrongs. Spontaneously, in 1808, Spain burst into a flame of religious, patriotic hatred of her French conquerors, and became the graveyard of Napoleonic armies. Austria attempted a national revival, but failed. Meantime, statesmen and poets planned and nursed to maturity a patriotic spirit in Prussia, while the English people kept up their dogged opposition to Napoleon. When, with his megalomaniac dreams he finally went down to defeat, the story of his brilliant successes and of his final failure could have been written largely in terms of Nationalism.

For the next hundred years, from the Congress of Vienna to the Congress of Versailles, national interests and national sentiment were to account for a major portion of the external history of European civilization. Metternich vainly tried to disregard popular feeling when he restored the old regime and remade the map of Europe. But his real services to the cause of peace and order were neutralized by national outbreaks in Greece, Belgium, and South America. Years before the final shipwreck of the Metternich system, in 1848, the revived memories of Napoleonic glory were preparing the French people for another experiment in Nationalism. About the same time Mazzini was firing the Italians with a determination to fight for national autonomy. The more practical Cavour capitalized, by devious and questionable methods, this dynamic sentiment and virtually achieved the unification of a national Italy. The Franco-German war found Bismarck's Vaterland glowing with national hate for France. From its close dates a new Germany, and also a new France and a new Italy. Forty-three years of peace and Bourgeois prosperity were to lull national feelings. But the Kulturkampf, the Roman Question, and the Anticlericalism of the Third Republic, not to overlook Alliances, Ententes, trade rivalries and colonial empires, reveal that the slumbering national spirit was by no means dead.

Excesses of Nationalism

Love of country is a virtue, founded in natural human instincts. Nationalism is a vicious thing, generated by the exaggeration of a virtue and further corrupted by elements of hatred, cruelty, snobbery, and often enough a kind of idolatry. *Deutschland über Alles* is a noble sentiment as the poet first penned it. Like the *dulce et decorum pro patria mori*

it expre_   eme gift of self for a higher cause. But
reinterpreteu   nperialistic sense it aroused the wrath
of the non-Germa_   rld. Patriotic inspiration has produced
much of what is fines_ in literature and in life. Chauvinism,
Junkerism, Jingoism, or by whatever name we may call its
perversions, have written their story in blood and tears. And
the sad fact is that education and all the tricks of propaganda
have been employed to develop precisely the worst features
of national character. Nor did this begin with the Nazis or
the Fascisti. Mussolini and Hitler had, in fact, to originate
very little. They merely applied with greater efficiency and
improved technique and in more favorable circumstances the
methods and aims of earlier times.

But what of the universal Church in a Nationalist world?
What of the divine institution which was founded to uphold
the rights of God in a world where the State arrogated to
itself unlimited power? The lay State in Italy and France,
and the Protestant State in Germany, almost inevitably came
to regard the Church as the enemy. When Gambetta, in 1877,
shouted his battle cry: _le Cléricalisme, voilà l'ennemi!_ he
made no distinction between a few misguided politicians
among the clergy and the Catholic Church herself. But the
point to stress here is that the statesman could exploit
nationalist sentiment against a Church which was mis-
represented as a foreign power. Throughout Europe at one
time or another the Papacy was attacked as the enemy of
the national state. Not only was there no question of co-
operation with the Holy Father on the part of Christian
governments, but there was a fairly constant and general
attitude of opposition.

Nationalism involves a sin against reason as well as a sin
against faith. It has been defined as the system, doctrine,
or movement which gives the national state the highest place
in the hierarchy of values; and this is, perhaps, the most
satisfactory definition we have. Whether in its Hegelian, its
Nazi, or any other form, the absolute state is a violation of
nature and of reason. And the Church is likely to pronounce
it so, whenever the anterior rights of the individual or the
family are not respected, or whenever the Church herself is

prevented from exercising her functions. It is possible that Nationalism, clearly defined, of course, may yet be officially declared a heresy. But the strength of Nationalism does not lie in the truth or half truth of its principles. Its strength lies in its appeal to emotion and to mob instinct. And this emotion and instinct are found even in the best of Catholics. Hence the triumph of Nationalism created extreme difficulties for the universal Church.

Various Isms

What precisely were the most striking features, the dominant characteristics, the main currents of nineteenth-century history? The answers to this question will vary according to one's philosophy of life and according to his previous study or reading. Nationalism and Democracy will find a place in every list. Imperialism as logical outgrowth of Nationalism, and Liberalism, so nearly related to Democracy, will also be mentioned. To those for whom history is past economics, the Industrial Revolution and its associated phenomena will loom large. Economic Individualism, business enterprise or, to use the term most familiar to the modern reader, Capitalism, will be the most characteristic feature. Some will insist that in the light of later developments the Class struggle and the rise of Socialism are among the most vital elements in the century. Others point to the march of science, to the idea of constant and inevitable progress. Still others will regard the spirit of tolerance, social reform, and humanitarianism as extremely important. One author undertakes to group all historical incidents around one grand progressive tendency toward a unified commonwealth of democratic national states. Another writes his history under the significant theme title: Freedom versus Organization. It may be that in a decade or so Materialism, Secularism, and Anticlericalism will be given due prominence.

Self-Satisfaction

The nineteenth century was nothing if not satisfied with itself. With Hegel it saw itself at the term of a long evolution of human freedom; with Comte it looked back on the slow march of the mind of man from the "theology" of its infancy and childhood, through the "metaphysics" of its rebellious youth, to the full-blown scientific *Positivism* of its maturity. Providence was ruled out in favor of *Progress*. And there was no doubt that man had progressed. In politics, Democracy and Nationalism represented to the men of this time an advance over all preceding ages. In the business world, economic Individualism with its sacred laws sanctifying the mania for money-making was producing a race of supermen. Utilitarians of various hues were convinced that they had found in pleasure and pain the sovereign norms of ethical conduct. In religion, if religion was mentioned at all, Indifferentism was rated a noble thing and the agnostic was proud of his larger freedom.

True, the self-satisfied age was not without its critics. Ruskin and Carlyle were eloquently contemptuous of achievements that ministered to animal appetites, and subordinated moral to material values. Others refused to accept material Critics ease as the quintessence of civilization. Long before Oswald Spengler, pessimist writers, forgetful of the undying Church, were proclaiming that the same process which brought Europe to its vaunted maturity would end in old age and decrepitude. "Europe," it was said, "is inevitably hastening to become what China is." Even before the Great War it was observed that all our marvelous inventions were *aussi puissantes pour le mal que pour le bien*. But there were even more powerful critics of the social system, men who, while professing to attack the smug philosophies of the dominant Bourgeois world, were in reality carrying its Materialism, its Liberalism, or a composite of the two, on to a logical conclusion in Marxian Communism and in Anarchism.

In this Century of Revolutions there was indeed a great deal of revolving about unstable centers, mostly in the pursuit of shadows. Naturalism had excluded the supernatural from the realm of human thought and succeeded only in creating an artificial fool's paradise of make-believe. Of course, no one will deny that there was a tremendous release of energy, that applied science made wonderful progress, that the industrial world produced a mass of material goods which by their quantity and quality softened the hardships of life and ministered to general well-being. Man's mounting dominion over nature has, to be sure, a spiritual significance. It should have resulted in a greater freedom from material cares, and by providing leisure it should have promoted the expansion and development of the soul and its faculties. On the whole, however, it seems to have had just the opposite effect. By immersing the mind in mechanical pursuits it left little time or inclination for things of the spirit. The mad rush of muscular activity is explained partly by the joy of getting results. But the attendant gyrations of muddled thinking must be ascribed largely to the fact that the mind deprived of any secure anchorage in metaphysical truths was unable to find rest on the shifting sands of false philosophies.

But we have barely mentioned as yet the most appropriate tag for the nineteenth century. It was *par excellence* the century of SECULARISM. In his study of earlier centuries the college freshman, if he does not resent the emphasis placed on religion in the treatment of public affairs, is at least mystified by it. When, however, he comes to the nineteenth century he can get a fairly accurate knowledge of what are considered the great movements of the time and of the actors in them without more than a casual reference to religion. The dynamic forces of the century were displayed on a stage from which religion was quietly ruled off. It influenced the lives of great men and of the masses, but it did so as a private supererogatory affair that had no place in public life, in the councils of state, in business, or in the centers of thought. There were good men and women, within the Church and outside of it; there were saints, canonized and uncanonized; the Church herself was renewing her youth; but the prevailing visible trend was toward social atheism. Battlers for the rights of God and revealed truth were regarded as discordant elements marring the harmony of "Civilization." If one religion was as good or as bad as another, there was no sense in wrangling over creeds. What a man believed and how he worshiped, if he worshiped at all, was his own affair. The world had outgrown the age when religion could be deemed important in political or social life. Practically, the State acknowledged no dependence on God. Politics and economics, literature and education were emancipated from the Church that presumed to speak in the name of God.

Thanks to Kantian philosophy man had become *autono-*

Secularism

mous; he had been becoming so since the dawn of the modern era when the Renaissance turned its face backward to classical paganism. In the Middle Ages, when the Church was supreme in the Christian Commonwealth, God was Lord in State and society, in town and school, but, in the simple formula of Karl Adam, the *Los-von-der-Kirche* of the sixteenth century evolved through the *Los-von-Christus* of the eighteenth century into the *Los-von-Gott* of the nineteenth century. Or, to quote Peter Wust, another among the corps of valiant German thinkers who are pleading for a return to sanity, the times are marked by "the advancing desecration of the world and of nature, the progressive profanation of man, of his body, his soul, his mind, his thought, his science, his art, his religion, his whole culture, in a word, by the reducing of the eternal to time, the naturalizing of the spiritual and the dethroning of God in His universe." With the triumph of Individualism a worldly, earthly society supplanted the Christian society. But amid the glamor and din and imminent chaos the Church still stood a strong bulwark of Christianity, of European civilization, of Humanity. She was there to lend her aid, as she had done in the past, toward the recovery from the passing frenzy of Social Atheism and of the *autonomous* individual.

Autonomous Man

THE CHURCH IN THE CENTURY

IV

THE PAPACY

THE CATHOLIC CHURCH IN THE NINETEENTH CENTURY claimed to be the "One, Holy, Catholic, Apostolic Church" of the Nicene Creed as reworded in A.D. 381. Her unity is best manifested in the Papacy, not so much because of the virtues or merits of the popes themselves as on account of the spontaneous loyalty and obedience which united clergy and laity throughout the world with the Holy See. The holiness of the Church is so bound up with her nature and essential purpose that even in periods of decline it must be present. The tares may sprout among the wheat, but however overgrown with weeds, the field must remain a wheatfield, and the divine seed must be all the while yielding a harvest. In the nineteenth century there was, as always, much hidden holiness, and the list of its men and women who attained to eminent sanctity is a long one. The Church may be criticized for not being what her Founder never intended she should be, and thousands or millions of her children may fail to use their liberty to conform their lives to the divine plan, but only when, if this were possible, the saints desert her will she no longer be the Church she claims to be. In the nineteenth century she welcomes the test of sanctity. She can fearlessly submit to be judged by her "fruits."

> One, Holy, Catholic, Apostolic

The Apostolicity of the Church is a matter of historical record. She still clings to the original "deposit of faith," and her chief Pastors still proceed in an unbroken line from the Prince of the Apostles. But she is apostolic in another sense. Her Catholicity, which means, as a minimum, the innate urge to spread over the earth, to "teach all nations," "to preach the Gospel to every creature," supposes an apostolic spirit at all times, and according to circumstances, apostolic action. The Church is essentially a mission Church. And in her missionaries, at home and in foreign parts, one may find the best gauge of her vitality. The Vatican Council offered the challenge of the moral miracle: Unity, Stability, Fecundity. The last of the Ecumenical Councils might have used the "One, Holy, Catholic, Apostolic" formula of the second. The cloister, the school, the parish church and the Catholic home generated the vitality of the living Church which is best revealed in her supreme pontiffs and in the active Catholics, clerical and lay, who support them, in her saints, where these can be known, and in her foreign missions.

A history of the popes comes very near to being a history of the Church, but only insofar as the popes are intimately connected, almost identified with the Church. Analogies between a social quasi-organism (the most perfect example of which is the Church) and the real human organism should not be pressed too far. But there is some warrant for applying to the visible Church under the Vicar of Christ the metaphor employed by St. Paul to clarify the relation existing between Christ Himself and His Mystical Body. How long the Church would continue to function in the abnormal state of being without a head is an ideal speculation.[1] As a result of tendencies at work in the nineteenth century the contact of the pope with the faithful throughout the world and his direct influence upon them have been augmented to a point not known since the age of Innocent III who, however, ruled over a much smaller Church. The urge toward greater centralization was a sign of health and vitality in the ecclesiastical body. Still it is one of the commonplaces of history that such development may be carried too far, that the increased efficiency of a centralized absolute government often blinds its beneficiaries to a corresponding decrease of vitality in distant local units. The obvious safeguard against such unwholesome development lies in the use of central control to whip up greater activity in outlying departments. "Catholic Action" is now the accepted technical term for the "apostolate of the laity under the direction of the hierarchy." The present pope with an influence unknown to most of his predecessors is a

Papacy

---

[1] At the height of the papal power, in the thirteenth century, there were, in fact, two unusually long interregna, 1268–1271 and 1292–1294.

promoter of ordered life in the furthest corners of his spiritual empire.

Since the year 1800 nine popes have sat on the Throne of Peter.[2] No one of them is negligible, though Leo XII reigned less than six years, and Pius VIII less than two. As a whole, the series is the most remarkable for its unbroken succession of men of high character, energy, and ability, in all the "august dynasty" since its beginning nineteen hundred years ago. It is a debatable question who has been the greatest of these modern popes, and it may be conceded, though not too readily, that a medieval Innocent, a Gregory, or a Leo surpassed in the qualities that should adorn the Vicar of Christ any of his more recent successors who bore the name of Leo or Pius. But it will be hard, in fact, impossible to find a hundred years in history in which the providential role of each pope has been so providentially supplemented by the others.[3] From Pius IX to Pius XI each pope appears as the nearly perfect instrument moved by the Hand of God. Each seemed to depart from the scene too soon, yet each had a successor who fitted almost ideally into a changing world. In

---

[2] The classic work on the modern Papacy is Joseph Schmidlin's, *Papstgeschichte der neuesten Zeit*. This monumental work, listed later as a continuation of Pastor's great *History of the Popes*, displays an immense erudition and an acquaintance with all available sources. Cf. also Ludwig Andreas Veit, *Die Kirche im Zeitalter des Individualismus*, 2, 126.

[3] Joseph Schmidlin, *op. cit.*, III, 1–4, traces the alternating supremacy in the Roman Curia and in the conclaves of two opposing currents of opinion. *Zelanti*, bitterly conservative and impatient with everything that bore the stamp of the Revolution, contended with more diplomatic cardinals who showed a willingness to understand the modern world. Each succeeding pope, from Pius VII to Pius X, seemed to swing toward the extreme furthest removed from the policy of his predecessor. Pius VII, mild, big hearted, and conciliating endeavored to heal the wounds of the Revolution; Leo XII assumed an intransigent attitude; Pius VIII was all for peace and understanding; Gregory XVI was rocklike in his rejection of Liberalism; Pius IX began as a "Liberal pope," but was forced by sad experience into an antimodern camp; then appears Leo XIII, smiling and eager to rebuild broken relations with the modern world; to the conciliating Leo succeeded the pope of purely spiritual outlook who would have no traffic with the enemies of truth; with Benedict XV came a revival of the spirit of Leo; in Pius XI we have a wholesome synthesis, a commingling of the best elements in either extreme. The "dialectic" of papal history does not appear too strained, and it affords a long view of an important historical process.

our time, if ever, "the popes die, but the pope never dies."
Even the weakest, the most unworthy of the two hundred and
sixty occupants of the Holy See has been powerless to stop
the vital flow of energy in the long line. This is a point of
capital value in Apologetics, and one of no little interest to
the historian. But by a strange paradox, the presence of a
Higher Power and Its continued positive influence was never
more palpably evident than in the age which has closed its
eyes to the supernatural and benumbed its sense of divine
things.

Prestige of the Papacy

To the seers of the middle nineteenth century the Church,
which was practically synonymous to their minds with the
papacy, was an "imposing ruin," a broken vase from which
the perfume had departed, a surviving but tottering relic of
bygone times. Ranke, to whose oracular dictums most historians bowed assent, apologized for his classical study of the
modern popes. "The day of papal power," he wrote in 1837,
"is gone forever." Forty years later he was surprised to find
that "the Papacy has entered upon a new epoch." It is a
pleasure to note that an American chargé d'affaires to the
Papal States was not so blind when he wrote officially in 1848:

> The Papacy is not only a great, but venerable fact around
> which the shadows of nearly twenty centuries gather in awful
> array; which has witnessed the rise and fall of many empires;
> which has survived thrones and principalities and powers.
> Young liberty should not exhaust her efforts against this rock
> of ages. She should conciliate what is an immense, if not
> irresistible moral power.[4]

This reads like a paraphrase of Macaulay's rhetorical essay
on von Ranke which had been published twenty years earlier.
If for these divergent views an explanation is wanted, it lies
in the striking contrast of the sinking material power of the
popes and their steadily rising moral prestige.

The "triumph of failure" would be a not inappropriate
title for an essay on the popes of the past century. Out of
impotence, defeat, and humiliation the prince of a petty

---

[4] Jacob L. Martin to President Buchanan, August 20, 1848. Cf. Leo
Francis Stock, *United States Ministers to the Papal States,* p. 15.

JEAN-BAPTISTE LACORDAIRE, O.P.

Fighter for liberty and foremost preacher
of his time (1802–1861)

THE COMTE DE MONTALEMBERT

The great historian of Western monasticism
(1810–1870)

MOST REV. JOHN HUGH[ES]
First Archbishop of New Y[ork]
(1797–1864)

RIGHT REV. JOHN ENGLAND
First Bishop of Charleston, S. C.
(1786–1842)

FRIEDERICK VON SCHLEGEL

Philosopher and critic (1772–1829)

From a painting by
A. von Buttlar — Bettmann Archive

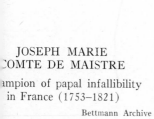

JOSEPH MARIE
COMTE DE MAISTRE

ampion of papal infallibility
in France (1753–1821)

Bettmann Archive

ORESTES A. BROWNS[ON]

Convert and outstanding Am[erican]
Catholic layman (1803–1[876])

MARTIN JOHN SPALDING

Archbishop of Baltimore and supporter
of the doctrine of infallibility
(1810–1872)

Italian state emerged as the acknowledged spiritual father of Christendom. The victim of 1870 is the infallible supreme pastor of the same crucial year. But the fall of papal Rome before the armies of Victor Emmanuel, and the exaltation of Pius IX by the Vatican Council, with the consequent violent freeing of the pope from temporal cares and the simultaneous universal acknowledging of his spiritual prerogatives provide a juxtaposition of nadir and zenith that is characteristic of the whole century. Pius VI had been dragged off to prison and death in France; Napoleon negotiated a Concordat with Pius VII. Pius VII was badgered, isolated, and mentally tortured by Napoleon; he was consoled by an outburst of spontaneous loyalty, and the fall of his persecutor restored him to Rome. The Revolution had realized the dream of Gallicans who wished to exclude the pope from France; but by a stroke of the pen Pius VII dispossessed eighty-six bishops of their sees and settled for all time the right of the pope to direct intervention in a national Church. Strong opposition threatened to prevent the decree of papal infallibility; and thereby the decree was made imperative. Within the Church the remains of Jansenism, Josephism, Febronianism, and a resurgent Gallicanism called for an exercise of authority which put the papal primacy in a clearer light. Catholic Liberalism produced the reaction of extreme Ultramontanism, which finally led to the balanced "common-sense" attitude of Leo XIII. Modernism, or the flirting of Catholics with pseudo-science and pseudo-philosophy, brought out the clear-cut defense of revelation and the supernatural by Pius X. The strong Papacy of today is the result of constant struggle.

Triumphs

A double definition of the Papacy has been given.[5] For the Catholic it denotes "the ecclesiastical system in which . . . the Vicar of Jesus Christ governs the Church as its supreme head." For most historians, and for non-Catholics generally, "it signifies the papal influence viewed as a political force." But the nature of papal political influence has changed during the past hundred years. Even the discharge of his primary

Spiritual Power

---

[5] G. H. Joyce, in *Catholic Encyclopedia*, XI, 451.

function of safeguarding Catholic truth and condemning error
was once looked upon as meddling in politics. Now the pope
stands forth as a spiritual and moral teacher freely pronounc-
ing on economic, social, and political questions, and his
authority and competence are acknowledged by all but the
hopelessly ignorant and ill-disposed. The general disillusionment of thinkers who see the hollowness of modern thought,
and especially the instinct of self-preservation in a society
tending toward anarchy, have brought about a more sympathetic attitude toward the Papacy. And the record of fearless
defense of sound principles is there to show that the popes
have deserved the moral prestige they now enjoy. Throughout the nineteenth century the secularizing policies of most
governments gave abundant grounds for protest and lamenta-
tion on the part of the popes. But strangely enough, out of it
all has come ample compensation in the shape of more immediate contact between the Holy Father and his subjects,
bishops, priests, and laymen.

The history of Pius VII up to 1814 is almost entirely the
story of his relations with Napoleon. After the Emperor's fall
the irony of history made him the chief protector of the
Bonaparte family, and the only advocate among the princes

Pius VII
of Europe for the prisoner of St. Helena himself.[6] The last
ten years of his pontificate fell in the period of the triumphant
Restoration. The genius of Consalvi at the Congress of Vienna,
the prevailing spirit of conservatism, and memory of his own
heroic stand against the tyranny of Napoleon substantially
repaired his earlier losses. One of his first positive acts, and
an extremely significant one, was the restoration of the Society
of Jesus, on August 7, 1814. *Motu proprio* he rehabilitated
throughout the world the militia which the enemies of the
papacy had forced a former pope to dissolve forty-three years
before to the great loss of Catholic life and with almost fatal
consequences to the foreign missions. The erection of thirty

---

[6] Cf. L. Marion, *Histoire de l'Eglise*, IV, pp. 364, 365, note: Mme. Letitia
addressed a sorrowful letter to Consalvi, May 27, 1818. Among other things
she says: "His Holiness and Your Excellency are the only ones in Europe
who make an effort to soften the hard lot [of Napoleon]." "The Pontifical
government is our only asylum and support."

new dioceses in France and seven in the United States, the conclusion of agreements regulating ecclesiastical affairs in Bavaria, Prussia, and the Upper Rhine Provinces, and the condemnation of secret societies, in particular of the Carbonari, were among the more important acts of Pius VII. The anticlerical revolution in Spain in 1820 was a cause of anxiety, as was also the stirring of Jacobin Liberalism. The pope had reason to fear the forces opposed to Metternich, but his repudiation of the Holy Alliance, in which the pietistic Czar attempted the impossible union of Catholic, Schismatic, and Protestant powers, stands as evidence of his fidelity to principle as opposed to political expediency.

Of Leo XII it has been said: "There is something pathetic in the contrast between the intelligence and masterly energy displayed by him as a ruler of the Church and the inefficiency of his policy as ruler of the Papal States."[7] In his inaugural encyclical *Ubi Primum,* of May 5, 1824, he condemned Bible   Leo XII
societies and the spirit of Indifferentism; he celebrated the Jubilee year, 1825, thus reviving the practice discontinued in 1800; he restored the Germanic and Roman Colleges; he set up a special Congregation of Studies to promote scholarly work. But far and away the most significant event in this short pontificate was the reorganization of the Church in the new Republics of South America.[8]

The twenty months of the short pontificate of Pius VIII fell in momentous times. In England and Ireland Catholic Emancipation began a new era on April 13, 1829. In France   Pius VIII
the July Revolution of 1830, with its immediate consequences

---

[7] Leslie A. St. L. Toke, in *Catholic Encyclopedia,* IX, 168.

[8] When successful revolution severed the political ties which bound the South American colonies to Spain and Portugal it created a delicate situation for the Church. Over a period of three hundred years there had been little direct connection with Rome. The Patronado had rendered inestimable service, but at the price of servile dependence on the Crown. It was the task of Leo XII to provide a new hierarchy without offense to Spain (and Portugal). South Americans sought the papal blessing for their revolution. The Pope thought only of the welfare of souls sadly in need of spiritual care. The story is told by Pedro Leturia in several monographs. Cf. *El Ocaso del Patronato* (Madrid, 1924), *La acción diplomatica de Bolívar ante Pio VII* (Madrid, 1925), *Bolívar y Leon XII* (Madrid, 1930).

in other lands, shattered the Metternich system. Belgium broke the chain of servitude that bound her to the King of Holland. In the Germanies the problem of mixed marriages was calling loudly for a solution. Poland was restless under the yoke of the Czar. In Italy and in Rome itself the Carbonari were preparing an insurrection. The Roman trouble was forestalled, and the pope laid down the norms for bishops and clergy in Germany regarding mixed marriages. For the rest, he could scarcely do more than remain passive and hope for the best.

Gregory XVI was a monk who felt little sympathy with the moving world about him. His mind was cast in a more autocratic mold, and he distrusted the political theories and the practical policies advocated by the dominant Liberalism **Gregory XVI** of the day. It would, perhaps, have been better had he understood his times. But even without the later experience of Pius IX it was clear enough that no pope could possibly work in harmony with the wild tendencies of an unrestrained Liberalism. The conciliating attitude of Leo XIII lay fifty years in the future. In the 1830's the futile attempt of the youthful enthusiasts who followed Lamennais to effect a working compromise between the Church and modern liberties showed that the time was not ripe for an understanding. Gregory was not a diplomat. Much less was he a politician. But he was a strong pope at a time when the first duty of the pope was to defend the right at the cost of sacrificing popularity. "He respected not the person of man," says Wiseman, "and cared nothing for the strength of those whom he had to encounter. . . . He spoke the truth plainly and publicly; and generally reaped the fruit of his straightforwardness and courage."[9]

Metternich protested that Gregory "did not know how to govern." This has all the appearance of an *a priori* judgment, for Metternich, along with the other Powers, undertook to tell the pope how to rule the Papal States before he had **Papal** had time to begin. Gregory had been pope less than three **States** months when a conference of the Powers met in Rome, and on May 21, 1831, issued a memorial which was to inaugurate a new era of better government. The collaboration of auto-

---

[9] Cardinal Wiseman, *Recollections of the Last Four Popes,* pp. 402, 403.

cratic Austria and Liberal France makes one suspicious, but
when they invited Czarist Russia, bureaucratic Prussia, and
"amphibious" England to share the wardship of the Church
one could be sure that their motives were not entirely
altruistic. This Catholic, Protestant, Greek Schismatic alliance
certainly could not unite on a basis of religion. Metternich
did, however, have at heart the peace of Europe, which to
most of the participants in the conference meant protecting
their own interests. Some excuse, of course, there was in the
known character of the monk-pope, and in the revolutionary
turmoil with which he had to deal.

The memorial outlined reforms in all branches of the
judiciary, and in local and municipal administration; it
provided for popular elections and for a predominant lay
participation in the papal government. Gregory, through his
secretary Bernetti, agreed to introduce reforms, but refused
to abandon his rights of sovereignty. Guizot, commenting upon
the decrees issued by the pope on this occasion, maintained
that all the chief points laid down by the conference were
being met in a satisfactory way.[10] There was, in fact, no lack
of good will on the part of Gregory XVI. He was not a statesman chiefly because he was so wholeheartedly a spiritual ruler.
If he opposed the introduction just then of railroads and
frowned upon "scientific" congresses, it was because he saw
in them the means of spreading revolutionary ideas, and
consequently a danger to the faith.

Gregory XVI has been judged by his limitations in a field
which was foreign to his spiritual functions. He was at best
a mediocre ruler in circumstances where an abler man might
have failed. But he was a strong, if not a great pope. His   A Strong
consistent support of the struggling Catholics in Prussia was Pope
always correct, and it was ultimately successful, as we shall
see in our discussion of the Cologne Affair. His attitude toward
the Catholic Liberals of France seemed at the time somewhat
cruel. But the good intentions of individuals did not warrant
the risk of committing the Church to unsound doctrines. A

---

[10] Cf. Fernand Mourret, *Histoire générale de l'Eglise,* IX, pp. 173–817,
and Schmidlin, *op. cit.,* I, pp. 528–539.

glance at Gregory's encyclical *Mirari Vos,* of August 15, 1832,
shows that he had to worry about a veritable flood of errors,
all more or less connected with Liberalism. There was an
"ugly conspiracy against clerical celibacy." Liberals were
proclaiming "one religion as good as another"; they argued
for separation of Church and State; they made a specious
plea for license of opinion and unrestrained "freedom of conscience," which meant in practice a repudiation of the law
of God. Lamennais, Lacordaire, and Montalembert had a
case when they journeyed to Rome in 1831, but the wild
ravings of the Liberals made it unwise and impossible to
approve their work at that time. The pope's worst fears were
confirmed and his caution justified when, two years later, the
excesses of Lamennais forced him to issue a direct condemnation of the man and his *Paroles d'un croyant.*[11]

Hermes

At the Prussian University of Bonn, Georg Hermes had
infected students, among them many candidates for the
priesthood, with an original and daring synthesis of Catholic
truth, Kantian speculation, and Rationalism. He pretended
merely to counteract a decadent Scholasticism. He had filled
the minds of those who heard him or read his books with
doubts and distorted ideas about God, revelation, and the
Church, about faith, grace, and original sin. Hermes died in
1831, but his books were still a danger to their readers. Hence
Gregory condemned the books by a Brief, *Dum acerbissimas,*
on September 26, 1835. The condemnation gave the Catholic
author a posthumous glory among Protestant Prussians.
Hermesianism refused to die, and Pius IX had to confirm
the condemnation of Gregory XVI in 1846. The case of Louis
Bautain, a well-meaning professor of Strassburg, is somewhat
different. Warned by his bishop, he went to Rome of his
own accord in 1840, and subscribed to six orthodox propositions dealing with faith and reason.

Pius IX

Gregory XVI had been elected on the morrow of 1830, and
his pontificate ran parallel with the triumphant Bourgeois
Liberalism of the July Monarchy. Pius IX became pope in
1846, on the eve of 1848, when Liberalism was about to yield

---

[11] *Singulari vos,* June 25, 1834.

the stage to the kindred but more virile system of Nationalism. *Il papa liberale* had a Liberal background. "In the house
of Mastäi Ferretti," Pelegrino Rossi is reported to have told
Guizot, "everybody is a Liberal, down to the family cat."
It was the general feeling of the Conclave of 1846 that the
new head of the Church should have greater regard for the
popular will. And when Count Mastäi Ferretti was elected an
explosion of popular approval from the most unexpected
quarters gave grounds for rejoicing, and for anxiety. The
days of rigor and opposition to "progress" ended with the
death of Gregory; the way was now clear for an ordered
Catholic liberty!

But Pius IX found himself in an anomalous position. He
was resolved to make every concession to material progress,
popular liberties, and participation of the people in the government of the Papal States. But there was a danger that
the "permanent insurrection of ovations" might turn his head;
that in the din and confusion he might not, as Guizot warned,
discern the "limits between change and progress, between the
practical and the impossible, between the salutary and the
perilous." But the greatest danger lay in the insincerity and
the dishonesty of Italian Liberals. Mazzini spoke insultingly
of "smothering the fatted steer with flowers." Louis Veuillot
drew a picture of "sedition laden with flowers, prostrate before
the pope and howling to be blessed by him." Most alarming
of all, a hidden hand seemed to be manipulating popular enthusiasm for the destruction of the Papacy. Nothing would
please the Masonic Lodges better than to ensnare the pope
by means of his own generous disposition. Pius IX was an
Italian and a patriot. He was to be driven into a Nationalist
campaign against Catholic Austria. The conflict between his
patriotism and his duties as head of the universal Church was
shortly to become painfully evident. He had begun with an
almost reckless rush of liberal measures: amnesty for political
prisoners, provision for material improvements, the appointment of Pelegrino Rossi as prime minister, with an elected
assembly empowered to control taxation. Before the end of
1848 Rossi was assassinated, a wild mob besieged the Quirinal,
and the pope fled in disguise to Gäeta. The orgy of Mazzini's

*Pius IX
Disillusioned*

six months' Republic ended when the French troops under General Oudinot restored order, and a disillusioned pope came back to Rome to make a new start in a pontificate which was to see the destruction of the Temporal Power and a corresponding marvelous regeneration of spiritual forces.

The chief events and movements of the period: the Syllabus and the Vatican Council, the Unification of Italy and the German Kulturkampf, are such as to require separate treatment elsewhere. But there was, aside from the better known historical facts, enough activity in other lines to fill out a busy pontificate. The re-establishment of the Catholic hierarchy in England in 1850 and in Holland in 1853 was an unmistakable sign of expanding life in the Church. A long series of concordats[12] and conventions with governments in Europe and America would fill a significant chapter in the changing relations of Church and State. The fact that in the Denzinger-Bannwart collection of doctrinal pronouncements Pius IX is given over six times as much space as Gregory XVI and nearly four times as much as the four preceding popes together is another indication of papal activity. A hundred formal approvals of religious congregations must be interpreted as evidence of vigorous life throughout the Church. Finally, the surge of pilgrims to the Eternal City for canonizations, beatifications, and several jubilees, especially at a time when the Papal States were crumbling before the advance of Victor Emmanuel and his motley supporters, may be taken as a proof of the personal popularity of Pius IX. Much more than this, it also means the Catholic world was awakened and on the move.

The activity of Pius IX in doctrinal matters is admirably summed up in the Syllabus and in the decrees of the Vatican Council. But the verdicts of the Syllabus are directed against errors which are more fully treated in encyclicals, allocutions,

Doctrinal Errors

---

[12] Angelo Mercati, *Raccolta di Concordati su Materie Ecclesiastiche tra la Santa Sede e le Autorità Civili*, devotes approximately half of his compilation of agreements between the Holy See and various governments to the nineteenth century. The number of states involved is an index to the political division of Christendom. The unity and universality of the Church is likewise apparent.

and apostolic letters, extending over nearly two decades. From the beginning of his pontificate, even during what may be styled his "Liberal period," Pius IX was using strong terms to condemn typical nineteenth-century aberrations. In his first encyclical of November 9, 1846, and again in his allocution of December 9, 1854, he attacked the Indifferentism that glossed over the distinction between virtue and vice, truth and error, as well as the Rationalism that dragged religion down to a purely human level, and the "Progress" that refused to set limits to unaided human aspirations. More specifically, he had to deal with Catholic philosophers who were infected with the virus of Rationalism, or who resorted to unsound arguments in their effort to combat it. He renewed the previous condemnation of the Hermesians who subjected faith to reason, and repudiated on two occasions, in 1857 and 1860, the closely related semi-Rationalism of Anton Günther. In 1862 he condemned the intellectual Liberalism of Jakob Frohshammer, who presumed to penetrate divine mysteries without the aid of revelation. The well-meant vagaries of the Ontologists were also rejected in 1861. On the other hand, Pius upheld human reason against the Traditionalists. But the pope was not working alone. During this pontificate Catholic scholars were actively engaged in the re-establishing of Scholasticism. The antimetaphysical philosophy of the century had produced a Neo-Scholastic reaction. A strong Jesuit group in Italy, Kleutgen, Scheeben, and several others in Germany, and a scattered few elsewhere were preparing the way for the *Aeterni Patris* encyclical of Leo XIII.

An estimate of the character of Pius IX would be easier if the unrestrained panegyrics of his admirers and the spiteful calumnies of his enemies had not heaped up so much literary rubbish to be cleared away. Pius was a thoroughly good man whose lot was cast in evil times. He was ardently devoted to the spiritual work of his high office; but he had little real understanding of the political currents that surged around him. He was keenly conscious of dangers to souls; he was out of touch with worldly affairs. "His heart," remarked Cardinal Bernetti, "was greater than his head." He was often sentimental, emotional, impulsive, almost feminine in his

Character of Pius IX

reactions when the situation seemed to call for a calm, cool judgment. His gaze was fixed on the past when the world was moving forward. He himself realized this. "Let my successor," he told Msgr. Czacki, "be animated by my love for the Church and my desire to do good. For the rest, all is changed around me; my system, my policy have had their day; but I am too old to change."[13] It is doubtful, at least, whether the Church and the world would have been better if Pius had been different. At this distance, he appears as a providential pope. Leo XIII could undertake his brilliant work of conciliation with the world largely because Pius had fought a hard, courageous fight. It is certain that the age of Pius IX witnessed a marvelous growth of the Church, and in that growth the "martyr" pope who, if he was not a diplomat or a statesman, was in the truest sense of the word a great shepherd of souls, had an enviable share.

Was Leo XIII the greatest of the modern popes? The question is a debatable one, but for an admirer of his immediate successor and of the present Pontiff it is difficult to give an affirmative answer. They have done a work which he would hardly have done so well. But no mere historian will deny that Leo was in the fullest sense of the word a great pope. And it is hard to see how any other in his place would have accomplished his individual task better than he accomplished it. As a diplomat, as a statesman, as a peacemaker he was superb. He was a progressive pope who never sacrificed principle to expediency. He was a scholar possessed of rare literary ability. He was at home in the field of economics and social theory. He was a promoter of learning and a patron of science, art, history, and philosophy. He could appeal with equal assurance to reason, to revelation, and to the record of his predecessors. He was a providential pope.

Gioacchino Vincenzo Pecci, the sixth of seven sons, was born on March 2, 1810, at Carpineto in Italy. At the Jesuit college of Viterbo he laid the foundation of his later proficiency in Latin and Italian. His ecclesiastical studies were

Leo XIII

---

[13] Schmidlin, *op. cit.*, II, 109 note.

made at the Academia dei Nobili and the Gregorian University. Ordained to the priesthood on the last day of the year 1837, his varied experience during the following forty years of active life gave him an intimate first-hand knowledge of the problems he was to meet as Head of the Church. As Governor of Benevento he had to bring order into a chaotic, brigand-infested province. Next, as Delegate in Umbria he displayed surprising ability in combating anti-papal propaganda, in removing causes of social discontent, in administering justice, and in building up material prosperity. In 1843 he was consecrated titular Archbishop of Damietta and sent as Papal Nuncio to Brussels. Here he learned the arts of diplomacy during three years of daily contact with delicate political problems. He also gained a personal insight into French and English affairs by a brief residence in Paris and London. Called back to Italy in 1846, he became Archbishop of Perugia. Here, during thirty busy years, he was a devoted pastor of souls, preaching, catechizing, promoting retreats and missions, sponsoring literary and scientific studies among his clergy. Here, also, his Academy of St. Thomas was a landmark in the revival of Scholasticism. In 1853 he was created Cardinal, but, very likely through the influence of Cardinal Antonelli, kept at a distance from Rome. In 1877 he went to the Vatican as Camerlingo, and on February 20, 1878, he was elected pope.

Wide and varied experience had prepared the sixty-eight-year-old Pontiff for the responsibilities ahead of him. But more important still were the qualities of character, natural or acquired, which he possessed. His well-known portraits reveal a tall, thin, "diaphanous," distinguished-looking nobleman of exquisite poise and dignity; a man of delicate constitution, but of iron will and tireless energy; a likable, witty, winsome individual who was at the same time conscious of the greatness of his office. His rather remarkable countenance, with its firm, angular features, high forehead, and wide mouth wore an expression of austere majesty clothed in an affectionate smile. This was the Pope who was called upon to restore calm after the stormy days of Pius IX. Clarity of vision, firm principles, intellectual acumen, brilliance in discourse, keen

Character of Leo

political insight, and a habit of initiative were the human equipment of this leader of men who was to be known as *Lumen in Coelo*.

In the critical, almost desperate state of religion and the Church, Leo found his great opportunity. At this distance the historian can admire the wisdom of Pius IX in clearing away

A Conciliat-
ing Pope

the debris of error and in laying the solid rock foundations of a more aggressive, more centralized modern Papacy. But sixty years ago the "martyr pope" had seemed to take his hopeless stand athwart the path of Progress. He had lost his own Temporal Power; he was at war with the dominant political and intellectual forces of Europe. Liberalism (this is the most convenient all-embracing term for our purpose) was contemptuously triumphant in State and society, in business, in thought, in religion. Nationalism was riding high in Bismarck's Germany, in anticlerical France and Italy. In the rest of Europe there was little to console the Vicar of Christ. His fearless defense of right and truth was regarded as a futile and foolhardy reversion to medieval obscurantism. His anathemas, when they did not arouse a rabid hate, were treated with pitying contempt. To Leo XIII the self-glorified nineteenth century pretended to look for "understanding." And the new pope did understand. He knew what was wrong with the world, and he buoyantly assumed the grateful task of making it right. His attitude was one of conciliation, but this was not to mean undue concessions nor weak compromise where there was question of principle. He announced quite plainly that he would carry on in the spirit of his predecessor, and continue his general policy in all its essential elements.

The story of Leo XIII falls naturally into two major divisions: his relations with the various peoples of the world and their governments, and his masterful teaching, embodied in his great encyclicals. Both of these topics will be treated in later chapters.

V

CLERGY AND LAITY

AS A RESULT OF THE STRONG ULTRAMONTANE REACTION against the disintegrating tendencies of Liberalism and its more ancient kindred isms, the vital currents in the Church became more and more centripetal.[1] The semiheresies, Gallicanism, Febronianism, and Josephism, like the heresies of the remote past, served the providential purpose of bringing out the essentially monarchical character of the Church, though, strangely enough, its democratic features were never more evident. The Vatican Council in its convocation, preliminary aligning of forces, prolonged discussions, and final doctrinal decrees represents the climax of a long development toward the definite formulation of the dogmatic position of the pope. But scarcely less important was the consistent exercise of powers which, theoretically, might still be questioned. Any doubt as to the extent of papal power, or more precisely of the juridical authority of the popes, in France in particular, but also in other countries, was settled by action rather than by arguing when, at the beginning of the century, Pius VII deposed a third of the French episcopate. He and his successors made thirty concordats with the governments of Europe. Royal *placets, exequaturs,* and *Appels comme d'abus* are things of the past. The progressive secularization of the civil power contributed by way of reaction to the exaltation of the spiritual power among Catholics. Historical circumstance explains much of what happened, but throughout the nineteenth century the Hand of God moved among the human actors in the religious and the irreligious drama.

Ultramontanism

---

[1] Veit, *op. cit.,* p. 106 and *passim,* discusses what he calls the "Ultramontanizierung des Denkens." The Church in Germany, it was remarked as early as 1829, was becoming steadily "more Roman and more hierarchical."

But no pope can rule the Church alone. However unlimited in theory or in dogmatic definition his power may be, he cannot be an autocrat. He teaches and rules and administers a divinely instituted Church through a divinely instituted hierarchy of bishops. The bishop, too, is a monarch in his own diocese, a father of his people, and the pope addresses him as "Venerable brother." But besides the element of aristocracy in the episcopate the Church has also its essentially democratic features. Every thinking Christian knows he has certain inalienable rights. He knows that liberty, equality, and fraternity were characteristic of Christianity many centuries before they became the sacred illusions of a Godless revolutionary society. He knows that popes and bishops and priests are subject to the same moral and divine positive law to which the boys in the parish school are taught to submit. He knows that in the sight of God the soul of a beggar in rags may be more precious than that of many a purple-robed dignitary in Rome. For him the Vicar of Christ is also the *Servus servorum Dei*.

Democracy in the Church

There is nothing incongruous in the fact that the century which witnessed the phenomenal rise of the papacy was also the century of strong action of the laity, even of lay theologians, in the Church. To complete the harmonious picture of a resurgent Catholicism, it was likewise the century of an invigorated and aggressive hierarchy. Chronologically, the laity were early in their spontaneous gravitation toward the Holy See. In the century of Democracy there was an upsurge of life from below. An elite among the faithful turned toward Rome, not in revolt against an imaginary tyranny, but to reassert their loyalty and to beg the blessing and approval of the Supreme Pontiff. And at the end of the century Leo XIII was gratified to find himself hailed as the "Pope of the people." Meantime, in every section of the Catholic world great men were bringing a new prestige to the episcopate. In the old feudal days kings had combined with the commoners to curb the nobility. In the nineteenth century, by an imperceptible process the Spirit of God brought the ecclesiastical monarchy, aristocracy, and democracy into a well-integrated, smoothly functioning whole.

The Laity

At least a dozen great cardinals may be singled out among those who made the Church what it was in the nineteenth century. A few of them, in keeping with the original purpose of the cardinalate, did their work close to the Holy Father as his secretaries, ministers, and diplomatic agents. Among these the first in time and the model for all was Ercole Consalvi. Arrested and imprisoned by the Revolutionary invaders of Rome in 1798, Pius VII made him Secretary of State in 1800. He matched the diplomatic skill of Napoleon in the strained negotiations for the Concordat of 1801, suffered for his loyalty to Pius VII during the despotic years of the Empire, won back virtually the whole of the Papal States at the Congress of Vienna, concluded agreements with the German princes after the Restoration, prepared the way for an understanding with the English government, and by his charm and tact exerted a wholesome personal influence upon the leading statesmen of Europe. He was "one of the purest glories of the Church of Rome." Less lovable and far less popular, but trained in the diplomatic school of Consalvi, was Luigi Lambruschini, the Papal Secretary under Gregory XVI, whose energy and ability were employed chiefly in repressing revolutionary elements in Italy. Under Pius IX the guiding spirit was Jacopo Antonelli, a cardinal who was not a priest. Cordially disliked in Liberal circles and slandered by his enemies, he was largely responsible for the consistently uncompromising attitude of Pius IX. But he resented the comparison of his zealous services to his chief in the spiritual order with the imperial ambitions of Richelieu. When Leo XIII succeeded to Pius IX cardinal secretaries still performed their daily tasks, but in the eyes of the world the pope was his own prime minister.

Cardinal Secretaries

When one considers the cardinals as makers of history in the nineteenth century he involuntarily thinks of great prelates who were primarily archbishops, and only accidentally as it were, members of the cardinalate. America had its Cardinal Gibbons; England besides Newman, its Wiseman, Manning, and Vaughan; Switzerland had its Mermillod; in France several able prelates of the middle century were thrown into the shade by the brilliant Dupanloup, who was never raised

National Cardinals

to the purple, but under Leo XIII the name of Cardinal Lavigerie is written large across the pages of French history; in Germany Hergenröther, the outstanding cardinal was a great historian. The cardinal-archbishops were great national figures, but in the case of most of them the affairs of the whole Church divided their attention. Newman stands in the fore-front of thinkers who diagnosed the ills of the century; Wise-man, too, was a scholar whom intellectual non-Catholics admired; Hergenröther, not so flashy as the antipapal Döllinger, was more than his match in argument; Gibbons, Manning, and Mermillod were leading sponsors of social Catholicism who collaborated with Leo XIII in the solution of the thorny question of labor and capitalism; Vaughan was a promoter of foreign missions; Lavigerie was himself an active missionary bishop, though he is best known as the "voice of Leo XIII" in his effort to convert the blind Royalism of the French Catholics into a policy of constitutional defense. As cardinals all of these prelates brought Rome closer to the peoples among whom they labored; as bishops they ruled, each in his own diocese, as successors of the Apostles.

The Church can be proud of its popes and its leading prelates in the nineteenth century. But the revival of religious **Priests and Laymen** life was not wholly due to them. Lacordaire, as a simple priest and later as a member of the Dominican Order, is a more imposing figure in the Church of France than any contemporary bishop. So is Balmes in Spain. The same may be said of Daniel O'Connell, Montalembert, Görres, Donoso Cortes, or Garcia Moreno in their respective countries. These laymen represented the best in the Catholic Church before the outside world. They did pioneer work when the natural spiritual leaders of the people had not the genius, talent, training, or energy to fire the enthusiasm of an enervated, badly battered Christianity, or to meet the attacks of a revolutionary age which had lost all reverence for the clergy. In the type of work they did and in the general character of their contribution to the Catholic cause there is little to distinguish priests and laymen. Lacordaire will ever be remembered as the eloquent preacher of Notre Dame. O'Connell was a magnetic molder of popular

KARL VON VOGELSANG
Austrian editor and social reformer
(1818–1890)

FREDERIC OZANAM
Apostle of practical charity
(1813–1853)

FR. JAIME BALMES
Spanish philosopher and publicist
(1810–1848)

JAMES CARDINAL GIBBONS
One of the leading sponsors of Social Catholicism (1834–1921)

opinion. But both are easily classified with a score of others whose apostolate of the pen and the spoken word was carried on in the same spirit and with methods that differed only by reason of accidental circumstances.

Taking the nations in order is probably the best way to view the activity of the individual Catholics who influenced the course of ecclesiastical history. In Ireland Daniel O'Connell towers like a giant above all others. There were strong men among the bishops, MacHale and Cullen for example, and a whole army of devoted priests carried on faithfully throughout the century. But in the public eye O'Connell's great achievement of Catholic Emancipation, in spite of the political failure that saddened his declining years, is without a parallel. England, too, profited by his victory. Thanks chiefly to the Oxford Movement, England had her Newman and Manning, but also her W. G. Ward, Faber, and Dalgairns among the converts. These along with Wiseman and Vaughan from the ranks of the Catholics by birth gave her a corps of able spokesmen and leaders. Across the sea in English-speaking America the phenomenal growth of the Church was the work of unsung heroes among the secular and regular clergy and of unsung heroines in the teaching congregations of women. Of the hierarchy Cardinal Gibbons is the best known, but he was hardly a greater man in his own sphere than John Carroll or Simon Bruté among the pioneers, or John England and John Hughes in the days of anti-Catholic bigotry. The convert, Orestes A. Brownson with his formidable pen and his bellicose spirit was America's outstanding layman.

Germany presents a score, at least, who deserve to be mentioned. From the Münster Circle, which gathered in the salon of the remarkable Amalie von Gallitzin, came Leopold von Stolberg and Friedrich Schlegel. In Bavaria King Ludwig I, under the influence of Bishop Michael Sailer, attracted the best talent of Germany to form his Munich School. Here, the incomparable Joseph Görres was the acknowledged leader, though among the other able scholars there was one, at least, Johann Ignaz Döllinger, who, if he had not forsaken the colors after a brilliant youth, might claim a nearly equal distinction.

Ireland and England

Germany

The founders of the Center Party who, under the leadership of Ludwig Windthorst, fought for Catholic liberty during the Kulturkampf made another chapter of Catholic history. William Emmanuel von Ketteler was not only the foremost among the bishops of Germany, but he inaugurated a social Catholic drive and inspired younger men to fight for social justice. To complete the list of the most eminent Catholic Germans it suffices to add the two historians, Hergenröther and Hefele. But from the beginning to the end of the century Germany had an unbroken line of writers, whose tireless literary activity supplemented that of the leaders. The Church in Germany was admirably served by her great Catholics, half of whom were laymen.

France

In France, the land of extremes and contrasts, great leaders, lay and clerical, waged the endless war of defense and attack against the de-Christianizing forces, born of the French Revolution. Chateaubriand, de Maistre, and Lamennais filled the stage during the first three decades. Out of the school of Lamennais came the picturesque pair, Lacordaire and Montalembert. Most flawless of them all, Frederic Ozanam did his quiet but effective work during the twenty years before his premature death in 1853. For forty critical years under three governments Louis Veuillot, "more Catholic than the pope," wielded his Ultramontane pen to the discomfiture of his friends and the indignation of all Liberals. In the closing decades of the century Albert de Mun, social reformer and eloquent pleader for justice to the laboring classes, was a Frenchman after Leo XIII's own heart. The hierarchy had its able men, Dupanloup and Lavigerie before all others, but in point of interest to the historian they were outnumbered by the laymen and simple priests.

Switzerland, Austria, Spain

Switzerland had her Cardinal Mermillod. Aside from him only one name, that of Gaspar Decurtins, who was his great lay collaborator, need be mentioned. In Catholic Austria the second decade of the century revolves around the powerful figure of a canonized saint, Klemens Maria Hofbauer, whose apostolic zeal transformed a diseased and drooping Church, and virtually crushed the remnants of an inherited Josephism.

Toward the end of the century it was Baron von Vogelsang who did most to stir Catholic life to action. Spain, also, is poor in Catholic champions. Jaime Balmes, the young priest who died at the age of thirty-eight, was the most promising writer, while Donoso Cortes was a model of aggressively Catholic laymen.

VI

SAINTS AND NEAR-SAINTS

The Saints

IN ANY "WHO'S WHO?" FOR 1938 ONE WILL FIND academic degrees, merited and unmerited, by the thousand. Statesmen and financiers rival in this adornment the professional men and college professors. Were a similar book compiled for students of the Middle Ages, the great mark of distinction would be an "St." before many of its important names. Alongside Charlemagne, Barbarossa, and Innocent III would stand the saints, Gregory, Boniface, Bernard, Francis, Louis, and Thomas, whose sanctity was a factor in the influence they exerted. Even the great, though certainly not saintly, Charlemagne was a candidate for canonization. In the nineteenth century Europe has as many saints as she had in the thirteenth. The statement may surprise the reader, but the difference between the two centuries lies not in the number of men and women who have drawn closer to God, but in the apostasy of those who directed public affairs during the past century. Politics, business, science, and literature for the most part stood in opposition to the Kingdom of God. There was, nonetheless, a thriving spiritual life which is not recorded in history books.

When Constantin Kempf wrote his *Holiness of the Church in the Nineteenth Century* abundant authentic records were at hand to make the task comparatively easy. The Roman Congregation of Rites had published a catalogue of processes of beatification and canonization in progress in the year 1901, and a similar catalogue in 1907. Since each process began with the gathering of data the writer had plenty of available material. This does not, however, lessen the value of the book, which consists in bringing before the public an army of Christians who amid the whirl and rush of the nineteenth century lived their religion heroically. And what is more, their story creates the presumption that countless others, not so well known, have also done the things that only the saints do.

As in the Age of the Martyrs, there were mass executions in which thousands died for Christ in China, Japan, Korea, Uganda, and Paris. In most instances these people have no individual history. Their names and their number are known to God alone. But there are scores of detailed accounts which recall the *Acta* of the Roman persecutions. Finally there are the full-length biographies of many whose sanctity and apostolic zeal were known before they won the crown of martyrdom. The reader will hesitate whether to admire more the constancy of veteran missionaries who met the final test after a long life of service, or the fervor of neophytes, very often mere children, whose luminous and cheerful faith defies a natural explanation. — Martyrs

The Church has ever had a maternal fondness for her martyrs. But the confessors of the faith who lived for Christ have more to offer the historian. Taking only those who appear in Father Kempf's book, we have one pope, ten bishops, seventeen secular priests, nineteen of the laity, and over a hundred from the regular clergy and congregations of religious women. In their variety of age, sex, and natural character, as well as in the circumstances in which they labored, they present a good cross section of the Catholic population. In their common devotedness to the Church and all that she stands for they should be her best defense against the attacks of a hostile world. It is to them that the Vatican Council referred when it appealed to the "eminent sanctity" by reason of which the Church is a "sign raised aloft among the nations." But official recognition such as they have received should not obscure the fact that unnumbered others practiced heroic virtues unrecognized, and that the possession of sanctifying grace, the essential sanctity of millions of Christians, lies in a realm beyond human observation. Another fact to bear in mind is that the introduction of the process of beatification often depends upon accidental conditions. There have been thousands of potential saints who lacked only a promoter to give them the necessary publicity. — Confessors

A final point, one which should startle the nineteenth cen-

tury, is that being raised to the altars means nothing less than
the working of miracles. The faith, the innocence, the charity,
chastity, and humility of these prospective saints is a standing
rebuke to the incredulity and atheism, the pride of mind and
moral depravity in the society about them. The evidence of
miracles which challenges scientific investigation is a conclu-
sive answer to half of the popular isms of the century. The
candidate for the honor of sainthood, or rather those who
champion his cause, must meet the objections of a "Devil's
advocate," whose duty it is to "defend the faith" by exposing
mercilessly any irregularity of doctrine or conduct or character. They must also produce facts which can be explained
only by an intervention of the Author of nature, and which
consequently show the divine approval of the Christian in
whose favors the miracles are worked. And when the Church
accepts or rejects, as she frequently does, the evidence in each
case she acts with the utmost caution, conscious that critical
eyes, aided by the best historical technique and sharpened by
a skeptical philosophy, may review the process in search of
flaws. In the schools the ordinary procedure is to begin the
study of miracles with the rational grounds for the possibility
of miraculous intervention on the part of God, but for an age
that is so pitiably weak in reason there is the simpler method
of examining the testimony of witnesses to phenomena perceived by the senses. The immediate purpose of the Church in
her canonizations is to determine whether this or that human
being is now in the enjoyment of heaven, and incidentally to
preserve from error those who would honor his or her supreme
success in life. But for the inquirer of open mind there is
enough in any one of a hundred judicial hearings preparatory
to canonization to upset the unreasoned foundations of nineteenth-century materialism and its related false philosophies.

The posthumous glory of Thérèse Martin, a Carmelite nun
who lived her twenty-four years unknown to the reporters of
social and political events, and died in an obscure convent
without causing a flutter in the village street, is an enlightening commentary on the times. The angels may record the
extent of her beneficent influence, but there are millions who
know her better than they know any of her contemporaries.

Miracles

St. Thérèse

Other millions have seen her image in homes, in parish churches, in mission chapels, or hung about the necks of soldiers at the front, and they have wondered at the spontaneous affection she has awakened without guessing the spiritual reality behind it. She was beatified with Cardinal Bellarmine in 1923, canonized with Peter Canisius two years later, and made patroness of the Foreign Missions along with St. Francis Xavier. The great pope who did most to honor her makes no effort to hide his devotion to her. If we judge the significance of the past by its effect on the present surely this Little Flower of Lisieux deserves a place in the history books. At least, an understanding of her and others like her is essential to any complete evaluation of the Church in recent times.

St. Thérèse, unlike the great Carmelite whose name she bore, had little contact with the world outside the cloister. Other saintly souls in the past century made their presence felt among those who knew them on earth. Klemens Maria Hofbauer, the first German Redemptorist, is remembered as the apostle of Vienna in the second decade of the nineteenth century. He was a power for good among disheartened and apathetic Catholics, a guide and friend of convert Jews and Protestants. Around him the ecclesiastical life of the Austrian capital revolved until his death in 1820. John Baptist Vianney, ordained two months after the battle of Waterloo, made the little village of Ars during thirty years the focus of a great spiritual revival. The crowds of pilgrims who darkened the roads leading from every corner of France kept him sixteen or seventeen hours daily in the confessional, around which they waited two and three days for a hearing. In inverse ratio to his scanty meals and his nightly sleep of an hour or two at most, altogether out of proportion to his natural talent and scholastic endowments, was the spiritual power which radiated from his frail form. Idle curiosity brought sinners to Ars. He sent them away with the love of God in their hearts. When the Curé of Ars died in 1859 another wonder-worker was caring for the street gamins of Turin. Ideal priest, friend of boys, born educator, social reformer and founder of two religious congregations, Don Bosco has been called the best "representative of the Church in the nineteenth century." His active life

Three Priests

covered the period from 1841 to 1888. The male and female branches of his Salesian Congregation are in charge of some six hundred houses, any one of them an answer to those who claim that the Church has not befriended the poor.

The apostle of Vienna, the Curé of Ars, Don Bosco, and the Little Flower are typical examples of what is, after all, the real life of the Church in the nineteenth century. But there were hundreds of others, a few of them scarcely less well known. The cause of Pius IX may or may not be carried to a successful issue. It is significant that a pope who seemed to represent everything that was distasteful to the anticlerical century is considered a likely subject for the severe scrutiny of the Roman authorities. Among the bishops listed for beatification is John Nepomuck Neumann of Philadelphia. Another hero of the American Church is the Vincentian, Felix de Andreis, who labored as a pioneer in and around St. Louis, until his death in 1820.

Saintly
Women

The most numerous category in the catalogue of potential saints is that of Religious Men. But it is doubtful whether their abiding influence is equal to that of the nearly equal number of Religious Women. Phillipine Duchesne, Anne Thérèse Guérin, and Elizabeth Seton, differing widely in character and mental ability but animated by the same apostolic spirit, burnt out their own lives in the service of souls, and left behind them Americanized religious congregations to continue their work.[1] Three nineteenth-century foundresses of teaching congregations have been canonized. Two of them, St. Madeleine Sophie Barat and St. Julie Billiart, have their spiritual daughters solidly established in America. St. Madeleine Sophie's active life as a nun covered the first sixty-five years of the century, and when she died at the age of eighty-six, four thousand of her Religious of the Sacred Heart were teaching young girls in every quarter of the globe. Only those who know what the Church in America owes to her teaching Sisters can attempt to estimate the value of services rendered

---

[1] Joseph B. Code, *Great American Foundresses* (New York, 1929) devotes thirty pages or so to each of sixteen women whose life and labors, sanctity, and enduring influence contributed greatly to the upbuilding to the Church in America.

ELIZABETH ANN SETON

Foundress and first Superior of the Sisters of Charity in
the United States (1774–1821)

From a portrait made in 1796

FR. ISAAC HECKER

Founder of the Paulists and a central figure in the
"Americanism" controversy (1819–1888)

by thousands of saintly women who have merged their identity in institutions and made their lives a ceaseless giving for others. But for pure heroism without the alloy of natural satisfaction that comes to the successful teacher, or even to the nursing Sister in the hospital, the Little Sisters of the Poor in their homes for the aged present the best example of selfless service.

In our own halls of learning some of the finest scholars are men who never won an academic degree. In the spiritual history of the nineteenth century chapters have been made by men whose names are not yet on the roster of the canonizable. There are admirers of John Henry Newman, Henri Lacordaire, Frederic Ozanam, and Garcia Moreno, to choose only striking examples, who contend that the attempt should be made to raise them to the altar. Uncanonized

Each of these men was a figure in the great, milling, external society the movement of which is recorded in history. But each had also an intimate interior life from which he drew the strength and inspiration for his outward exertions. They were what they were in their relations with men because of their union with God. The writer, the pulpit orator, the apostle of practical charity, the political crusader, each was a man of prayer, a man of God. Ozanam has been called *le grand Catholique* of his age. This brilliant lecturer of the Sorbonne, who is best known as the founder of the Conferences of St. Vincent de Paul, possessed "the eminent virtues of a true saint." When he died prematurely at the age of forty the world lost a scholar and the Church an able defender. A glance at his correspondence reveals the soul of a near-saint. Newman, too, lived close to God. As a mere boy he wrote letters which show this, and all through his long life his moral earnestness was patent to all. Lacordaire, a great public figure, a fighter for liberty and the foremost preacher of his time, drew his power to move an incredulous generation from his hours of prayer and interior recollection. The martyred president of Ecuador, whose public career was replete with thrilling incidents that make it read like a work of fiction, followed a rule of life worthy of a fervent religious. As a soldier he was a hard, resourceful fighter, as a statesman he did more than any other to raise the economic and cultural level of his people, but he consecrated Ecuador to the Sacred Heart, and strove to imitate Jesus Christ in all his actions. He died for his country and his Church.

These men, and others like them, Daniel O'Connell for example, may never receive the supreme distinction of official canonization, but they are not out of place in the company of those we call "saints."

VII

CATHOLIC THINKERS

THE NINETEENTH CENTURY WAS A PERIOD OF TREMEN-
dous intellectual activity. The remarkable advance along
material lines was the result of an application of mind to
the mysteries of nature, and the mastery over nature has in
itself a spiritual significance. But the nineteenth century
turned its back upon the supernatural. It did more; it
employed its mental powers to discredit the supernatural.
And this, too, meant intellectual activity. It philosophized on
a basis of false principles, but at least it philosophized. It had
its new systems, political, economic, and social, and was
eloquent in their defense. It built its utopias, in part at least,
of elements borrowed from Christianity. But logical or
illogical, rational or sentimental, its leaders did a great deal
of thinking. What, then, is to be said of Catholic thought,
of the intellectual life of the Church?

Intellectual Life

Inevitably, the writings of Catholics were largely apologetic
and controversial. In the first half of the century, particularly,
the Church was on the defensive. Faith was attacked in the
name of Reason; grace and the supernatural were supplanted
in the public mind by Nature. The conquest of material forces
opened up limitless vistas. It was the task of the Church to
set limits to the pretensions of reason, and to insist that there
was a life beyond the reach of man's natural powers. The
same Church might have felt the satisfaction of a sweet
revenge when, in the second half of the century, she found
herself defending the legitimate claims of reason against the
spiritual heirs of the old exaggerations.

But besides her adversaries outside the Fold the Church
had to deal with deviations, more or less serious, of Catholic
thinkers. The undue exaltation of individual reason had driven
well-intentioned men like de Bonald, Lamennais, Bautain, and

Errors of Catholics

Bonnetty into the extreme reactionary error of Traditionalism, which derived human ideas from a sort of heritage handed down to the helpless intellect. On the other hand, there were Germans like Georg Hermes and Anton Günther who made sincere but misguided efforts to defend religion, each in his own original way. Both became entangled in the maze of post-Kantian speculation. Both shared the contempt of their contemporaries for the old Scholasticism. At Louvain, Ubaghs and Laforêt expounded a revived Ontologism. In Italy an apostolic soul, Antonio Rosmini-Serbati, formulated his system of knowledge, which was vitiated by the same Ontologism. The obvious remedy for all these erratic tendencies was a return to the common sense of Scholasticism. And so a generation of able teachers set to work clothing the thought of St. Thomas in a language adapted to the nineteenth century. Kleutgen, Scheeben, Franzelin, and several brilliant Italians opened the way which eventually led to Leo XIII's *Aeterni Patris*. The poison of errors was ejected from the Catholic schools, and a healthy state of mind was created which would later stand the shock of Modernism. Catholics who submitted to the supreme magisterium, and who clung to the sane tradition of the older Scholasticism, had to deny themselves the satisfaction of daring and original speculation. But amid the noise and rush and confusion of modern thought they constructed the one secure refuge of philosophy.

Among the champions of the Church a long line of Frenchmen met the attacks of a Revolutionary society effectively. At the head of any list of Apologists would stand the names of Chateaubriand, de Maistre, de Bonald, Frayssinous, Lamennais, Lacordaire, Montalembert, followed in the next generation by the dynamic and irrepressible Louis Veuillot and by a group of able bishops, Dupanloup, Freppel, Pie, and others. England had her remarkable cardinals, Wiseman, Manning, Newman; Spain had her Balmes and Donoso Cortes; America had Brownson. In Ireland, Maynooth was a center of thought. In Germany was found the best historical scholarship. Besides the epochal *Symbolik* of Möhler, which demolished Protestant argument, and the multiform writings of Görres, there was the work of Döllinger and the rest

Intellectual
Leaders

of the Munich School. And when Döllinger wrecked his brilliant career by his apostasy, Hergenröther and Hefele more than supplied the last erudition. But the pioneer in scholarly history among nineteenth-century Catholics was an English priest, John Lingard.

The historical arguments against Christianity, including, of course, attacks upon the Sacred Scriptures, constituted a real danger, out of which, however, much good was to come. Catholic research uncovered the solid historical foundations of the Church, and eminent historians made the best results of their study available for seminarians in a series of historical handbooks. So sure was the Vatican Council of the historical position of the Church that the Fathers offered this as evidence of her divine character, while Leo XIII, a few years later, opened the Vatican Archives to all scholars. The answer to false philosophies, and in particular to the pseudo-scientists who mixed good science with bad philosophy was the great Neo-Scholastic revival.

At the beginning of the century the Church had virtually nothing in the way of institutions of higher education. Wholesale confiscation and secularization had wrecked the languishing school system of the Old Regime, and had left the Church without the means of rebuilding. Besides, in France Catholic education was crippled by the University monopoly which dated from Napoleon. This monopoly of primary, secondary, and university education was broken successively in the years, 1833, 1850, and 1875. Throughout the world the Church had an uphill fight against disheartening odds. The courage, the generosity, and the spirit of sacrifice that went into the slow construction of the present system are a standing proof of vitality in the Catholic body. The first landmark in the recovery of higher learning was the founding of Louvain University in 1834. The establishment of Catholic universities in Freiburg and Washington in 1889, following closely upon several French foundations, belongs to what may be called an organized official effort of the hierarchy to promote advanced learning. But fully as important were the diocesan seminaries where the young clergy were trained, and the expanding institutions of the Religious Orders, notably of the Jesuits.

Institutions

Negatively, the intellectual movement in the Church kept the faith free from errors of the age; positively, it bore rich fruit in the doctrinal decrees of Pius IX and in the encyclicals of Leo XIII.

The Munich School

The "Munich School" deserves special mention. In the second quarter of the century the Bavarian capital was the home of high scholarship, frankly and aggressively in the service of the Church.[1] A group of able men, aided and protected by a powerful patron, devoted themselves to teaching, writing, and discussion of religious questions in an atmosphere that stimulated original, but withal strictly orthodox, thinking. Most of these scholars were laymen; several of them were converts. Their acknowledged leader was Joseph Görres; their patron was the Wittelsbach king, Ludwig I, romantic, ardently patriotic and, until his passion for a Spanish dancer turned his head, a militant Catholic. The king had grown up in a Bavaria in which the *Aufklärung* and the French-inspired folly of an autocrat Minister had crippled the Church and brought the clergy to a sad state. But the wholesome influence of a great teacher, Johann Michael Sailer, and contact with German Romanticism prepared the king to lead a movement for reform. Catholic Bavaria had played a sorry role in spreading the poison of the Revolution. Ludwig made Munich the center of Catholic thought for Germany and, to a notable degree, for the whole Catholic world.

In 1825 the University was transferred from Landshut to Munich. Görres was called from his exile in Strassburg to a kind of informal leadership of the brilliant assembly which the king was gathering wherever talent could be found. Görres was then effectively giving to Germany a "Catholic voice," as he had given her a "political voice" before the crash of Napoleon's power. He had already exhorted Ludwig to be a Christian, a pillar of the faith, a protector of liberty of spirit. He had urged him to make Bavaria a refuge for religion and truth, and to build a culture based on God, not on the shifting sands of human opinions. In 1827 he threw his own

---

[1] Cf. Georges Goyau, *L'Allemagne religieuse*, II, pp. 54–111, for the best brief account of the Munich School. We have drawn freely from Goyau in this and the following paragraph.

tremendous energy into the work, and during twenty years this layman spent himself in a fruitful effort to raise the level of clerical studies, integrate the science of the time into a better apologetic, make Catholics proud of their heritage and, incidentally curb the pride of Prussian bureaucrats. Around him gravitated the young Döllinger, for whom the priesthood was but a means toward scholarship; the canonists, Moy and Phillips; the philologists, Lasaulx and Windischmann; Allioli, who gave to Germany a Catholic Bible; Brentano and a group of Romanticists; and Görres' own very likable son, Guido. In the Görres home was established the famous "Round Table," which resembled not so much an academy or a salon as a spiritual family.

The Munich School radiated a good influence throughout Germany. It was felt beyond the frontier in France and England. Montalembert, Lacordaire, and Lamennais were drawn to Munich; and at a later period Newman recognized the immense erudition of Döllinger. The Reformation had provincialized Christianity. Görres aimed to reknit the scattered parts, and to arouse an echo in other lands. He was a historian who was rather a philosopher of history. His was an eagle's-eye view of time and space. A journalist who delighted in the excitement of political controversy, he viewed the turmoil of human affairs around him as Augustine or Bossuet or Aquinas might have viewed it. His volumes on Mysticism were "the most vigorous protest of modern Catholicism against Rationalism." The jibes of critics he welcomed as an opportunity to emphasize Catholic truth. He would have fought gladly as a lone knight. Circumstances made him the inspired and inspiring leader of an elite group, which we know as the Munich School.

The influence of Catholic thought was exercised in Germany, as elsewhere, largely through a vigorous press. Before his call to Munich the pen of Görres had made the *Katholik* a powerful champion of the Church. In Munich he found a new vehicle for his ideas in the *Eos*, aptly named, for it was in fact a product and a cause of the new "dawn" in the Fatherland. But the peculiar creation of the Munich School was the courteous, but uncompromising *Historisch-politische Blätter*, still extant and known as *Das gelbe Heft*. It may seem like straining a point to connect the Ludwig-Missionsverein and its beneficent activities with the intellectual revival in the Bavarian capital. But both owed their vitality largely to the initiative of the romantic, patriotic, and religious-minded king. The militant Catholics who refused to be ignored in the sphere of culture or of politics, also fostered and promoted an apostolic spirit.

VIII

THE MISSIONS*

THE MISSION SPIRIT IS AS OLD AS THE CHURCH HERSELF. The Mission Spirit
But its manifestation in the succeeding ages of the world is
as varied as the external history of the unchanging Church.
Throughout, we can see, under the hidden hand of Providence,
the same heroic zeal of apostles, the same self-immolation,
similar human mistakes and blunders. In three or four fairly
well-defined periods,[1] it can readily be observed how the
mission spheres of activity, organization of forces, and
methods of evangelization have varied. There are times of
greater or less spontaneity, of more or less rigid organization.
Similarly, too, there are instances of special dependence on the
secular arm or of more purely ecclesiastical action.

The nineteenth century prepared the way for the harmonious
synthesis of all that was best in earlier times. The apostolic
fervor of the primitive Church made every Christian a potential, when not an active, missionary. He was conscious of
possessing a divine message, and the objects of his zeal were
all about him. There was individual aggressiveness and freedom, but little direction from above. Later when the Church
had conquered the dying Roman Empire, and still more so
when she became the State-Church of the Middle Ages, there
was a greater reliance on the Christian prince, with its
attendant advantages and its inevitable loss of an exclusively
spiritual appeal. The individual sanctity of the great national

---

* The major portion of this chapter appeared in *Thought,* X (September,
1935), 286–297.

[1] Cf. Joseph Schmidlin, "Die Missionsunterschiede der drei kirchlichen
Zeitalter," in *Zeitschrift für Missionswissenschaft,* XIII (1923), p. 18 ff.

Professor Schmidlin's *Missionsgeschichte* (English translation, *Catholic
Mission History,* edited by Matthias Braun, 1933) is the most up-to-date
work of its kind.

apostles who converted the barbarian world counteracted to a large degree the dangers in the system, but the human element needed close watching. Mass conversions could be produced by doubtful motives, and the external flow of baptismal waters did not always assure internal transformation. Numbers mounted when whole tribes followed their chieftain into the Church, but it took centuries of slow pastoral care before the Faith took root in individual souls.

At the opening of the modern period the Church found herself committed to a policy of co-operation with the leading colonial powers. For good or for evil the king's ships and the king's soldiers were called to aid in the work of spreading the Gospel. Or shall we say, rather that the soldier of the Cross was enlisted in the work of extending the king's domain? But the "colonial mission" was soon to give way to the "ecclesiastical mission." In 1622 Gregory XV set up the Congregation de Propaganda Fide, a sort of central commission or ministry to supervise and control the whole mission field. In the thousand years before this date papal or Roman initiative had been a rare phenomenon. True, the State had sought the approval of Rome and individual apostles had been fortified by the blessing of the Holy Father. Indirectly, too, the Holy See had worked effectively through the great Religious Orders, which owed to the popes their existence and their commission to labor for souls. But with a few scattered exceptions the record of Rome was not one of aggressive activity. The new Congregation should have brought about a decided change. But the fact remains that the first two centuries after its foundation the story of the Catholic missions is not an imposing one. The best features of the Propaganda policy, at once magnanimous and narrow, were limited to a preparation for a long future and to non-interference with a few flourishing missions already established. The sickly century that preceded the French Revolution was a sad one for the Church and it was almost fatal to the Missions. It registered no great achievement, and its crowning disaster was the destruction of the Jesuit missions everywhere.

Dark clouds and confusion hung over the beginning of the

The Modern
Period Opens

nineteenth century. The mission field lay in ruins; laborers were few or nonexistent; all the sources of supply were like so many fountains gone dry. But the catastrophe of the French Revolution had engulfed abuses and disorders as well as beneficent institutions of the Old Regime. The Church, held in bondage under Bourbon despotism, was again free; the diseased mentality of the *Aufklärung* had given way to a healthier state of mind; the denatured Christianity of an ornamental nobility had succumbed; there was a hunger for the supernatural and for the realities of religion; the dawn of a new democratic age held high promise for clergy and laity alike. The times demanded a new outburst of energy, but they also provided the opportunity for it.

Rising to
a New Life

Among those who seemed to control the destinies of the world there was a marked tendency toward paganism and irreligion. But the issues were clearly enough defined, and the struggles ahead of the Church were to provide a training ground on which new strength would develop. Then, too, there was stimulation in the universal atmosphere of progress which Catholics could share for better ends. Even the Protestant churches awoke to new life and began a new era in mission activity. Humanitarian and Romanticist half truths aided the process of regeneration. On the material side, the prosaic ambitions of the businessman and the statesman's dreams of empire opened up world-wide communications and provided a necessary means for evangelizing distant peoples. With all this there was born in the lowliest of Christians a consciousness of their common duty to extend the Kingdom of Christ. In a democratic age the Church, too, could call on a limitless reserve of power, and bid her laity to take an active interest in the missions. The materialistic century went its own feverish and often futile way, but its third decade was to find the breath of a new life stirring vigorously in those who promoted and organized the first mission aid societies.

We shall here center attention on the American scene, with the advantage of avoiding the distractions of a wider field, and the same time revealing the Mission character of the Church in the United States.

As an early fruit of the revival of Catholic life in Europe,

and at the same time as a stimulus and a means toward richer
vitality, we have, aside from a dozen or more kindred organizations,[2] the three outstanding mission societies which most
effectively aided the American Church: *la Propagation de la
Foi,* the *Leopoldinen-Stiftung,* and the *Ludwig-Missionsverein.*
All answer to the definition of a mission association: "An
organization depending on voluntary enrollment and having
for its object the welfare of the missions abroad and the
creation of a basis at home." Their purpose was to support
the missionary by prayer no less than financial aid. In no
sense did they appoint or send the priest or nun or brother
who labors in the mission field; they did not even attempt
to control the work which their almsgiving rendered possible,
nor have they in practice presumed to dictate how their
money shall be spent; neither did they undertake to train
candidates for the work. It is hard to see how a self-interested
or merely human motive could enter into any part of the
process. It was all unselfish giving for the sake of the good
they could do and felt that they ought to do. They had the
approval of the Church authorities, but the Church assumed
no obligation in their regard. It was a one-way contract; they
gave, and, aside from the often expressed gratitude of their
beneficiaries, looked only for a reward in another world. If
their vanity were flattered by any lurking thought of their
own magnanimity, there were the immensely more wealthy
Protestant organizations whose donations outweighed their
own perhaps ten to one.[3] Yet they could take a justifiable
pride in the results of their generosity, while at the same

[2] Bernard Arens, *Manuel des missions catholiques,* pp. 294–351, gives
pertinent data for over 300 mission aid associations in twenty or more
countries between 1816 and 1924. Many of them are now negligible. But
their number, variety, and wide distribution indicate the spirit behind a
popular movement. The tabulated contributions of the Propagation de la
Foi, *ibid.,* pp. 292, 293, show a steady increase during its first half century
from nearly two million francs for its first decade to over five million
annually. The nearly constant figure of approximately six million over
a period of fifty years, including the World War, is evidence of excellent
organization. Running parallel to the Propagation de la Foi, but about
half as effective financially, was the Work of the Holy Child.

[3] Schmidlin, *op. cit.,* p. 564, note, gives $50,000,000 as the annual
Protestant contribution to the Missions. The Catholic estimate ranges from
$4,000,000 to $12,500,000.

Mission Aid
Societies

time they must have been conscious of a deepening of their own spiritual life through participation in the great business of saving souls.

It may be invidious to say that on the whole France has taken the lead in this field. But in the order of time, as well as by the extent of influence and the volume of collections made, this is true. Hence we turn first to the Society for the Propagation of the Faith. About its origins we have a wealth of interesting facts; still when there is question of apportioning credit or of designating the real founder we are face to face with an insoluble tangle. This difficulty is in itself an index of the spirit in which its organizers worked. There is not the slightest hint of any claim of honor or of a seeking of personal satisfaction through publicity. High-minded souls were intent solely on doing a work of zeal which they felt had to be done. A simple recital of the steps by which the society came into being will make this clear.

"The Propagation of the Faith"

The movement which culminated in the formal founding of the Society on May 3, 1822, had been initiated by a young woman of twenty, an elderly widow, and a successful businessman. Outside inspiration had come from the American Bishop of Louisiana, Msgr. DuBourg, and from the seminary of the Foreign Missions in Paris. Each of these was a factor in the work which was the fruit of their combined though largely independent efforts. But somehow, historians who treat the subject in a summary way tend to look on Pauline Marie Jaricot as the foundress of the society and its most typical member. The picturesque but self-effacing role she played will appeal most strongly to the general reader. Historical truth, however, demands that others be given credit for a substantial share in the work.

Pauline Marie Jaricot was born at Lyons, July 22, 1799. At an early age she turned to a life of piety and self-abnegation, taking a vow of perpetual virginity when she was seventeen. If we may judge by her pictures, she was a beautiful girl. Her crowded life of varied and ceaseless activity reveals a social worker on a very high level, an ardent soul whose grandiose dreams of a world conquest for Christ hovered over and around her practical plans for the betterment of her im-

Its Founders

mediate surroundings. She reformed the vicious lives of factory and servant girls, taught them to pray, and then enlisted their support for the foreign missions. Hers was the *sou par semaine* idea, and the plan of organizing penny collections through groups of ten, a hundred, and a thousand, which with later modifications has remained a characteristic of the Society. It may be doubted whether she had heard of the penny-a-week contributions of the Anglicans. It sufficed for her that this was an efficient means to the end she had in view. She never claimed originality, and she was definitely influenced by her constant correspondence with her brother Phileas, who was a student at the seminary of the Foreign Missions in Paris, and whose letters never allowed her interest in apostolic work to lag.

But Mlle. Jaricot had been anticipated by Mme. Petit, whose mission zeal displayed itself among the well-to-do classes of Lyons. Mme. Petit had lived in America. In 1794 she came to Baltimore, a penniless exile from her home in San Domingo. The comfort and sympathy she found in another San Domingan, the youthful Abbé DuBourg, won her enthusiastic support for the missions in America. She returned to Lyons in 1803, and when, twelve years later, DuBourg arrived as the newly consecrated bishop of New Orleans she was ready and eager to aid him by collecting alms for his poverty-stricken diocese. Among her first conquests was a prominent merchant of Lyons, M. Benoit Coste, whose main contribution to the Society was to give it a universal character. Mlle. Jaricot's attention was fixed on the Orient; Mme. Petit thought only of America; M. Coste gave the work a broader scope to take in the whole world. This idea, accepted from the beginning of the organization, received a definite and final consecration when, in 1840, Gregory XVI formally erected it into a universal pontifical society. Sixteen years after the first meeting the Society received welcome assistance from a second American Bishop. All France was aroused by the eloquent pleading of Bishop Flaget of Bardstown, who toured forty-six dioceses, preaching in from six to fifteen parishes of each. "Everyone," he told his hearers, "admires this mite of the poor with the power of miracles . . . which crosses the sea . . . to produce marvels which allow the infant and the aged, the poor and the unfortunate to believe themselves apostles." Flaget made the missions better known, dispelled doubts as to the expenditures of alms, convinced the donors that they were bringing relief to a great distress, and roused a new pride in the work. The preaching of Flaget was rich in returns for America.

Before we turn to the other mission societies, and before we consider the results of their work in America, a word must be said about the spirit of the Society for the Propagation of the Faith, as it is revealed in its *Rule*. According to the revised Rule of 1834 this "Society of piety and charity called the Propagation of the Faith has for its sole object to aid by its *prayers and alms* the Catholic missionaries charged with the preaching of the Gospel in lands beyond the sea." Daily prayer was to call down graces from heaven; weekly alms would aid the missions financially. The union of these two means is important. Mere money gifts could not do supernatural work. In fact, to prayer was added another force, which may leave the historian a bit cynical, but of the value of which the founders had no doubt. That very Christian force was the sacrifice or abnegation which almsgiving entailed, and which they felt would win the blessing of Almighty God on the human efforts of the missionary. Other articles in the Rule provided for the assembling and distribution of alms, for the gratuitous service of officials, and for the publication of mission news in the *Annales*. There were two self-recruiting Councils, one at Lyons, the other at Paris, each with its president elected for five years and its cashier elected for life. Alms were to be sent, not directly to individuals, but through the constituted authorities in the various missions. The *Annales* were to publish annual statements of collections and disbursements, and at the same time keep the members informed as to how their money was spent. While the Frenchman is notoriously a patriot, there is nothing in the Rule, and surprisingly little in the conduct of the officials, to indicate discrimination against other nations. When, early in the history of the Society, charges were raised of secrecy or politics or misdirection of funds the integrity and single-mindedness of the Society stood out the more clearly.

Its Spirit

We are not concerned with the grand total of the Society's contributions during the first century of its existence. Judged by mere figures, the hundred million dollars and more of the Society are pitifully overshadowed by the huge sums of the Protestant organizations. Moreover, only a fraction of this (namely, seven million dollars) went to America, and America has more than returned what she received. The most noteworthy feature of the Society's finance is the marvelous stretching, so to speak, of the sums dispersed. A few thousand dollars have been made to support a whole mission. At the end of the century seven million francs were being apportioned among seventy thousand workers, which gave an average of one hundred francs for each missionary.

Results

It was the timeliness, let us say, of the gifts that multiplied their value. Just when the American frontier was calling most desperately for spiritual aid and when the impoverished missionaries seemed to be tied to the home base, the Society of the Propagation of the Faith (and its sister societies in Germany and Austria) began to function. There was no question of salaries or of profits for those in the field. All they asked was in many instances transportation, a bare temporary sustenance, or, quite frequently, the means of adding a little additional solemnity and color to public worship. There were, of course, heavier demands for the building of churches and schools, or the liquidating of debts that impeded progress. But wherever the money was applied, none of it was ever wasted. On the contrary, its returns were augmented manifoldly by the intelligence, industry, and singleness of purpose of the men and women who were spending themselves with no ambition for personal gain. They appreciated the sacrifices of their benefactors in Europe; but they could not possibly realize as clearly as we do the value of the pioneer investment they were making.

The Austrian Foundation

Too much, perhaps, of our limited space has been devoted to the Society for the Propagation of the Faith. This French society was first in the order of time and the first to aid America. It was the most universal in its scope and most generous in the amount collected and dispersed to the missions. For Americans, however, the Vienna foundation has a peculiar

POPE PIUS XII

The one man with moral courage to defy the power
of Napoleon (Pope 1800–1823)

CARDINAL CONSALVI

Secretary of State to Pius VII and
"one of the purest glories of the
Church of Rome" (1757–1824)

JOSEPH GÖRRES

Journalist, philosopher of history, and leader of the "Munich
School" (1776–1848)

REV. JOHN LINGARD

English priest; pioneer in scholarly history in the nineteenth
century (1771–1851)

LIBRARY OF LOUVAIN UNIVERSITY

The founding in 1834 of Louvain University marked the beginning of the Church's recovery of higher
learning (the above photograph represents the Library as rebuilt after the Great War)   Keystone

interest. It was founded exclusively for America. The idea
and the first impetus came from Father Frederick Rese, a
Cincinnati priest. Its contributions all went to America, and
its published reports dealt with the American Church alone.
The annual, or nearly annual, *Berichte* carry on the inside
cover: *"Statuten des zur Unterstützung der katholischen
Missionen in Amerika gebildeten Vereines unter dem Namen
Leopoldinen-Stiftung,"* in which America is named as the
favored field of the Foundation. In the triple purpose laid
down in the first statute first place is given to "the further-
ing of greater efficiency in the Catholic Missions of America,"
subsidiary objectives being the "edification of the faithful
and their participation in the spread of the Church of Jesus
Christ in distant lands, and the erection of a monument to
the memory of the imperial Habsburg princess, Archduchess
Leopoldina of Brazil. "The remaining statutes give a fair and
authentic idea of the means and methods employed for the
ends in view. In general they were prayer and almsgiving,
daily prayers and a *kreuzer* (two and a half cents) a week.
Greater sums were solicited from the more wealthy. Membership was voluntary both as to entering and leaving the organization. Groups of ten handed their contributions to collectors,
who in turn passed the sum on to the pastor. Through the
local deans the total sum eventually reached the bishop, who
delivered it to the central bureau in Vienna. Disbursements
were regulated by needs, as the directors saw them. Quite
naturally, a major share of the alms went to Germans, but
there was no flagrant discrimination. During the first ten years
Cincinnati was the most favored diocese, receiving as much
as Detroit and Charleston combined (97,000 florins or about
$40,000). This is explained by the fact that the impetus to-
ward the founding of the society came from Cincinnati.
Detroit ranked second, since it was the diocese of Bishop
Rese, the founder. But practically every diocese received attention, Vincennes and St. Louis following close upon the better
known Detroit. The whole story is very similar to that of
the Lyons society even down to the low cost of administration
and the voluntary services tendered gratis. The forebodings
of Samuel F. B. Morse, who feared for the future of America

and wrote a book to reveal a deep plot of Metternich, had no foundation in fact.

Munich

The Ludwig-Missionsverein of Munich also has a glorious record, though perhaps in its origin and in its functioning somewhat less idealistic and somewhat more vulnerable to the attacks of critics. It is significant that the founder, again Father (or Bishop) Rese, thought it well to appeal to the anti-French feelings of King Ludwig; it is also significant that Ludwig in the beginning saw no utility in the prayer features of the older societies. The Propagation of the Faith charged the organization with a lack of the right spirit, and the King showed on more than one occasion that he could be ultra-nationalistic. But the Church in America has reason to be grateful to Munich, and Ludwig has found valiant defenders. He may have been sincere in his belief that close contact with the Fatherland was the best means of preserving the faith of emigrants. Others, like the famous missionary, Father Weninger, were convinced that the "language keeps the faith." King Ludwig himself was a generous soul, and Bavaria could count on no material return for the million dollars sent to the United States. But money contributions do not represent the full, or perhaps even the chief, assistance given by the Ludwig-Verein. This includes the intangible but immense labors of the teaching sisterhoods who owed their first foundations and their early prosperity to the financial support and the direction of the Munich society.

Financial Aid to America

A mere summary of statistics, though it is far from telling the whole story, may help to clarify the picture. The tabulated lists of the Ludwig-Verein, for example, show a steady increase in the total disbursements of the society and a parallel decrease in the amounts allotted to America. The best set of figures covers the years 1844–1916, and gives $892,989.23 as the American share. Up to 1862 America's percentage of the total ranged from 37½ per cent to 81 per cent. In 1875 it had dropped to 18 per cent. Five years later it was 12 per cent. During the last quarter of the century, while the society's annual donations were steadily mounting from about $56,000 to about $135,000, our share remained fairly constant in the neighborhood of $10,000. During the first three years of the

World War, 1914–1916, the total disbursements remained constant (about $100,000), while our share sank from $2,000 to $50. The striking feature in these last figures is not the small contribution but the fact that Germany was still, as late as 1916, aiding the Catholics of America.

Turning to the French society, we find America receiving $7,000,000 out of a grand total of $100,000,000 in the hundred years between 1822 and 1921.[4] It is interesting to note the slight setbacks in the more turbulent years of French history, 1830, 1848, and 1870. With few exceptions the annual collections advanced at a uniform rate from 22,915 francs in 1822 to 8,000,000 in 1918. But more interesting for us is the distribution of these funds to the various dioceses in America. Four dioceses, Charleston, Galveston, Indianapolis (including Vincennes), and Santa Fe received over $200,000; twenty-three others (among which the Philippines and Hawaii are listed) received over $100,000, and fifty-seven received less than $100,000. The older dioceses were quite significantly dropped from the list in the 1860's. Albany, Alton, Baltimore, Boston, Brooklyn, Buffalo, Chicago, Cincinnati, Columbus, Dubuque, Fort Wayne, Hartford, Indianapolis, Louisville, Newark, Philadelphia, Pittsburgh, and Portland, Maine, were apparently able to stand on their own feet before 1870. St. Louis received its last subvention as late as 1872.

But once again, and in conclusion, the importance of the Catholic Mission Aid Societies cannot be measured by the amount of money they gave. The strategic placing of their limited funds is an extremely vital element in their charity. Every dollar was stretched, as it were, to its utmost efficiency. There was little or no waste and no marginal profits for middlemen. Donations frequently acted like a catalytic agent to release greater energies. And over and above the cash subventions there was the incalculable service rendered by transporting missionaries, men and women, to the fighting front. The effective work of a teaching sisterhood, for instance, bore no proportion to the relatively small sums required to set them up in a frontier community. In the hands of a missionary

---

[4] Cf. Edward John Hickey, *The Society for the Propagation of the Faith* (Catholic University, 1922), Appendix, pp. 187–189.

giant like the Austrian Jesuit, Father Weninger, the generous alms of the Leopoldine Foundation (about $25,000 in twenty-five years, 1852–1887) were multiplied many times over in their effects.

A historian of the Lyons society, writing in 1912, gives an insight into the spirit in which the mission work was carried on.

> An astonishing fact, he tells us . . . marks the close of the century. Speculators and economists laud the resources, salubrity and charms of a country; they do not always succeed. The publications of the Propagation of the Faith speak of nothing but privations, perils and struggles; the more they darken the picture, the more they enkindle zeal for the Missions, especially if they open the sombre perspective of martyrdom.[5]

The Mission Spirit

In all ages the spirit of the missions is the spirit of the Church at its best. And the spirit which animates an institution is the most important thing in it. There are those, however, who prefer to study results, achievements. For them we have from the pen of the Bishop of Cincinnati a typical, though incomplete, résumé of a variety of activities. Nearly one hundred years ago, in 1839, Bishop Purcell wrote:

> Constant as has been the drain on the charity of Europe by the nascent churches of the East and the West, that charity is still inexhaustible. It has enabled us to liquidate a large portion of the debt which we had contracted in the building of churches throughout the state, in the purchase of the orphan asylum, in the support of the seminary and the maintenance of the clergy. It has furnished vestments for the sanctuary and paintings to decorate our churches. It has replenished our libraries with books of science, learning and piety; it has added to the number of our missionaries.[6]

When he acknowledged the "charity of Europe" the Bishop may have had other agencies in mind, but what he wrote can be applied directly to the Mission Aid Societies. They were largely responsible for the optimism and the sense of security

---

[5] Quoted by Hickey, *op. cit.*, p. 140.
[6] J. H. Lamott, *History of the Archdiocese of Cincinnati*, p. 188.

that had arisen since the first Bishop of Cincinnati, Edward Dominic Fenwick, appealed to Europe sixteen years earlier. At that time the Bishop, with a few scattered churches in his immense diocese, almost despaired as he matched his annual revenue of eighty dollars against a crushing debt and the needs of his six thousand poor immigrants. Thirteen years later, in 1852, the diocese had emerged from the nursery stage and was beginning, in its turn, to aid the foreign missions by a donation of 10,000 francs to the Society of the Propagation of the Faith. *Mutatis mutandis*, the story of Cincinnati is true of a hundred other dioceses. Since the birth of the Republic the Catholic Church in America has multiplied its membership by nearly one thousand and spread its influence to every corner of the land. In that tale of progress the Mission Aid Societies have written an essential chapter. They arose at a time of renewed vitality in Europe; through their "pennies of the poor" they produced a remarkable vitality in America and particularly in the communities along the American Frontier.

NAPOLEON AND AFTER

IX

THE CHURCH AND NAPOLEON

ON AUGUST 22, 1799, PIUS VI DIED AT VALENCE IN France, an exile and a prisoner of the Revolution. He was buried by his helpless friends in a common graveyard, and the Administrator of the Department of Drôme reported to Paris: "The late pope has just died; we have seen the last of them and the end of superstition." The exultant boast was echoed from Berlin: "We shall have no more popes!" During the Revolution the Church had been robbed of her property, persecuted in her faithful clergy, attacked in her divine constitution, supplanted by a new cult. Voltaire, to all appearances, had triumphed in his work of destruction. The disciples of Rousseau had ruled out the supernatural to transform a denatured Christianity into a new religion for humanity. The hour was a dark one for the Church of Christ. But it was the gloom before the Resurrection.

Easter Sunday, 1802, the grand old cathedral of Notre Dame was bright with color and gay with happy faces. Lights blazed on the high altar, and the banners of France floated over the crowded nave. Napoleon Bonaparte was there with his fellow consuls and his ministers. Foreign ambassadors and officers of the army assisted at the solemn Mass and joined in the *Te Deum* for the Concordat and the restoration of religion in France. Pius VI had been succeeded by another Pius, and the Directory had given way to a victorious general who was to bring order out of chaos. Popes may die, but the Pope never dies. The Church could be driven into the Catacombs, but she would emerge purified and with the principle of life still strong within her.

Much had happened since the death of Pius VI. While the friends of the future arbiter of Europe were preparing and executing the *coup d'état* of Brumaire, twenty-four of the

The Concordat

95

thirty-six living Cardinals were gathering at Venice under the protection of Austria. There the conclave opened on November 30, 1799, and on March 14, 1800, Cardinal Barnabo Chiaramonti, Bishop of Imola, was elected Pope and chose the name of Pius VII. On July 3rd he was safely installed in Rome, and Napoleon Bonaparte was moving toward an understanding with him.

Napoleon[1] had no special love for the Church of his baptism. He was a Mohammedan in Egypt; he would be a Catholic in France. From political and interested motives he took the initiative in restoring the old religion. If this is a tribute to his statesmanship, it is also evidence at once of the vitality of Christianity and of its value to the nation. The satanic Revolution had failed in its efforts to kill the Church. It had forced the clergy and the people to choose between fidelity to conscience and allegiance to the new regime; it had made its most fateful and inexcusable blunder in demanding the oath to support the Civil Constitution of the Clergy. From that criminal move had flowed the division of the nation, the flight of the king, and the worst features of the Terror. Its blasphemous cult of Reason was mere madness; its Theophilanthropy, a ridiculous fad; its Constitutional Clergy, a pitiable and ineffectual anomaly. Napoleon took in the situation at a glance. France needed the internal peace which could come only through reconciliation with the Vicar of Christ. Napoleon the genius among statesmen did what Napoleon the nominal Catholic would not have done. He turned to Rome because he saw in the Church an indispensable ally in his work of regenerating France and, perhaps also, a powerful prop of his future Empire.

On the eve of the battle of Marengo he assembled the clergy of Milan, and delivered an address which was intended to prepare the ground for later negotiations. "A society without religion," he told them, "is like a ship without a rudder. As soon as I can confer with the new pope, I hope to have the happiness of removing whatever obstacles may stand in the

Napoleon
Restores
Religion

---

[1] There is a steadily expanding volume of literature on Napoleon. For his relations with the Pope the Memoirs of Cardinals Consalvi and Pacca are especially helpful. No attempt is made in this chapter to alter the more obvious and generally accepted view of the subject.

way of a complete reconciliation of France with the head of the Church." Immediately after the battle he sent Cardinal Martiniana to Rome with a message that proved he was in earnest. He wanted religion in France; he was determined to brush aside the remains of Gallicanism; he would have a renovated clergy. If the Pope was "reasonable," he would grasp the situation and realize that working in harmony with the First Consul he could bring the French nation back into the Church. "Go to Rome," he concluded in his grandiose manner, "and tell the Holy Father that the First Consul desires to make him a present of thirty million Catholic Frenchmen." The first step had been taken that was to lead to the Concordat.

The Concordat of 1801 marked the dawn of a new era for the Church in Europe and in the world. Aside from the fact that it swept away the Civil Constitution and stopped the persecution in France, thereby enabling a renovated and purified Church to begin anew its labors for a spiritually starved nation, it inaugurated a policy which was to be characteristic of nineteenth-century relations between Church and State. There had been important concordats before. That of 1516, between Leo X and Francis I, had notwithstanding its evil features been supremely important in keeping the kings of France free from the major temptation of greedy princes during the religious upheaval of the sixteenth century. But the nineteenth century was pre-eminently the age of concordats with its thirty or more such agreements modeled on that of Napoleon and Pius VII.

In earlier centuries when Canon Law was in honor throughout Europe a concordat was regarded as a series of concessions made by the superior spiritual power to an inferior civil power. But in the nineteenth century the prevailing tendency outside purely ecclesiastical circles was to reverse the roles and to consider the concordat a grant of privileges made by a sovereign prince or his government to a Church which was ranked with other subordinate corporations within and under the omnipotent State. The changed conception is indicative of a new mental attitude which was characteristic of the nineteenth century. Ever since the drafting of the Civil Constitution of the Clergy the Church has had to struggle against the

The New Era

tendency to treat her as, at best, a mere department of state. In general, however, the Church has been willing to co-operate with the civil power as she finds it. In the presence of material strength and in the absence of a saner mentality on the part of rulers, the concordat has been the only feasible means of avoiding disorder and continual conflict. The Holy Father has been practically forced to waive some of the prerogatives of a divinely appointed head of Christendom and to descend to a level of equality with upstart princes who control his rebellious or helpless children. He has generally been content when the essential rights of the Church are secured by a sort of bilateral contract entailing mutual obligations on the part of the contracting parties. It is, furthermore, a sad commentary on the political morality of the modern world, to say nothing of its spiritual degeneracy, that civil authorities, forgetful of elemental justice, have too often evaded or ignored the terms of an arrangement which should be accorded at least the dignity and binding force of a treaty between sovereign powers. Such was the condition in the nineteenth century that the papal acceptance of concordats as the lesser of two evils often proved to be only a temporary makeshift. Pagan principles and a lack of fundamental sincerity frequently perturbed the relations of Church and State. But for all that the Napoleonic Concordat was to continue to regulate ecclesiastical affairs in France down to its arbitrary and unwarranted abrogation by the Third Republic in 1905.

One can imagine the difficulties with which Pius VII had to contend when he undertook to treat with the new Caesar who now pretended to play the part of a new Constantine. Three years previous, as Bishop of Imola, the future pope had given expression to his own conciliatory attitude. Revolutionary democracy, he had written, needed Christ. France was now a nation worth saving, and he was willing to forget the past. But such dispositions were rare among his entourage. Those who had suffered during the nightmare of the Revolution were little inclined to acknowledge the wisdom or justice of any concession to those who had robbed and persecuted the Church. There were prelates who looked upon themselves as confessors of the Faith, and who were averse to any sacrifice

Obstacles

of their former rights and privileges. There were the Bourbon princes and the emigré nobles who posed as champions of the ancient Church and protested against any arrangement with the usurper of the Bourbon throne.

But an even greater obstacle was encountered by Napoleon in the rabid antagonism of the Jacobin element in France. It was hard for the disciples of Voltaire to admit a return to Christianity and the consequent overthrow of their godless principles. Add to this the fear of having to disgorge the sequestered wealth of the old Church and we have as so often in the past, motives sufficient for the determined opposition which the First Consul had to meet among the supporters of his popularity. Napoleon could disregard the whining of the Constitutional Clergy who had betrayed their conscience to make a weak compromise with the Revolution. In his eyes they were merely contemptible. But it was not easy to quiet the reclamations of powerful infidels who regarded a restoration of religion as treason against the principles for which the Jacobins had fought and of which the First Consul was considered the heir and protector. Nonetheless a religious pacification was necessary, and Napoleon was determined to bring it about for the sake of France as well as for the increase of his own prestige and power.

Bonaparte had made the first advances, but it did not suit his policy to let his initiative appear too openly. Hence his next move was to insist that the negotiations take place in Paris. On the other hand, Cardinal Consalvi, the papal Secretary of State, a master of diplomacy equal to the First Consul himself and superior to any of his ministers with the possible exception of the astute Talleyrand, was on the alert to safeguard the dignity and interests of the Holy See. The battle of Marengo had been won on June 14, 1800. On September 4 a letter from Talleyrand to Cardinal Martiniana intimated that the Pope would have to send his representatives to Paris. Archbishop Spina and the General of the Servites, Father Caselli, were accordingly sent with instructions to discuss matters and report to Rome, but without plenipotentiary powers. Consalvi had thus effectually checked any attempt to deceive or browbeat the papal envoys, and had saved the

Negotiations

Pope from the humiliation of treating on equal terms with the slippery apostate, Talleyrand. The Concordat was eventually signed at Paris, but only after Consalvi himself had appeared on the scene.

Preliminary negotiations began on November 8, tentative projects being submitted by both sides. The First Consul insisted on getting for himself the Bourbon prerogative of nominating all French bishops; Monsignor Spina countered with a demand for recognition of Catholicism as the religion of the State. Talleyrand set himself to obtain special concessions for the married clergy with an eye, of course, on his own sacrilegious union. Here, Pius VII intervened to assure the First Consul that such cases would be dealt with in a kindly manner, but according to the rules and ecclesiastical discipline. This was not to the liking of Talleyrand, and even before the Pope's final decision on the case of the married clergy could reach Paris, the wily intriguer had prevailed upon Bonaparte to forward an ultimatum, threatening to break off all discussion if his terms were not accepted within five days.

The ultimatum arrived in Rome on May 29, and was presented by Cacault, the French agent. But Cacault was determined that the business of the Concordat should not fail. It was at his suggestion that Consalvi set out for Paris, where he arrived on June 20. Talleyrand had retired, and Bonaparte was face to face with a diplomat whose coolness and presence of mind was a match for every subtle art his genius could command, with a priest before whom his sallies of rage and his threats were impotent, with a man whom he had to admire in spite of himself.

Projects and counterprojects continued. Bonaparte forgot his ultimatum, and finally, on July 15, 1801, this battle of giants ended with the signing of a concordat satisfactory to both parties. This solemn treaty between the spiritual and the temporal power was to have, after the formal sanction of the Pope and the French Government, the force of law in Church and State. It was not a realization of the Christian ideal, but under the circumstances it was a consummation worthy of the *Te Deum* at Notre Dame the following Easter Sunday.

The Concordat Completed

The text of the Concordat comprises a preamble and seventeen articles. In the preamble the Catholic religion is declared the "religion of the great majority of French citizens and in particular of the Consuls." Article one secures freedom of public worship, but contains the famous "police regulations" clause which was later to nullify, in the "Organic Articles," much that was agreed upon in the Concordat itself. Article two calls for a new circumscription of dioceses. Article three demands a spirit of sacrifice on the part of those bishops who shall be asked to resign their sees for the good of the Church, or in the event of refusal, shall be deprived of their sees by the Holy Father. According to article four the First Consul is to nominate the bishops and archbishops of the new dioceses, and the Holy Father is to confer canonical institution following the forms of the Old Regime. The next two articles impose an oath of fidelity on the bishops and clergy of second rank. In articles nine, ten, and eleven the bishops are accorded the right to delimit parishes, appoint parish priests, and establish a cathedral chapter as well as a diocesan seminary. Articles thirteen and fourteen promise the restoration of church buildings but provide an amnesty for the possessors of confiscated Church property. For the rest, the Government undertakes to support the clergy and to permit pious foundations. The First Consul is to have all the prerogatives of the Bourbon kings; in the event, however, that he should not be a Catholic a new arrangement would be in order.

But the great Concordat, which was in many respects a step backward to the Old Regime, was soon to reinstate more explicitly the errors and abuses of Gallicanism. To it were added, under the pretext of necessary police regulations, seventy-seven "Organic Articles." Against these Pius VII protested in vain. For Napoleon some slight extenuation of this apparent trickery and insincerity may lie in the fact that he had to placate the anti-Christian Jacobins. The whole tenor of the Organic Articles was to nullify the beneficent provisions of the Concordat itself. Administered by an unfriendly Government, they could serve to rivet the chains of slavery on a helpless Church. Moreover, they would stand as a precedent and a model in future diplomacy.

But great as was the disappointment of the Holy Father

The Organic Articles

he could well congratulate himself on the prospect of brighter days for religion in Europe. The irreligious policy of the Revolution had been definitely abandoned. The "Son of the Revolution" had disowned the Civil Constitution and publicly proclaimed that the Nation could not get on without the Church it had tried to destroy. It is more than a coincidence that at the moment when the Concordat was solemnly published Chateaubriand's *Genius of Christianity* appeared to warm hearts chilled by the cynicism of Voltaire and to guide minds led astray by Rousseau, and that this defense of the old Faith was favorably reviewed in the *Moniteur*, the official publication of the new regime. It was tantamount to a sanction of Napoleon in favor of the revival of religion.

The Imperial Coronation

Two years later the Cathedral of Notre Dame was again the scene of a gorgeous ceremony. The First Consul had become, by senatorial decree, Emperor of the French, and the Pope had, after much distressing opposition from Bourbon supporters, made the painful journey to Paris to grace the occasion with his presence. Consalvi's Memoirs tell the story of humiliation and studied insult at the hands of the new Charlemagne. The Holy Father was forced to play the part of a mere imperial chaplain. The whole affair was prophetic of the ten years of unbridled impudence that were to follow in the dealings of Napoleon with the Head of the Church. It betrayed also something akin to petty jealousy in the upstart Emperor, who would not share his new glory, much less his power, with another. He knew that the Pope had "traversed France through a population on their knees." After the coronation he shunned the company of the Pope. "The people," he confessed, "will travel one league to see me, they will go thirty leagues to be blessed by the Pope." Even the most elementary marks of civility were boorishly denied the Vicar of Christ. On the morning of the coronation he was needlessly forced to wait an hour and a half, to yield the place of honor to Napoleon, to look on like a mere spectator while Napoleon crowned himself and Josephine. He had come to Paris with the hope of effecting modifications in the Organic Articles and of otherwise improving the relations of France with the Church. In everything he seemed to fail, but there were real, though intangible, good results. The sincere sympathy of the people was aroused by the unjust treatment he received, and religious fervor was awakened by his saintly bearing and his self-effacement.

Open conflict between the Pope and the Emperor was inevitable. Pius VII put his conscience and his duties as Father of Christendom above every personal consideration; Napoleon regarded the Pope as a mere servant and the Church as an appendage and a prop of his Empire. Pius VII would not purchase peace by betraying the interests of the Church;[2] Napoleon demanded a cringing, sycophant attitude in those under his power. Opposition to the Emperor meant progressively greater sufferings as the ambitions of the tyrant soared to dizzy and more dangerous heights. **Conflict**

Difficulties multiplied. Aside from the tension created by the Emperor's high-handed treatment of the French clergy and his almost blasphemous revision of the Catechism, there was the chain of specific tyrannies during the ten years following the coronation. Trouble started with the Pope's refusal in 1805 to dissolve the marriage of Jerome Bonaparte and his American wife. Confiscation of Papal territories broadened the breach. Then Napoleon launched his desperate and foolhardy Continental Blockade, and whatever sympathy there may have been for the helpless victim of imperial aggression was turned to admiration for the Pope who dared to stand alone against the orders of the master of Europe. Pius VII refused to close his lands to the commerce of England. General Miollis entered Rome at the command of Napoleon, and a year later, May 17, 1809, the Papal States were incorporated into the Empire. The answer of the Pope was an excommunication in general terms of all who had violated the rights of the Church. Napoleon had met the one man who had the moral courage to defy his power. The date of this definite and final rupture is to be noted. Napoleon's star was apparently still in the ascendant. He could con- **Pius VII Resists Tyranny**

---

[2] Bourbon supporters who were opposed to the Concordat contrasted what they considered the weakness of Pius VII with the strong resistance of Pius VI. Pius VI *per conservar la fede perde la sede:* Pius VII *per conservar la sede perde la fede.*

temptuously sneer at papal excommunications which would not, he trusted, make "their weapons fall from the hands of my soldiers." The haughty words would be recalled after the dramatic disaster on the frozen snows of Russia, but historians trace the beginnings of retribution to the national rising in Spain, and that rising was largely the work of the Spanish clergy indignant at the injustice done to the Head of the Church.

Five years of exile and suffering awaited Pius VII. The excommunication bore the date of June 12, 1809; on July 6 the

Pius VII Prisoner

Pope was a prisoner, and by the middle of August he had been dragged over a painful route to Savona, on the frontier of France, while twenty-six of the Cardinals were removed to Paris. Military orders had been executed with Napoleonic speed and thoroughness. It was the apparent triumph of brute force. Pius VII was to remain a prisoner cut off from his advisers and bullied by the Emperor until the collapse of the Empire in 1814. His courage was to break momentarily in 1813, but Napoleon really never had the satisfaction of feeling that he had subdued the spirit of this lonely and defenseless old man. It was not sufficient for Napoleon's purposes to incarcerate the Pope. He needed a co-operation, either voluntary or coerced, which he failed to get. Even as a prisoner Pius VII possessed the power of weakness; he could resort to passive resistance. By simply doing nothing he could make the situation very unpleasant for the Emperor.

Twenty-seven dioceses deprived of bishops through the firm

Passive Resistance

refusal of the Pope to confer canonical institution stood as visible proof of the limitations of despotic power. The ingenuity of the Emperor was effectually balked. The Catholic Church would not function without her Head. Napoleon tried various expedients. He appointed an ecclesiastical commission in 1809; he assembled ninety-five prelates in a "National Council" in 1811; he tried to win the authorization of the Pope for an arrangement whereby canonical institution might be conferred by the Metropolitan. The National Council proved too loyal to the Pope, and was dissolved after three weeks. After another three weeks a rump Council met to

decree the validity of canonical institution at the hands of
the Metropolitan. Pius VII was hoodwinked into a sort of
approval of the decree, but expressly insisted on the provision
that the Metropolitan should act merely as his delegate and
in his name. Napoleon at the height of his power, and employing every unscrupulous means, was never more than partly
successful against an old man with justice on his side and
with a singleness of purpose that regarded only the salvation
of souls.

On April 2, 1810, Napoleon had married the Archduchess
Maria Louisa, daughter of the Habsburg Emperor. The
marriage was preceded by a divorce. The whole affair makes
an interesting and significant chapter of ecclesiastical history.
Back in 1796, before he had become famous, the young general had contracted his civil marriage with Josephine Beau-
harnais, an influential young widow who was in a position
to aid his advance to power. In 1804, on the eve of his
imperial coronation, Josephine informed Pius VII of the
irregularity of the union, and the Pope insisted upon a valid
marriage. Napoleon acquiesced only on condition that the
revalidation take place in secret. Cardinal Fesch, armed with
all the necessary dispensations, performed the ceremony.
When Napoleon, with Europe at his feet and desirous of an
heir to his Empire, which Josephine could not give him,
resolved on a union with the House of Habsburg he appealed
to the diocesan court of Paris, urging defect in form and
lack of consent as grounds for annulment. The case was
decided in his favor, and later confirmed by the Metropolitan
court. The wily Emperor had, it seems, foreseen this eventual-
ity and had, if we accept his questionable testimony, actually
withheld his consent five years earlier, thus rendering the
union with Josephine null from the beginning. But the crux
of the matter lay in the traditional direct jurisdiction of the
Pope in the matrimonial affairs of princes. The Emperor's
experience with Pius VII in the attempted divorce of his
brother Jerome made him wary of a similar check on this
occasion. Pius, however, was not so easily thrust aside. He
protested against the whole procedure, with at least this

Napoleon's
Divorce

significant result, that thirteen of the twenty-seven Cardinals who were to add color to the ceremony did not take their places in the cathedral on the morning of the marriage with Maria Louisa. The wrath of the Emperor asserted itself by depriving them of the means of support and of their cardinalatial robes. Hence the appellation: *Black Cardinals*.

The darkest hour for Pius VII came with his removal to Fontainebleau in May, 1812. Napoleon on the eve of his Russian campaign planned to curb the "obstinacy" of the Pope by throwing himself personally into the struggle. Had not his dream of world dominion been blasted it seemed humanly impossible to prevent the destruction of the temporal power of the Papacy and, what was even more serious, the introduction of Gallican principles into the very Constitution of the Church. According to Napoleon's plan the Pope was to become a mere French subject with a Curia subservient to imperial demands. Disaster in Russia moderated the pretensions of the Emperor. But one of his first acts after his return was the extorting of the so-called Concordat of Fontainebleau, which he declared a part of the civil law and forced the clergy to celebrate with a national *Te Deum*. The triumph was of short duration. The weakness of the Pope vanished with the first remonstrance of the Cardinals still faithful to him, and he retracted his concessions. What might have happened had not the War of Liberation engaged the attention of Napoleon is left to conjecture. But the front of brass had feet of clay. The Empire of the megalomaniac was about to crash. A month before his own abdication the Emperor had set his prisoner free; and on May 24, 1814, the Pope was again secure in the Eternal City.

The Congress of plenipotentiaries in their gold braid and lace which shortly after met at Vienna that same year to remake the map of Europe, to re-erect its sprawling thrones, and to repress the anarchy of the Revolution was more intent upon apportioning square miles of territory and millions of mere human beings than it was upon a restoration of religion. But apart from the new vogue of Romanticism, the experiences of the recent past had made apparent the need of religion even in the great game of politics. Moreover, the courageous conduct of Pius VII and his sufferings at the hands of Napoleon were an eloquent argument for a hearing of his representative at the Congress. That representative was Cardinal Consalvi, the saintly priest who was at the same time one of the ablest diplomats of the age.

X

AFTER NAPOLEON

THE EXTERNAL HISTORY OF THE RESTORATION PERIOD can be told briefly. After the scare of the Hundred Days the defeated Emperor was safely confined to his island prison, and the Bourbons set about the task of wiping out as far as possible even the memory of the revolutionary era. In 1817 an effort was made to abolish the Concordat of 1801 and to replace it by that of 1516. The effort failed, but the Organic Articles were for the most part dropped. The Divorce Law of 1792 was abrogated and Sunday observance reintroduced. The Charter of Louis XVIII had declared Catholicism the religion of the State. A closer union of throne and altar marked this return of the Old Regime. But this was far from an unmixed advantage for the Church. It meant a renewal of the slavery of the "Gallican Liberties." It meant also a share in the common hatred of all disappointed Liberals. Louis XVIII was a clever politician, and until his death in 1824 he rode the waves of revolution and reaction with remarkable dexterity. But when his brother, Charles X, a man of less political prudence but of more rigorous moral principles, came to the throne, the Bourbon monarchy went rapidly to its doom. The immediate cause, or rather occasion, of the fall of the Bourbons was the issuing of the July Ordinances of 1830. It was a foolhardy attempt to curb the opposition. Moreover, Charles X had not been an uncompromising defender of religion and the Church. His courage had failed, and he had weakened to the extent of permitting the Martignac ministry to attack the seminaries and the teaching congregations. Whether or not it was possible for him to save his throne and the Church in the face of the Liberal opposition is doubtful. But the fact remains that his bungling ruined the monarchy and caused much suffering to the Church. And yet, should we not rather blame the short-

The Restoration

sighted Gallicanism that sought to lean supinely on the
cushioned support of an unstable throne?

If we have devoted much space to the story of the Church
in France this is not merely because Bourbon France had
during two centuries held a central and dominant position in a
shattered Christendom. It is rather because the Revolution
gave France a ruler who was at the same time master in Italy,
in Germany, and throughout Catholic Europe. His name is
woven into the sad chapter of religious history in the German
lands, for the Church of the old Empire was to be an instrument and an aid in his plan of domination over the Habsburgs. The central event of this period was the great Secularization of 1803. Whether we regard this act of robbery as the
natural consequence of the Febronian-Josephist betrayal of
the Church or as a just punishment of Heaven on a worldly
clergy, it stands out on the very threshold of the century as
characteristic of a new spirit in the relations between the civil
and ecclesiastical powers. Divine Providence could, of course,
draw good out of evil, but the first effect of this high-handed
injustice was the prostration of religion; the more remote
results are evident in the predominance of Protestant, or rather
Liberal and anti-Catholic, culture in nineteenth-century Germany. The Church in Germany was to know humiliation and
persecution. In its present dark hour it can look back with a
consciousness of unconquerable vitality to at least three
attacks on its life that might have been fatal, but which in
fact gave birth to a new burst of energy.

The major responsibility for the Secularization of 1803 must
be laid at the door of Napoleon. To explain his action a double
motive may be assigned. He wanted to bind the petty princes
of Germany to his Empire, and this he could do in no more
effective way than by satisfying their greed. Following the
age-old policy of the Bourbons he was determined to weaken
the Habsburgs, and the withdrawal of Church lands from the
already tottering Habsburg Empire presented itself as an easy
expedient. In all this Napoleon found ready accomplices. In
fact, the idea of confiscating ecclesiastical property seems to
have been suggested by Prussia as early as 1795, when the
treaty of Basle was signed. The enervated condition of the

*The Church
Prostrate in
Germany*

*Robbing
the Church*

German Church was an open invitation to the spoilers. In the utter absence of moral scruples, which was peculiar to the period, nothing stood in the way of an arrangement that promised general and enthusiastic co-operation among the powerful, as well as stability for the future Empire of Napoleon. Rome was quietly ignored. Josephism had constituted the prince a sort of national pope in his own domain. Febronianism had smoothed the way for any bishop who wished to be pope in his own diocese. One might almost say that the Church which was being so roughly handled was not the Catholic Church at all.

The peace of Campo Formio in 1797 gave the left bank of the Rhine to France. The dispossessed secular lords, gathered with Napoleon's leave at Rastadt, to discuss indemnification. There had been precedents enough since the religious revolution of the sixteenth century. Protestant States had, in fact, been built up largely by a process of secularization. In the England of Henry VIII, in the course of the "Reformation" in Germany, at the signing of the treaty of Westphalia, in the conquests of Frederick the Great, and most recently in the French Revolution Church lands had been sequestered. At the conclusion of the Napoleonic Concordat, as earlier under Mary Tudor, the pope had been virtually forced to leave the robbers in undisturbed possession as the price of peace. If the princes had any scruple in the matter lawyers were at hand to justify the act by legal theories. In 1801, when the treaty of Lunéville confirmed and amplified the spoliations of 1797, provision was made for indemnities. At no cost to himself the victor could thus win the support of the vanquished.

A delegation met at Regensburg and in February, 1803, a decree of this imperial delegation, the *Reichsdeputationshauptschluss* legalized the robbery. Austria had acquiesced helplessly; behind the scenes Prussia, Bavaria, and the smaller States had bartered with the agents of Napoleon. It requires no effort of the imagination to picture the gloating of the Jacobin element over this blow at the Church. The losses of the Church have been tabulated: three electorates and twenty-one million florins. Prussia's gains were three times her losses to Napoleon; Baden was still more fortunate with a gain six

EMPEROR JOSEPH II OF AUSTRIA

"The Imperial Sacristan" (Emperor 1765–1790)

KING LUDWIG OF BAVARIA

Supporter of the missions (King 1825–1848)

From the painting by W. von Kaulbach — Bettmann Archive

times her loss; and Württemberg was twice as well off as before Napoleon's conquest.

Not all this, perhaps, should be counted a direct loss to religion. A portion of the ecclesiastical property had served worldly purposes. But as usual the robbing of the Church meant the robbing of the poor and the ruin of culture. Libraries and schools suffered, and on the whole, the Catholic loss ministered remotely to Protestant "Progress." There is a certain consolation in the picture of Febronian mitres tumbling into the Rhine. "Good Catholics," Cardinal Pacca wrote, "attributed the spoliation to just chastisement of Heaven drawn down by irreligion and the loose morals of the clergy." A purified and spiritualized German Church would struggle out of the agony against powerful opposition. The maladies of the Church were no longer internal; Febronianism was all but dead and Josephism was an external danger. Most important of all, Rome had to be called in, and with Rome came new vitality.

Over the distracted and crippled Church of the German lands hovered the dark shadow of Napoleon. If, as in France, his genius for order, for discipline, for organization cleared away much of the debris of the Febronian pretensions of a worldly-minded episcopacy and their luxury-loving clergy, the purpose of the conqueror was political, certainly not religious. If Napoleon showed a willingness to treat with Rome, it was only that he might secure a firmer hold on the German people. Backed by Napoleon, the Holy Father had been able to depose all who proved recalcitrant among the one hundred and thirty-five French bishops. With a stroke of the pen he had cut the ground from under a potentially schismatical Gallican Church. This was a significant preliminary move in the direction of the unquestioned primacy of the Pope which the Vatican Council was to assert so effectively in 1870. In German lands there was no such assertion of papal authority. But the political ambitions and the high-handed practice of the Emperor resulted eventually in a similar beneficent though still remote rehabilitation of integral as opposed to national Catholicism. A kind Providence was to draw ultimate good out of oppression and injustice, but this was no part of the plans of the oppressor.

Rome to
the Rescue

In the chaos and confusion, with whom was the pope to deal? The futile claim of the decrepit Habsburg Empire to speak for German Catholics may be dismissed, as it was dismissed by the complete dissolution of the Empire at the hands of Napoleon in 1806. But Napoleon himself was not easily waved aside. In France *his* Concordat had brought peace to *his* Church. His iron hand was now stretched across the Rhine. His passion for unity and uniformity in all that fell under his despotic sway naturally continued to show itself. For him it would be much easier and more in accordance with his character to control a united German Church than to bother himself with semidependent units. After 1806 he was Protector of the Confederation of the Rhine. Let the pope, then, negotiate with him. But time and the rapid movement of events were against him. The individual states of Germany and their people were powerless to move toward an understanding with the Head of the Church without the permission of the Emperor. But with the launching of his wild career of European conquest all hope of initiative on the part of Rome was frustrated. Soon the pope was a prisoner, and all that was left to the suffering Church of Germany was patience and a passive resistance to schismatical tendencies and nationalistic machinations of Dalberg, Wessenberg, and Metternich.

With the overthrow of Napoleon the way was prepared for a series of concordats. But if the Emperor was gone, his

More Concordats

spirit remained, for good and for evil, to influence negotiations with the Holy See. Prussian policy was belligerently Protestant, while in nominally Catholic regions there was plenty of antipapal, anticlerical "philosophy," whether we call it Jacobin or Josephist, to poison the minds of statesmen and ambitious clerics. The example given by Napoleon, therefore, is not the only, nor even, perhaps, the chief explanation of unfair and insincere dealing with the Church. Still, the fact remains that the French Concordat of 1801 and its Organic Articles served as a model in Germany.

The State-Church theories of Protestant officials have their

State Absolutism

roots at least as far back as the religious upheaval of the sixteenth century. Catholic imitations of these theories abounded since the *Aufklärung*, when the Sacristan Emperor

Joseph II made "Reason" his coregent, and rebellious prelates regarded the pope as a sort of elder brother with whose services they could readily dispense. With this background, in spite of the sobering effect of the Revolution, it is easy to surmise in what spirit the new powers rising out of the great Secularization of 1803 would function. The immense dissipation of ecclesiastical wealth entailed a notable loss of prestige for the Church and seriously hindered her work. But along with poverty came dependence upon the State and a shackling of spiritual activity that seemed to forebode the utter destruction of the Catholic faith. It looked like a reversion to pagan absolutism which made the prince a *Summus Pontifex,* a supreme dictator over the bodies and souls, the external movements and the consciences of his subjects.

A dozen technical terms were invoked to justify the arrogance of Catholic rulers who felt that some justification was needed. The so-called *jus circa sacra* was supposed to include a *jus reformandi, jus advocatiae, jus cavendi.* More specifically, the prince claimed a right of inspection and supervision over the smallest details of ecclesiastical life. To this was added the royal *Placet,* or censorship of decrees and ordinances, and the *Appellatio ab abusu,* which might reverse any judicial decision. Finally, the State controlled the hierarchy through its right of nomination to higher dignities, and the shrunken property of the Church through a sort of eminent domain. In a word, there was no limit to the power of the omnipotent State to meddle in the affairs of an enslaved Church. An Imperial decree of 1803 guaranteed, it is true, some legal protection to religion. But even in the realm of theory the protection was a shadowy thing. In practice, the various Governments were free to interpret it to suit their own pompous notions. And they did interpret it with a disregard for God and man that was Napoleonic.

Bavaria, Baden, Hesse-Darmstadt, and Nassau rivaled bureaucratic Prussia in reducing the Church to the status of a mere department and thwarting all independent action. In matters concerning marriage and all that it implied, in education on all its levels the State might be presumed to have a vital interest. But there was to be no sharing of the field with the Church, except as a barely tolerated subordinate. Even in the purely ecclesiastical province of public worship and in the training and appointment of the clergy the State dictated the slightest minutiae. Fortunately, there was enough dissatisfaction and resentment and enough heroic resistance on the part of self-respecting men among the clergy and laity to make this wholesale oppression unworkable. This, and not any sense of justice on the part of officials, was the origin of the rapprochement to Rome and the ensuing concordats.

Bavaria was the first among the German states to reach an The Bavarian understanding with the Holy See. When Cardinal Consalvi Concordat and the Bavarian representative von Häffelin signed the first draft of the Concordat on June 5, 1817, negotiations that had stretched over fifteen abortive years came to a happy ending. But a jealous government was still to revise and qualify its provisions, and finally, after the royal and the papal signatures had been duly affixed to the document, it was to be published as a mere appendix to the Bavarian Constitution of 1818. Concessions to royal absolutism, to antireligious Liberalism, and to possessors of stolen Church property had to be made. But even so, the State was not content with the hard bargain it had forced on the Church. On a smaller scale a device similar to the Organic Articles of Napoleon went far toward nullifying the freedom granted to the Church. But by 1821 an obnoxious minister, the anticlerical Montgelas, had been dismissed and a *modus vivendi* was found which smoothed the way for a Catholic revival in Bavaria.

Efforts to put order into ecclesiastical affairs in the Rhineland led to endless negotiations between consistently selfish and overbearing states on the one hand and the long-suffering Papacy on the other. But no formal concordat was concluded. The struggle with the Prussian Government resolved itself into an effort to mitigate downright tyranny. The Prussian State was autocratic, and the Prussian State was Protestant. It had acquired a million and a half Catholics, mostly in the Rhineland and in Silesia, whose religious rights it had undertaken to respect. But by every kind of political cajolery and near violence a whole bureaucracy of officials endeavored to crush the limited Catholic autonomy. Through an educational system, arbitrary marriage laws, and political ostracism Catholics were to be brought under the exclusive control of the State. In 1821 a Papal Bull was accepted by Frederick William III. It had virtually the effect of a concordat.

THE CATHOLIC REVIVAL

XI

A NEW CATHOLIC ADVANCE

A BRIEF REPETITION MAY BE IN PLACE AT THE OPENING of this chapter to introduce us to the new turn of events. The genius and the meanness of Napoleon had prepared the way for a Catholic Revival. France was crippled and in need of religion. When Napoleon opened the negotiations that ended in the Concordat of 1801, he was paying an eloquent tribute to the vitality of the Church, even in her deepest degradation. The courtier prelates of the Old Regime had identified the Church with the absolute monarchy and its parasite nobility. The lower clergy had shared the misery of the people. The Revolution split the clergy as it split the nation. It soon entered upon an altogether unnecessary war with religion. The Church was robbed of her wealth, then attacked in her constitution. The robbery begot no martyrs, but the Civil Constitution of the Clergy forced sincere men to choose between their enthusiasm for the Revolution and their conscience. They were persecuted, guillotined, deported, forced underground or into exile. Systematic and determined efforts were made to de-Christianize France. Long before the Revolution Napoleon had seen the futility of such measures. Hence, his approach to Rome.

War on Religion in France

We have seen how, when Pius VII refused to be a tool in the enforcement of his economic war against England, he was arrested, carried off to France and loaded with indignities. The Church in her Head had reached the depths of humiliation and helplessness. But the duplicity and brutality of the emperor and the steadfast bearing of the Vicar of Christ fanned a flicker of sympathy throughout Europe. The pope could suffer persecution, but the Papacy could not die. Still, the outlook was dark and there was little enthusiasm in Catholic hearts.

Then, as we have further seen, the colossal empire collapsed. The Bourbons came back to Paris, the Pope returned to Rome, and the diplomacy of Cardinal Consalvi, the greatest churchman of the age, secured from the Congress of Vienna the restoration of the Papal States. In France the destruction done during the nightmare of the Revolution was repaired to some extent. The Catholic religion was declared the religion of the State. But the condition was not a healthy one. Everything was calculated to associate the Church with the attempt to rebuild the Old Regime. The leaders among the clergy had their faces turned toward the dead past. The Restoration in France was to be of short duration, and, notwithstanding a show of external grandeur, the situation was precarious. The vital forces of the nation seemed to be on the side of irreligion.

Looking then beyond the Rhine we have observed how the condition of the Church there was still less promising. Intoxicated in the person of her natural leaders by the *Aufklärung*, she had been enervated by Febronianism and enslaved by Josephism. In her weakened condition she had been robbed by the great Secularization of 1803 and laid prostrate at the feet of the petty princes and the Prussian Bureaucracy. Napoleon had set his heavy hand on the left bank of the Rhine. To "indemnify" the more easily manageable among the secular lords for what they had lost in the process and to secure their greedy, self-interested support he parcelled out to them the lands of the Church. It was one of those human crimes out of which Providence would eventually draw forth good. But in the temporal order it was to cripple Catholic worship, charity, and education, and at the same time to lay the foundation for the transfer of leadership in scholarly circles to the anti-Catholic and materialist North.

Josephism, which meant a State-controlled national Church, should have died with the sickly eighteenth century, but it lingered on in the courts where each little prince was pope, and in the bureaucracies where meddling officials regulated the details of religious discipline (and of doctrine) for political ends. But more deadly still was the virus of Febronianism, which struck at the divine constitution of the Church by setting up a hierarchy that could ignore the voice of Rome.

Conditions in Germany

Most of the shepherds of the flock were nonentities. A few have won an unenviable place in the history of the Church. Carl Theodor von Dalberg, for example, was not a vicious man, but in the several high offices which he held, he thought little of religion and much of enriching himself. He cringed before Napoleon, "licked his boots" we might say, and the emperor used his vanity and venality to the detriment of religion, and of the German people. Worldly Prelates

No wonder Cardinal Pacca reported to Rome: "The Church in Germany can be preserved only by a miracle." The sad feature was not that "mitres had tumbled into the Rhine." Good Catholics, to quote Pacca again, attributed the spoliation to a just chastisement from Heaven. Much worse was the fact that pseudo-philosophy was supplanting religion. Naturalism was crowding out the supernatural and the anemic Church seemed doomed to perish. Niebuhr, historian and statesman, pronounced the condition "irreparable." But where the leaders had betrayed their sacred trust there was still hope from two directions. The restored Papacy was knocking on the door of the sick society and, with the aid of a surge of vital energy from below, would ultimately bring relief and health. It is with this new vitality in the humbler members of the German Church that the following pages are concerned.

France and Germany were not, of course, the whole of Europe nor the whole of the Church. But they seemed to hold the future, and if they failed, it was hard to see from what quarter salvation could come. Metternich's Austria, it is true, still wore the trappings of the old Catholic Empire and it did render some service to the Church, but the day had passed when the Church could look to Austria for aid and protection. Italy was an uncertain quantity; the Spanish Peninsula was hopelessly decadent; the dark shadow of Russia rested upon Poland; the American Church was in its infancy; Ireland was under the iron heel of England. In the non-Catholic world there was energy and hope, but not for the things of God. Religion had been disintegrating since long before the upheaval of the sixteenth century. The issues were not so clearly defined as they are at present, but for the men who figure in the history books the Catholic Church was, for the

most part, an antiquated and slowly dying institution. Politics
and the building of states, business and industrial efficiency
were the things that mattered.

But the Spirit of God was moving among the people. Souls
grown weary of a chaotic world were turning back to the

The
Awakening
Middle Ages to build the future on the solid things of the
past. Rationalism had called up a rival in the new Romanticism. Writers sought inspiration in the past, and there
they found the glories of the nation bound up with religion
and the Catholic Church. They were chosen souls who could
appreciate the antidote to a deadening materialism and to
the radical doctrines of the French Revolution. Converts
came into the Church and wayward sons returned. Even
among those who remained outside the Church the reaction
against irreligion was a source of new life. But all this was
to be a spontaneous movement of the elite few.

Religion was sick, indeed, at the turn of the Voltairean
eighteenth century and on into the Voltairean early nineteenth
century. The malady was due to wounds inflicted upon the
Church by diabolic powers outside the fold, but even more,
perhaps, to internal disorders. The Church which the French
Revolution had tried to destroy was not a sound and healthy
organism. Its natural leaders had been weakened by long and
inglorious inaction in the debilitating atmosphere of a Gallican
court and by inhaling the poisonous fumes of "Philosophy."
A like condition prevailed in Germany, where under other
names similar diseases were at work. The bishops were
infected with Febronian, the princes with Josephist, ideas.
Both combined to set up a national Church, cut off from the
life-giving influence of Rome. Even at the capital of Christendom the condition was ominous. Pius VI had just died in
exile. His successor, Pius VII, was to have a hectic pontificate
until the dream of Napoleon was dissipated at Moscow,
Leipsig, and Waterloo.

But the Papacy was internally sound, and there was a

The Papacy
hunger for the realities of religion in souls that had been fed
on the unsubstantial trash of the "Philosophers." Napoleon's
eye discerned this double fact, and wisely realized the aid
he might receive for his projected restoration of sanity

in France from Chateaubriand's famous book, *le Génie du Christianisme*. In any other age it would have been received for what it was, a rather bombastic, uncritical appeal to emotion. But coming at the time it did, it was eagerly devoured by the spiritually starved nation. France was ripe for a reaction against the irreligious mania of the Revolution.

With Chateaubriand are linked the names of two other Frenchmen who supplemented his work, de Bonald and de Maistre. Reason and faith joined with mere eloquence. It was a union of the poet, the philosopher, and the prophet. Simultaneously with these champions of the Church in France, two German groups prepared the revival of religion in the Fatherland. They were the Münster Circle which drew inspiration and direction from Princess Amalie von Gallitzin and the South Germans under Johann Michael Sailer. During the Congress of Vienna the Bishop of Eichstätt headed an energetic defense of the Church. And at an earlier date the Redemptorist, St. Klemens Maria Hofbauer, already alluded to, carried on his remarkable apostolate at Vienna. But we are interested in laymen. To begin, then, with the writer of the book just mentioned:

Francois René Vicomte de Chateaubriand was an emigré noble who had traveled far in his wild youth. His conversion to better ideas, though not perhaps to perfect morals, occurred at the death of his mother in 1798. Through his tears he saw a new world. *J'ai pleuré et j'ai cru,* he tells us. With all the eloquence of Rousseau, with all the color and grace of the great masters, he penned his classic work on the Genius of Christianity. In it all the noblest ideals and achievements of the past were linked with the Church. Literature and art and the refinements of life, all that was best in man's dealings with his fellow man; divine truth and divine worship, which raised man nearer to God; individual freedom and virtue and vigor of mind — these are Christianity's gift to Civilization. The Bible was pitted against Homer as the great book of humanity. Catholics were taught to be proud of their Church. Admiration engendered love, and love led to belief. Voltairean cynicism was silenced; Rousseauvian sentimentality was christianized. The Revolutionary slogans:

Chateau-
briand

"Liberty, Equality, Fraternity," were claimed for Christian Democracy. Against the shallow Deism of the time was ranged in all its luster the revealed truth about God, Christ, and the Church. And pointing to the future, the author lyrically spread out the glories of the Church as mother of a chastened liberty in a Democracy made safe for the world by a high sense of duty. This was Romantic enthusiasm. It was not meant to convince by close reasoning. Rather it thrilled by its emotional appeal; it blinded by brilliance of imagery; it soothed like soft music; it made its readers *want* Christianity to be true. It was the book of the hour. It won what was needed most, a hearing for the Truth. We do not now go to it for objective history of the long progress of Christian civilization; we would not refer to it to settle an argument on a question of fact or of interpretation. The book is, itself, a historical document that reveals the mentality of the age in which it was so successful. Chateaubriand, with all his defects, was a maker of history.

Joseph
de Maistre

A kindred spirit was Joseph de Maistre. Every freshman knows his often repeated dictum: For three hundred years history had been a conspiracy against truth. At his hands the empty utopias of Rousseau and the hollow sneers of Voltaire were demolished. He regarded the Revolution as diabolic through and through, *satanique par essence*. He made an eloquent plea for authority, more specifically for the restoration of papal authority. In the Holy Father he saw the mainstay of society, the only support of the political and social order. Fifty years before the Vatican Council he flaunted papal "Infallibility" before the eyes of a world that had tried to ignore the pope altogether. Even Rome was astounded at the claims he made for the prerogatives of the Head of the Church. His chief work, *du Pape*, was written at St. Petersburg and published on his return, in 1819, to his native Savoy. It was full of exaggerations, but it served its purpose in gaining a hearing for Christianity. Joseph de Maistre deserves a place among the pioneers of Catholic thought in the nineteenth century.

Less known and less important, but still an influence in

the Catholic revival, was the Vicomte de Bonald. Where Bonald Chateaubriand spoke to the heart, he addressed himself to the reason. But his main appeal was to Tradition. His philosophical doctrine was later condemned. But his insistence on placing morals above money, and man above the machine was opportune in its wholesome effect, and showed the way to balance and a proper sense of values.

A word must be said about the early writings of Felicité Robert de Lamennais. Rough and often crude, this "irascible titan" entered the lists in defense of the universal sovereignty Lamennais of the pope. Against the Gallicans he wielded his powerful pen with telling effect. At first a hater of Democracy, he was later to become its champion. He was a priest, but more like a lay-man he fought for the freedom of the Church. He made serious mistakes, and his lamentable fall is one of the sad chapters in the story of Catholic polemics. Historians have seen in him a combination of Rousseau, Pascal, Bossuet, and Tertullian. With an "eloquence to raise the dead" he shouted to an apathetic world that there was "one true religion, only one, and that necessary for salvation." In 1817 was published his rousing *Essay on Indifference*. Even now we can meditate with profit on one of its memorable sentences. "A society is sick," he wrote, "not when it is passionate in the pursuit of error, but when it neglects and scorns the truth." His soul was aflame in its quest for truth, and for him truth and the Church of Christ were one.

Passing over to Germany, we encounter a remarkable gathering at the Münster home of Amalie von Gallitzin. This princess, "richest, grandest, most lovable soul," according to Leopold von Stolberg, recalls the French *salons* of the eight- The Münster Circle eenth century. She had shone brightly in the brilliant society of the *Philosophes*. But she was a mother, and she saw in the education of her children her first duty. Attracted to Münster and held there by two zealous educators, Fürstenberg and Overberg, she found her way back to the Catholic Faith. She made her First Communion in 1786 and began a new life as "mother of the poor and oppressed" as well as the guiding spirit of a new "Holy Family of sister souls," who gathered in her drawing room for mutual help and inspiration. When she died twenty years later, Münster had become a model for all Germany. Her son, Demetrius, had carried her name to America and was working as a pioneer priest at historic Loretto in western Pennsylvania. Her influence was spreading over Germany indirectly through men whose faith had been quickened at Münster.

Princess Gallitzin had brought to Münster her love of learning, especially of the philosophy of Plato. She owed her zeal for Catholic truth to the organizer and renovator of the Westphalian school system, Franz von Fürstenberg, and to the "teacher of teachers" and her spiritual father, Bernard Overberg. Educators can learn from Overberg and his methods. He was an efficient trainer of the clergy, director of a normal school, and an ideal catechist. Above all, he was a man of intense deep interior life, who regarded his teaching as a priestly office and who drew others by his example.

Among the members of the Gallitzin circle were men whose names stand out in German Catholic history. The future Archbishop of Cologne, Clemens Augustus von Droste-Vischering was to become the center, if not the active leader of a long struggle between the Catholic conscience and the Prussian government, which deepened the faith of Germans as no other event had done since the Reformation. Leopold von Stolberg, converted by the influence of Overberg and the princess, was to place his scholarship and literary talent at the service of the Church. His voluminous *History of the Religion of Jesus* presented Christianity in all its warmth and freshness to the learned world and won a hearing for the Church. Münster had its elite leaders who were not merely ornamental. Their spirit worked down to the lower classes and spread abroad to other leaders. Stolberg, through his writings, and Droste-Vischering in person were largely responsible for this. But there were also the occasional visitors who came to refresh and stimulate their faith at Münster.

Among these was Johann Michael Sailer. He had been a Jesuit novice, but was forced to turn to a new career when the Society of Jesus was suppressed in 1773. Practically, the change meant merely the dropping of a name, for his later activity down to the age of seventy-eight, when he became

Johann Michael Sailer

LEOPOLD VON STOLBERG

Convert and historian of the
Münster group (1750–1819)

ANCOIS RENÉ VICOMTE DE
CHATEAUBRIAND

Genius of Christianity aided in
ring sanity to France (1768–1848)

ST. JOHN BOSCO

The beloved "Don Bosco," friend of the urchins of
Turin and founder of the Salesians, is one of the
great figures of his age (1815–1888)

Bishop of Regensburg, was very much that of the Religious engaged in educational and literary work. As professor at Ingolstadt and Landshut, and even more, it may be, by his forty-odd volumes of published writings he "formed a school of holy priests, ready for the fray." He has been called the Francis of Sales of Germany. In his deep charity, his habitual serenity, and the vigor of his faith he bore an outward resemblance to the Saint Bishop of Geneva, though there is little likelihood of his canonization. He was an inspiration and a guide to Catholics and Protestants alike. He taught them 'how to pray," and in so doing deepened the faith of Catholics and brought non-Catholics unconsciously nearer to the Church.

Sailer's apostolate spread over Germany. He was instrumental in placing Droste-Vischering in the archiepiscopal see of Cologne and Melchior Diepenbrock in that of Breslau. But his hand is best seen in the formation of Ludwig I, King of Bavaria, who for a quarter of a century was the main support of Catholic activities in Germany. The name of Ludwig calls to mind the Ludwig-Verein and the "School of Munich," elsewhere discussed in this volume. Sailer's ambition was to prepare men for the nineteenth century, when ecclesiastics "must know more, be more active, and be ready to suffer more" than in former times.

Italy, too, had her great Catholics, overshadowed though they were by the great popes. Among them we may here recall Alessandro Manzoni, a poet; Don Bosco, the canonized teacher and social worker comparable to Vincent de Paul; and Giuseppe Toniolo, a professor of economics with a deep appreciation of spiritual values. Manzoni, in the first half of the century, used the novel to drive home very wholesome political, social, philosophical, moral, and religious truths. Don Bosco, previously referred to here, displayed a marvelous efficiency and resourcefulness in his efforts to safeguard the faith of street urchins, to bridge the gulf between the Vatican and the Quirinal, and to allay the anticlerical prejudices of Italian politicians. Toniolo flayed the injustice of economic Liberals, and preached a Democracy in which "the activity of all should tend to promote the well-being of all, and in particular of the

The Revival in Italy

lowest classes." To meet a de-Christianized modern culture
which had created "a yawning abyss between the Almighty
and the average man" Toniolo called for sacrifice, love, and a
sense of duty, for a leveling of the hierarchical social pyramid
which had placed a favored few at the apex of society. His
work lives on in the *Rerum Novarum* of Leo XIII.

Other names, perhaps, should appear in this brief survey
But the persons mentioned form a fairly complete list and
indicate clearly enough how the Spirit of God was working
Under the influence of the Romantic movement, or merely by
way of reaction against the radical Revolution, they laid the
foundations and determined the structure of later building, at
least for leaders among the laity. They had shown that the
Church was not slumbering. But the irreligious element was
also awake, and conflict was inevitable. There would be persecution at times, and always struggle. Old ghosts of ecclesiastical and papal tyranny would be dragged forth, but the
Church was clearly on the side of liberty. Montalembert
O'Connell, and Görres fought for freedom from oppression
and in defense of common rights and justice. No fair-minded
man at the present day would uphold the Penal Laws of England, or the pretensions of the Prussian bureaucracy, or the
University monopoly in France. In the name of Humanity, as
well as of Religion, Catholics can claim the approval of
history.

XII

CATHOLIC LIBERALISM

OCTOBER 16, 1830, MARKED THE INAUGURATION OF A most remarkable journalistic venture. During more than twenty years previous Félicité de Lamennais had fought the enemies of truth and religion. His prestige had won the ardent *L'Avenir* support of Charles Réné Forbes Comte de Montalembert, and the Abbé Henri Lacordaire, the future peerless orator of Notre Dame. The July Revolution had swept away the Bourbon Monarchy and set up the "citizen king," Louis Philippe. A charter of liberties proclaimed the dawn of a new Democracy. But France was the heir of a historic past, crowned and transformed by the cataclysm of the Revolution. In her veins the fever of Jacobinism and virus of Voltairean "philosophy" were rampant still. Catholics generally, and the higher clergy in particular, benumbed by the lethargic chill of Gallicanism, were yearning for a return of the Old Regime. The burst of new life after the Napoleonic Concordat on which we have dwelled, and the apparent recovery of religion under the Bourbons, had restored a measure of power to the Church, but had left her still clothed with the trappings of a bygone age to face the anticlerical forces that ruled the State. Conflict was inevitable; it was merely a question of methods to be adopted. Abroad, in Ireland, Daniel O'Connell had carried the Church into the political arena and won the battle for Catholic Emancipation, while in Belgium a dominant Catholic majority had fraternized with the Liberals to write a modern constitution. In the United States the Church was thriving in spite of, if not by reason of, her separation from the State. In these conditions the program of *l'Avenir* was formulated. Its principles and its general policy grew out of the needs of the time. Its problems arose as much from the inertia of Catholics as from the insincerity of the enemies of religion. Its ultimate failure was due to the exaggerations and lack of prudence and tact on the part of its leader as well as to such of its doctrines as, in the excited state of the public mind at that period, were positively dangerous.

This brings us to the subject of Catholic Liberalism with which this chapter is concerned.

Catholic Liberalism is hard to define.[1] The elusive term covers the tendencies, tactics, and theoretical system of those who, while striving to keep within the bounds of orthodoxy, accepted the so-called "modern liberties" and urged the Church to take her place boldly and, without leaning on the State, in the Revolutionary society of the early nineteenth century.

"You tremble before Liberalism," wrote Lamennais; "catholicize it and the world will be saved." But the mighty Titan, whose literary power did so much to galvanize the struggling Catholics of France into new life, failed in his enthusiasm to distinguish between Catholic Liberalism and the almost inevitable lowering of Catholic ideals, which is best named Liberal Catholicism.

It is well at the outset to state that the movement which was launched in 1830 was almost immediately disowned by the Church and that its leader died an apostate. Chastened and modified by papal condemnation, the cause was carried forward by two of the most lovable crusaders of the past century, Montalembert and Lacordaire. Opposition within the Catholic camp was intense and often bitter. For Louis Veuillot, the Catholic Liberal was neither Catholic nor Liberal, and this incomparable journalist wielded his uncompromising, vitriolic pen against every attempt to conciliate the enemies of Rome. The *Syllabus* in 1864 and the Vatican Council seemed

---

[1] Besides general Church histories and a number of monographs on the leaders of the Catholic Liberal movement there is an abundant periodical literature in English. Orestes A. Brownson wrote voluminously on this typically Brownsonian topic. But by far the best available account of the movement for historical sequence, interpretation, critical estimate, and use of primary sources, is that of C. Constantin in the *Dictionaire de théologie catholique*, IX, pp. 506–629. This long article is equivalent to a fair-sized book, and is a congeries of direct quotations from primary sources, particularly from *l'Avenir*. The subjoined bibliography contains all the best works in French. Needless to remark, the papal encyclicals are an indispensable source.

to vindicate Veuillot, but with changing circumstances Leo XIII adopted measures which would have delighted the heart of Montalembert and his friends.

But before proceeding further one should know the remarkable leaders who carried the banner of Catholic Liberalism in order to understand the movement itself. It is all but impossible to separate men so wholeheartedly in earnest from their work. Let us, however, begin by striving to obtain a summary survey of their ideals, particularly on the perennial problem of Church and State. To the age of Godless Liberalism they proclaimed a new era of God *and* Liberty.

Against a decrepit but still persisting Gallicanism they were aggressively ultramontane. Christt was the King of all nations, and the pope, His Vicar on earth. Social order, and consequently the State, depended on truth, justice, and religion. The Church must be free to pursue her divine mission of saving society. But she needed no privileges. She must cease to lean on the broken reed of official protection — an enslavement. The Concordat, and more specifically government nomination of bishops was repudiated. The most extreme of practical (or impractical!) demands was for the suppression of the Budget of Worship. True, the wholesale spoliations of the past had given the clergy a just title to support by the robber State; but, argued Lamennais, the Government had forgotten that it owed the clergy an indemnity and regarded its doles as pay for service and weak-kneed subservience. Finally, independence of action and renewed life could come only through complete separation of Church and State. A union of the two, resembling the union of soul and body, would be the ideal. But in the circumstances the ideal was impossible. Instead of a Church animating and inspiring the State, while the State placed its material forces at the service of the Church, Catholics were faced with the danger of a State-Church in which religion would be administered like agriculture, the customs, or the army. The Church needed only liberty; she must forget the past with its privileges and its slavery.

State Control Repudiated

But what would the Church get in return for relinquishing her historic position and renouncing in practice a portion of hed divine rights? The answer was that the power of truth and

Freedom Under the Law

a resurgent vitality within the Church would compensate for apparent losses. Catholics should take their stand on the *Charte* of 1830, and insist on their rights as Frenchmen. They should admit, and use to the full all the "modern liberties"; political and civil liberty, economic liberty, liberty of speech and of the press, liberty of teaching and of assembly, liberty of conscience and of worship. If this meant according an equal freedom to error and irreligion, this was regrettable, but had to be permitted. The slogan was: *toutes les libertés pour tous.* No man had an inherent right to believe and act as he liked; demagogy and mob fury, absolute popular sovereignty and amoral diplomacy were wrong. But for individuals and for nations arrived at maturity the unavoidable abuses of freedom had to be tolerated as a concomitant of wider liberty.

But the journalistic dictatorship of Lamennais and the influence of *l'Avenir* stirred up a storm of opposition. The whole

Opposition program was censured by the bishops and denounced to Rome. The three leaders (Lamennais, Lacordaire, and Montalembert) suspended publication and appealed in person to Gregory XVI. Their reception was chilling. On August 15, 1832, the encyclical *Mirari Vos* crippled the movement. The leaders were not mentioned by name, but their fundamental errors and dangerous tendencies were condemned. In the disturbed condition of Europe the Pope had to disown what looked like indifferentism in religion and rebellion in civil affairs. Most emphatically he reprobated the major thesis of Separation of Church and State.

In the subsequent history of Catholic Liberalism we find a lack of unity. Lamennais, at first submissive and then recalcitrant, was condemned in person in 1834 and spent the last twenty years of his life in bitter criticism of all authority. But his two disciples, loyal Catholics still, though valiant crusaders for liberty, were to give long years of service to the Church — Montalembert as orator, writer, and organizer in the House of Peers and on the public platform; Lacordaire chiefly in the pulpit of Notre Dame and as restorer of the Dominicans to France. Largely through their efforts the Revolution of 1848 found the Church enjoying a public favor she had not known in the earlier Revolutions. The *Syllabus* and the encyclical *Quanta Cura,* of 1864, seemed to reiterate the anathemas of *Mirari Vos,* while the Vatican Council was hailed as a triumph for the enemies of the Catholic Liberals. But with the end of the long "martyrdom" of Pius IX and the advent of Leo XIII much of what was good in the campaign for a *modus vivendi* with modern society was salvaged. In his masterly encyclicals Pope Leo was as clear and definite in defining and defending eternal truths as was any of his predecessors, but he will be remembered for his habitual readiness to work in harmony with whatever forces were not incurably evil in the modern world. The *Ralliement,* his urging of die-hard Royalists to rally to the support of the Third Republic, is a crowning example of his attitude in practical politics. On the other hand, the rabid anticlericalism of French Liberals and the eventual Separation of Church and State by arbitrary act of an atheist clique seemed to justify the intransigence of Catholic opponents of Liberalism, while the false philosophies that festered to a head in Modernism revealed only too clearly the prudence of the Church in curbing the enthusiasm of those who were too eager for a compromise with the nineteenth century.

Because the Catholic Liberals battled so bravely; because, in fact, of their very mistakes, it is easier for the Catholics of today, than it had been for Leo XIII, to adopt the proper attitude toward the modern world. They taught Catholics not to fear liberty and to fight for their rights in the political arena; they shook the Catholics of France loose from the enervating grip of the Old Regime; they deprived anticlericals of every pretext for hating the Church as the enemy of the modern State. At the same time, the check put upon them by the popes vindicated the dominion and the rights of God, and effectually stopped a drift toward indifferentism and social atheism.

XIII

THE CHURCH IN GERMANY

THE STORY OF THE CHURCH IN THE TERRITORIES UNDER Prussian domination a hundred years ago is typical of one phase of her history throughout the nineteenth century.[1] A despotic state in the person of an autocrat king and a group of rationalist ministers undertook to crush a Church without leaders or led only by a weak-kneed hierarchy. The struggle, which in the beginning had the appearance of a slow strangling of a half-willing victim, was concerned with a point of discipline and a point of doctrine. There was the moral question of mixed marriages and the intellectual or theological question of Hermesian philosophy, which has itself been called an attempted "mixed marriage" of Faith and Reason. Intrigue, deception, and a process of lulling to sleep of potential opposition was at first the successful policy of the government, and the outlook for religion was disheartening. But after some incidental bungling and slipping the bureaucrats turned to violence. Two archbishops were thrown into prison, and for a moment the strong-arm methods seemed to prevail. But excess begot defeat, and apparent weakness triumphed, Rome, already aroused, became more active. A Catholic Press stirred the popular indignation. The government was forced to yield. And the Church emerged from the conflict with new vitality, a fighting spirit, and a consciousness of something to fight for.

A deeper significance lies in this example of the recurrent

---

[1] The most recent authority on the Cologne Affair is H. Schörs, *Die Kölner Wirren*, Berlin, 1927. German historians, Brück, Schnabel, Veit, and others treat it fully. Georges Goyau, *l'Allemagne religieuse*, II, pp. 161–220 gives a graphic account. The *Athanasius* (1837) of Joseph Görres, of which 10,000 copies were sold in the first month, is the most remarkable contemporary work. Pertinent documents are printed in Carl Mirbt *Quellen zur Geschichte des Papsttums und des römischen Katholizismus*.

phenomenon of near death followed by a rising from the tomb, of dark days of helpless weakness, languor and inaction giving place to a more vigorous life. In the early 1830's the situation looked hopeless. On the one hand stood a strong State, neutral by profession, Protestant by long tradition, but in its principles, its policies, and methods anti-Catholic, and in its inspiration antireligious. On the other hand, a Church in which the shepherds of the fold had all but abdicated, and the faithful were very much like starving sheep exposed to the ravages of the wolves. The king, whatever religious sentiments he may have harbored, was an autocrat with a decided anti-Catholic bias. More important, his ministers were "enlightened" bureaucrats, who had inherited the Voltairean, Jacobin prejudices of the preceding generation, and who consequently held exaggerated ideas of State supremacy. They had learned practical methods in the school of Frederick the Great and, though they might be slow to acknowledge it, in that of Joseph II. Like Frederick they had their power complex, their skepticism and religious indifference, and their contempt for spiritual ideals; like Joseph they were ready to play the sacristan or to usurp the functions of the Holy See. They were predisposed to accept and to apply Hegelian doctrines of unlimited sovereignty, and their semipagan intelligence was utterly impervious to any appeal based on arguments of right, justice, or the salvation of souls. But, as often happens, the Church had far less to fear from the tyranny of her enemies than from the cowardice, neglect, and complacency of her own leaders.

Languid Leaders

Against an embattled bureaucracy with a definite program and a host of functionaries to execute orders unquestioningly the Church could oppose only a hierarchy with a tradition of servility and sycophancy, a hierarchy that was content to suffer in silence, to connive at the State's intrusion into spiritual affairs, even to collaborate in the sorry business of tying the Church hand and foot and delivering her over to Caesar. Georges Goyau has pictured a humiliating scene of bishops prostrate before the king and begging the permission of Rome to remain so. Prostration it surely was, but there was less effort to persuade the Holy Father to bless their abject

A Servile Hierarchy

neglect of high duties than there was to keep Rome in the dark, and to prevent the pope from prodding them into action. This enervated condition will surprise no one who recalls the previous half century of German history. Prelates, high and low, had been tainted by the *Aufklärung*. They had drunk in the poison of antipapal doctrines; they had been first debilitated and distracted by excess of wealth and worldly cares, then shaken and badly scared by the stormy and uncertain years of Revolutionary and Napoleonic conquest, and finally sickened by the dizzy scramble of politics. If the Imperial Sacristan had left a heritage to the Prussian bureaucrats, the hierarchy which tamely submitted to his meddling in the smallest details of ecclesiastical life had bequeathed their spirit of acquiescence to their successors. Febronianism had been a declaration of independence from Rome. But this self-assertion was purchased by a corresponding subserviency to Vienna, and later, by a logical transfer, to Berlin. The German hierarchy had placed itself in a false position by defiance of the pope. Its false position was given a certain permanency by its cringing attitude toward the king. The remedy could come only from a reversal of the earlier process. Spiritual anemia had been induced by wantonly breaking away from the source of spiritual vitality. Health could be restored only by resuming connections with the center of Catholic life in Rome.

The Cologne Affair

On the twentieth of November, 1837, the Archbishop of Cologne, Clemens August von Droste-Vischering was arrested by order of the Prussian government and dragged off to the prison fortress at Minden in Westphalia. Three months before this memorable date Msgr. (later Cardinal) Cappaccini reported on conditions in Germany from Vienna. He calls his report a *luttuoso quadro,* a sad picture. Three months later Metternich, writing also from Vienna, summed up the situation in the statement: "Germany has never been more Catholic." Allowing for some pessimism on the part of the papal under-secretary and for the freedom of epistolary correspondence in the remark of the Austrian Chancellor, one must accord to these contrasting reports an importance in keeping with the responsible sources from which they emanate. Nor is their connection in time with the Cologne outrage merely a coincidence. The Archbishop was not himself a heroic figure. He was not a fighter, nor a man to lead a revolution. But in the circumstances he became a symbol, and his passive resistance to tyranny aroused a long-suffering and indifferent people to action.

The attack on the bureaucracy of Berlin was led by one of the greatest battlers for liberty of that age, or any other. We shall have more to say of Joseph Görres. In the present instance it was his pen, a pen "worth four army corps," which converted a tactical blunder of a powerful ministry into the rallying cry for a persecuted Church. Görres "roared like a lion," and the echo was heard in the far corners of Europe. Before the tribunal of a "Liberal" age, Görres flayed the sins of an illiberal autocracy and pleaded the cause of a persecuted Church. Against the machinations and the muddling of a bureaucratic ministry he appealed to the consciences of the people. Against the maxims of absolutism he upheld the individual's fundamental rights to religious freedom.

On the surface the question at issue was an act of tyranny on the part of the State. The crisis had grown out of the deeper controversy on mixed marriages. But this involved a still more fundamental principle of state interference with religious rights. The mixed-marriage problem had its origin remotely in the gigantic robbery of the Church known as the Secularization of 1803. This was primarily a forced transfer of property from a weak, defenseless clergy to a greedy gang of princes whose support Napoleon wished to secure at no cost to himself. It also broke the power of the Catholic Church in sections of Germany where for a thousand years vast territories and revenues had been controlled by ecclesiastical lords. But Protestant princes, with Prussia in the lead, were not content with the loot nor with the consequent predominance which it gave to the Protestant party.

In the same year, on November 21, 1803, the Prussian king had issued a royal declaration on the subject of mixed marriages. This applied, naturally, only within the limits of Prussia as it then was. But the Congress of Vienna extended the rule of Prussia to include Westphalia and the Rhineland. To this Catholic territory the king wished to extend also the influence of Protestantism. The obvious means were educa-

Mixed
Marriages

tion, the officials sent out from Berlin, and royal regulations governing marriage and the religion of children. It availed little that paper guarantees of religious liberty had been recorded, or that the State made profession of official "neutrality." Orders from Berlin might be couched in terms that wore a harmless and even reasonable character. The purpose was clear enough. If the king could not apply the *cujus regio, ejus et religio* of former days for the forcible conversion of his Catholic subjects, he could throw the power of the State into a campaign for the slow wearing down of opposition, and thus effectually bring about a complete victory for the Evangelical Church of the Hohenzollerns, which dated incidentally, from 1822.

The Policy
of Prussia

In August, 1825, accordingly, the king's cabinet issued an order extending the edict of 1803 to the western provinces. Two points stand out: all children must be raised in the religion of the father, and premarital promises were, by the high command of the State, invalid and of no account. In this the State arrogated to itself an authority beyond its competence. But the one-sidedness of the measure appears when we recall that in practically all mixed marriages the Protestant party was the father, and that the Catholic woman would, as a general rule, insist upon the Catholic education of her children. As envisaged by the government, a whole army of young officials would invade the Catholic Rhineland and the Province of Westphalia, marry daughters of the better class families, and, when the wife was not perverted, at least secure the rising generation for the Evangelical Church.

This clever arrangement met with some opposition from the parish clergy who had the courage to enforce the ecclesiastical canons. But the bishops as a group were men of peace, who were ready to connive with the government. In 1828 the case was referred to Leo XII. But Leo died the following year, and Pius VIII, his successor, issued a Brief, dated March 25, 1830. The Brief went to the utmost limit in the way of concessions. It provided for the validity of marriages, even when illicit, and imparted wide faculties to the bishops, including the *sanatio in radice* for marriages performed by non-Catholic ministers. But it enjoined upon the parish priests a merely "passive assistance" at the marriage ceremony, along with the further duty of instructing the Catholic party in his or her obligations regarding the education of children.

With this the government was not satisfied. And at once the Prussian minister in Rome, Josias von Bunsen, began a long campaign of intrigue and duplicity to bring about a revision of the Brief. But Bunsen succeeded only in discrediting himself and his government with the new pope, Gregory XVI. Then the government resorted to another expedient. If Rome had a conscience, perhaps the German hierarchy would prove less intractable. The Archbishop of Cologne, Ferdinand von Spiegel, was called to Berlin in June, 1834. There it was agreed that the Brief should be considerably softened in its application. Instead of the parish priest being merely a witness to the "sin" of the Catholic party, he was encouraged to bless the union. This amounted practically to a nullifying of the Brief, which as a matter of fact had been so far kept secret by the Archbishop and his suffragans. In other words, papal orders were not to interfere with the Berlin program of 1825. The people and the clergy were to be kept in ignorance of even the minimum requirements laid down by the pope, and conversely the pope was kept in ignorance of what was going on in Germany. Only a miracle, it was said, could save the Church in Prussia.

But the hand of Providence revealed itself in a series of events that upset the plans of the bureaucrats and their **Rome Alert** accomplices among the hierarchy. In August, 1835, Archbishop von Spiegel died. In September, a special Congregation of Cardinals discussed the German situation, and informed the pope that he could in conscience no longer remain silent. They recommended a protest to the Berlin government and an encyclical to the German bishops. The press in non-Prussian Germany and abroad published disturbing criticism. Bunsen was recalled. In Liége an exile, Johann Laurent, undertook to open a channel of communication between the faithful in Germany and the Holy Father. Finally, a deathbed repentance of Bishop Hommer of Trier brought the whole disgraceful conspiracy of 1834 to the notice of Gregory XVI.

Meantime, a successor had to be found for the deceased Archbishop of Cologne. The government sought a candidate whom it could control, and who at the same time would be acceptable to the parish clergy. It made the providential mistake of choosing Clemens August von Droste-Vischering.

Clemens August was an old man. He was of a retiring disposition, intent, it seemed, more on his prayers and the perfecting of his own interior life than on politics and the affairs of the world around him. The government felt it could rely upon him to do what in the circumstances it most desired, namely to do nothing. And that was, in ultimate analysis, precisely what the new Archbishop did. But his "passivity" was of a kind the government had not expected. Instead of permitting the iniquitous Convention of 1834 to determine the activities of the clergy the Archbishop referred those who asked for direction to the Brief of 1830. Even before his election to the See of Cologne he had shown a similar attitude on the question of Hermesian doctrines. In both cases Rome had spoken; there was no need for further discussion. Passivity consisted merely in pointing to the decision of the pope. But the papal Brief was to be given its obvious meaning without gloss or constructive interpretation.

As coadjutor to the Bishop of Münster Clemens August had read the Convention of von Spiegel and his three suffragans, and had shown a disposition to agree with it. In his new responsibility as archbishop he had the curiosity to read the Brief which still lay among the secret papers of his deceased predecessor. With the Brief in front of him he saw the Convention for what it was, a betrayal of the Church. From that time on politics, the favor of Berlin, and all human considerations had to be balanced against a high sense of right and justice, against the duties of office, the laws of the Church, and the salvation of his own soul. The old man set his face like a rock, went into virtual retirement, withdrew the usurped faculties of his Vicar-General, who pretended to act as vicar of the Cathedral Chapter, and thus effectually blocked the plans of the government.

The bureaucrats tried coercion. They appealed to Rome.

They demanded the Archbishop's resignation. And then in desperation they ordered his arrest. They knew his Cathedral canons were not loyal to him. They thought he was unpopular with his clergy and people. But somehow the indifference they had counted upon turned to resentment and indignation. The papal envoy, Capaccini, had been objective enough in the sad picture he had drawn of a religiously starved people, neglected or led astray by a hierarchy lazy and unfaithful and completely under the thumb of an absolutist bureaucracy. But he had not seen, and certainly the king's ministers had not seen, the Spirit of God working in the souls of many faithful priests. Capaccini had noted the sham religion of the upper and, for the most part, of the middle classes, and although he gave the women of Germany credit for some religious fervor, he failed to see any human hope for the future.

But the path of despotic absolutism was to be a rough one. A suppressed and careless populace was stirred to action by the quiet nocturnal arrest of the Cologne archbishop. Rocks were hurled through the windows of the canons of Cologne. In Aachen, in Münster, in Coblentz the ministers witnessed a revulsion of feeling which government troops could partially control, but which nonetheless made them very uncomfortable. This feeling was nursed into vigorous flame by the eloquence of Görres and his fellow publicists. Clemens August became the new Athanasius. The story of centuries of persecution was retold, and its lesson brought home to the Hohenzollern court. The "neutral" state was unmasked. A battle of principles was brought out into the open, and before the bar of European intelligence Prussian absolutism had to stand trial.

Meanwhile events had taken a parallel turn in Prussia's eastern province of Silesia. There, the government had had its own way in its plans for de-Catholicizing the populace. But the Archbishop of Gnesen-Posen, Martin von Dunin, was roused to action by the example of Cologne. Previous success in Silesia had encouraged the government in its program for a Protestant victory in the west. The reverse happened. The blunder in the west wrecked plans which were well under way in Silesia. Before the arrest of Clemens August, Archbishop von Dunin had appealed to the ministry for permission to follow the Brief of 1830. Then, when a direct appeal to the king met with a refusal, he forbade his priests to bless mixed marriages under pain of suspension. For this he was prosecuted before the civil tribunal, which "suspended" him, ordered his arrest and the payment of all costs of the trial. But the king intervened and the Archbishop was called to Berlin. He returned to his diocese without authorization and was again arrested. By this time the people were fully aroused, and the whole province put on mourning. But the government stood fast until the new king, Frederick William IV, succeeded his father. However, the bishops of Ermland and Kulm had been induced to take the side of the Archbishop, and the renegade Leopold von Sedlnitzky, Bishop of Breslau, was forced to abdicate.

The accession of Frederick William IV provided a welcome occasion to break the impasse. He was of a conciliating disposition, and he wanted peace. He recognized the real grievances of his Catholic subjects as well as the futility of the old autocratic methods. He had experienced a general coldness on the occasion of a visit to Münster, where passive resistance had cast a chill over the amusements of the people. He had seen, too, a revival of the religious spirit on the one hand, and the exposure of official intrigue on the other. Clearly, it was time to acknowledge past errors. Besides this, the ministry was thrown into a panic by the prospect of having a dead archbishop on their hands. For Clemens August's health had broken under the strain and he had to be released from his prison. Finally, Pope Gregory XVI was revealing some hard facts, and the Catholic press was making the people more and more restless not only on the religious issue, but on other phases of Prussian administration.

But there were difficulties to be met. The government had proclaimed the Archbishop a traitor. It would not be expedient to permit him to return to Cologne. The Archbishop, on his side, demanded a recall of gratuitous charges made against him. Moreover, there were Catholics who preferred to have the Archbishop out of Cologne. Circumstances had made him

The
Dénouement

FÉLICÉTÉ DE LAMENNAIS

Journalist and fighter against the enemies of truth; his apostasy is one of the unhappy events of the nineteenth century (1782–1854)

WILHELM EMMANUEL VON KETTELER
Bishop of Mainz, social reformer, and model and precursor of
Leo XIII in his battle for the laboring man (1811–1877)

a hero, it is true, and his piety, his aloofness from public affairs, his carelessness of political or personal consequences had fitted him for the role he had had to play. But he also had his defects, among which was an autocratic and un-conciliating disposition. It was accordingly arranged that he should retain the title of Archbishop, while an administrator in the person of the bishop of Speyer, Johann von Geissel, should care for the Archdiocese. Geissel was appointed in 1842, and inducted into his new charge by Clemens August himself. Trier, Paderborn, and Münster also received new bishops. And while the hierarchy was thus being rejuvenated, a Catholic "Ministry of Worship" was established in Berlin in February, 1841. As a symbol of his benevolent feelings toward his Catholic subjects the king contributed liberally toward the completion of the five-hundred-year-old Cathedral of Cologne.

The historian can trace the steps by which a Church, beaten down and reduced almost to destruction, arose with a new vitality stirring within her. He may be going beyond his field if he tries to check the special intervention of divine Providence in the whole affair. But it had been said that the situation could be saved only by a miracle. Surely, there was a touch of the marvelous in this resurrection. The main factors at work on the side of religion were unquestionably the pope, the Catholic press, and an awakened conscience of the common people. As negative results, we have the curbing of the absolutist State with its Josephist traditions, its bureaucratic pettiness, and its Hegelian pseudo-philosophy. More important for the Church herself, we have the eradicat-ing of the lingering disease of Febronianism. Positively, there is the new seriousness in matters of faith, a fighting Catholic press, and an accession of high-class converts to the Church. Wilhelm Emmanuel von Ketteler abandoning in disgust the service of the Prussian State to begin, after his ordination to the priesthood, his great ecclesiastical career, is at once a compensation for losses during the struggle and a promise of a new day.

Wilhelm Emmanuel von Ketteler, Bishop of Mainz, aggres-sive and clear-headed social reformer, friend of the working-   Von Ketteler man, "precursor" and model of Leo XIII, and hater of absolutism in any form, may be taken to personify Catholic action in Germany in the middle nineteenth century. Ketteler was born in 1811 and died in 1877. The fighting spirit of his student days, which were more remarkable for his dueling propensities than for devotional practices, went with him through life. When in 1837 the Prussian bureaucracy outraged the Catholic Rhineland by arresting the Archbishop of Cologne, Ketteler turned from the service of the State to begin four years later his studies for the priesthood. Two years at the University of Munich brought his mature mind into contact with the best Catholic thought in Germany. Ordained in 1844, he threw his boundless physical energy into the hidden humdrum duties of a country pastor. The year 1848 found him among the deputies at the Frankfort Parliament. In 1849 he was rector of Berlin's most important Catholic church, and in 1850 he was made Bishop of Mainz. As a man of action, in the pulpit and with the pen, he battled for right and justice and the amelioration of social conditions. He fought State absolutism in the political arena, tore to shreds the bad philosophy of Liberalism, and combated Socialism by persistent efforts to bring relief to the suffering poor.

For him God was the only Absolute Being, Christianity was a permanent insurrection against all the tyrannies which menace the legitimate expansion of the individual and the legitimate rights of human personality. He was the declared enemy of "supermen" in parliament, on the throne, in business and industry. No king, no people, and no system could claim unlimited power. Absolutism, monarchic, bureaucratic, or "Liberal," meant simply the negation of human dignity. But if he hated the autocracy in government which destroyed personal liberty, he hated also the revolutionary lawlessness which broke the bond of unity in society. In modern Liberalism he saw the intellectual child and heir of the old monarchy and its bureaucratic tyranny. It exploited the worst passions of the mob in order to walk on the people; of its very nature it tended toward the omnipotent State. And the Socialist State was nothing else but modern constitutionalism under the control of a few clever leaders of the laboring classes. Ketteler understood the misuse of words and phrases, so characteristic of the nineteenth century, which camouflaged the revolt against God and essential human interests. He could be particularly bitter against Masonic Liberalism. He had apprehensions for the future of humanity if a clique of wealthy nabobs "who do not believe in God, or Christ, or the dignity of the human soul; who think only in terms of material interests and the pleasures of sense; and are buttressed by a secret hidden organization, should pass for the elite of humankind." During thirty years he fought the dominant anti-Christian, he might have said antisocial, forces of his time. Like a giant conscious of his power, he felt the joy of combat in attacking the bureaucratic State, a flourishing Liberalism, the magnates of industry, a revolutionary Socialism, and finally the mighty Bismarck himself.

But Bishop von Ketteler was not merely an iconoclast. He diagnosed the diseases of society, but he was more intent upon building up healthy social conditions. The Church, he insisted, was too well aware of the fallen state of man to put any confidence in social utopias; at the same time she knew the potential greatness of man, and could not excuse him from responsibility. It was heresy to exaggerate the strength of man; it was also heresy to exaggerate human misery. It was naïve to expect a return to a happy state of nature, or to look for social improvement without strenuous effort. Ketteler was sympathetic with Democracy, because his heart was with the poor. He studied the program of the Socialist leader Ferdinand Lassalle, and agreed with his criticism of economic evils. He read his St. Thomas and he clung tenaciously to traditional Christianity, but his gaze was fixed on the future, and his movements were all in a forward direction. In 1848 he pleaded for an interior reform of the soul. In 1864 he was still repeating that the Church and Christianity effected the reforms of society not by mechanical means, but by a change of heart in the individual Christian. But whereas in 1848 his reading and study had not yet revealed any practical way out of impoverishment and misery for the masses, by 1864 he was proposing his grandiose scheme of co-operatives financed by Christian charity; in 1869 he was outlining a program of

Ketteler, Social Reformer

relief for the workers, including specifically increased pay, shorter hours, Sunday rest, exclusion of children, young girls and women from the factories; and in 1873 he presented the Center Party with projects for social legislation which embraced everything from better sanitation to State aid in labor organization. Because a pastor of souls had an obligation to work for the betterment of social conditions, the Bishop claimed the right to intervene in political questions.

XIV

THE CHURCH IN ENGLAND AND IRELAND

ON APRIL 13, 1829, GEORGE IV GRUDGINGLY AFFIXED HIS signature to the Act of Emancipation, and his Catholic subjects were admitted to political rights which had been denied them since the seventeenth century or earlier. This act of tardy and partial justice put an end to the worst features of the old Penal Code which Burke had pronounced "as well fitted for the oppression, impoverishment and degradation of a feeble people and the debasement in them of human nature itself as ever proceeded from the perverted ingenuity of man."

Catholic Emancipation

Burke was speaking of Ireland, where bigotry, nursed by hatred and greed and perhaps by fear, enacted law after law in an effort to break the spirit of the people and to kill its soul. But the Catholics of England were not much better treated. In Ireland national feeling contributed greatly to the stanch faith of the people. Still, the martyred nation deserves all the glory that belongs to the heroic sacrifice of material advantages for spiritual ends.

The long ordeal, which made the Irish a backward people in material wealth and power, gave them a spiritual quality which is of the utmost significance for the nineteenth century. And in this the course of history in Catholic Ireland is typical of the history of the whole Church. Another historical paradox lies in the fact that the sufferings which reduced Ireland to the state almost of a Pariah among the nations sent her sons abroad to enrich the English-speaking world with spiritual ideals, and to leaven its increasing materialism with religious thought and sentiment. "They know not Ireland who only Ireland know." Irishmen in the nineteenth century have carried on a silent apostolate not unlike the *peregrinatio pro Christo* which planted centers of religion and culture on the Continent during the three centuries following Ireland's conversion to Christianity. It was providential that an apostolic nation should be at hand to spread over the globe in the wake of the Colossus of trade and industry whose ships plowed the seven seas to establish the mightiest empire of history. It was also providential that a handful of English Catholics, a hundred years ago, received liberty to live and multiply with the expanding greatness of England.

Fifty years before Catholic Emancipation there were some seventy thousand Catholics in England, and perhaps three and one half million in Ireland. The English clergy numbered about three hundred and fifty, the Irish about two thousand. Scotland had thirty thousand Catholics and forty priests. A series of Relief Acts awakened their slumbering hopes, and eventually gave them a fair share in the liberty which was the boast of the nineteenth century. The American War of Independence produced the first break in the old tyranny. The spread of liberal ideas and the military needs of England brought about the Relief Acts of 1778,[1] which permitted Catholics to own property in England and Ireland, and abolished the infamous trade of informer. Its aftermath in the disgraceful Gordon Riots of 1780 showed that bigotry was not dead and would be hard to kill. In 1793, under stress of the French Revolution, Irish Catholics were allowed to practice law. This was the year in which eighteen-year-old Daniel O'Connell returned from his uncompleted education abroad to choose a career for himself at home. O'Connell, the agitator, the organizer, the Liberator, was to personify the movement for Catholic Emancipation. The interesting story of the rebellion of 1798 and the destruction of the Irish Protestant Parliament in 1800, of the controversies among Catholics and the futile efforts of liberal-minded English and Irish leaders to obtain Catholic Emancipation would require more space than can be given to it here. The central figure of the movement that was finally crowned with success in 1829 was Daniel O'Connell.

O'Connell formed the Catholic Association for purposes of

Daniel O'Connell

---

[1] Relief legislation was not uniform in England, Ireland, and Scotland. In Ireland the years 1771, 1774, 1778, 1782, 1792, and 1793, each marked a step forward in the relaxation of the Penal Code.

peaceful agitation in 1823. In 1824 the poorest peasants were contributing their penny a week to the "Catholic Rent." When the Association was suppressed by the Government, in 1825, O'Connell reorganized it under a changed name. O'Connell proved himself a master in two ways. He roused the masses to organized protest, which might have been done by any demagogue. He controlled them within legal bounds, and for this vastly more difficult achievement he deserves to rank with the foremost popular leaders of all ages. At this time Catholics owning land worth forty shillings a year could vote only for Protestants, and in practice they had always supported the candidate of the local landlord. In 1826 the Ascendancy Party was jolted into a state of alarm by the election in Waterford of a candidate favorable to Catholic interests. The example of Waterford was followed by three other constituencies. Meantime, in England, hopes for Catholic emancipation were being shattered against the rocklike opposition of the House of Lords. The great crisis was reached when O'Connell himself stood for election in County Clare. Triumphantly elected, he knew he could not sit in Parliament as a Catholic. But this show of organized force and determination had the effect of convincing Wellington and Peel that refusal to meet Irish demands meant civil war. The House of Commons under the leadership of the reluctant Peel was ready to pass the Emancipation Act. Wellington's problem was to overcome the sullen opposition of the Lords and the "scruples" of the king, who feared for the Anglican Establishment.

On April 13, 1829, Catholics were granted the privilege of sitting in Parliament. But a sop in the form of irritating penal restrictions had to be thrown to bigotry, and, most important, the forty-shilling freeholders whose massed support of O'Connell had carried the day were disfranchised. O'Connell, moreover, who had indignantly refused to take the oath against Transubstantiation after the Clare election, had to be re-elected. But this merely served to reveal the bitterness of the opposition. He went to Parliament to continue his fight for the removal of Catholic grievances. The first of these grievances was the tithe by which Catholic Ireland was bled to support a useless and unwanted Established Church;[2] the second was nothing less than the Repeal of the Union. O'Connell, the master in legal agitation, now the "uncrowned king" of Ireland and the great "Liberator" whose example was an inspiration to Catholics fighting for liberty on the Continent, was to know in his declining years the bitterness of failure and defeat. But he had taught the people to fight, and the clergy to lead them. His work was carried to eventual triumph by the uncompromising perseverance of the present generation.

The Ascendancy backed by British power still continued to batten on its fair preserves in Ireland. Legalized tyranny, political chicanery, and merciless evictions fill out the sad story of the victim nation in its struggle toward the Gladstone Disestablishment of 1869 and the Irish Land Acts of 1870, 1881, and later. Home Rule, O'Connell's "Repeal of the Union," had to wait for its partial realization until after the World War.

The factors which brought relief to the Catholics of England and Ireland throw considerable light on the changing times. The Penal Laws were the product of an earlier age; they were utterly out of harmony with the new spirit of the early nineteenth century. Even apart from the titanic exertions of Daniel O'Connell and the marvelous vitality of the Church in Ireland forces were at work which must, however slowly, put an end to the pampered ascendancy of Established Anglicanism. Negatively, there was the dawning conviction that the Catholic Church no longer constituted a danger to vested interests which had been founded largely on confiscation of ecclesiastical property, or to the regime that had so often employed the "Popery" scare to build up its political power. Positively, there were the Liberal ideas of statesmen who followed the generous tradition of leaders like Burke and Grattan, of Canning and Fox. There were also the Radicals who thought all religion an anachronism, and who were too con-

Liberalism

---

[2] The Anglican clergy, more than one third of whom were absentees, collected an annual revenue of 800,000 pounds. The lowest paid Anglican bishop received an income over ten times that of the average Catholic bishop.

temptuously indifferent to religious beliefs to carry on a persecution that had served its purpose.

In effecting the change of mental attitude toward Catholicism the French Revolution had been a major influence. Partially, this was due to the exchange of ideas on religious tolerance which had been going on between England and France throughout the eighteenth century. But for the Catholic cause the presence in England of some ten thousand exiled French ecclesiastics during the early 1790's was of inestimable value. The generation of Englishmen which was to grant a measure of justice to the Catholic minority in 1829 had lost much of its inherited hatred of Rome through close contact with cultured Frenchmen whom it could not help admiring. No doubt, too, the warmth of a charity that befriended the unfortunate did much to melt the icy crust of a sectarian bias. Protestant England gave freely in public and private contributions to alleviate the distress of victims of persecution from "Catholic" France. And these priests, who were taken into the institutions and even the homes of the ruling class, did what they could to repay the kindness shown them. But in a larger way the people of England, whether they were moved by Christian charity or by humanitarian sentiment, received the Scriptural reward of their good deeds in the diminution or removal of an ingrained prejudice which otherwise might have prevented Catholic Emancipation.

The Oxford Movement was essentially a revival of spiritual life within the Anglican community. Unconsciously, at least in the beginning, its leaders drew nearer to the Catholic Church, though the greatest among them thought for years that the pope was Antichrist, and some of them never did overcome their antipathy for Rome. The movement was remarkable on account of its contribution to religion in England and throughout the world. As a reaction against Rationalism, Liberalism, and the Erastian State it throws much light on some of the characteristic features of the nineteenth century.

The Oxford Movement

The Movement centered in Oxford University and covered twelve critical years, extending from John Keble's sermon on "the National Apostasy," in 1833, to John Henry Newman's submission to Rome, in 1845. Its immediate purpose was to save the Church of England, to free her from a benumbing slavery to the State, to fight off threatened aggressions, to stimulate a renewal of fervor, to spiritualize an Establishment which had become a sort of philanthropic society, smug, satisfied, and sunken to a state of lethargy with no higher ideals than respectability and comfortable living in this world. The remedy for this condition was sought in a return to the Apostolic origins of the Church, and in a reassertion of her sacramental character. Personal holiness and the spirit of sacrifice, humility, charity, and zeal in the exercise of the ministry were the first practical means employed. The leaders were scholars eager to show their sincerity in action: in preaching, in the performance of liturgical devotions, in private direction, in literary activity. They were ready for personal self-efface-ment, but they did not shrink from vigorous propaganda through books, pamphlets, letters, and conversation. Their "Tracts for the Times" were especially effective, and among Anglican clergymen in remote corners of England the new apostolate was known as the "Tractarian Movement."

The head, the heart, the soul of the movement was John Henry Newman,[3] son of a London banker with a Bourgeois Calvinist background. Fellow at Oriel since 1822, Vicar of St. Mary's in 1828 and the University's most popular and in-fluential preacher, master of literary expression, a searcher of his own soul and a near-saint from his boyhood years. A hypersensitive soul that recoiled from pain, but never lacked the courage to struggle toward the light through difficulties and doubts and a heritage of antipapal prejudices, he was one of the greatest spiritual forces of the century. Henry Austin Adams was guilty of pardonable hyperbole when he ventured the statement that Newman possessed the most powerful intel-ligence that ever rested on Anglo-Saxon shoulders, but there is much truth in his further assertion that when the head of Newman crashed through the dark wall which separated Englishmen from Catholic truth it left a hole so big that

John Henry
Newman

---

[3] The literature on the Oxford Movement is voluminous. A number of studies came out in connection with the centenary in 1933. An indispens-able source is Newman's *Apologia*.

ignorance and bigotry have no excuse for not seeing through it. *Credo in Newmanum* was William George Ward's way of expressing his view of the place occupied by Newman in the Oxford Movement.

But Newman did not and could not work alone. "The true and primary author of it," he writes in his *Apologia*,[4] "as is usual with great motive powers, was out of sight. . . . Need I say that I am speaking of John Keble?" In Keble's National Apostasy sermon, preached on July 14, 1833, Newman saw the birthday of the movement. But the modest, retiring, and saintly Keble, whose piety is enshrined in his *Christian Year*, published in 1827, was as Newman said, a hidden source of inspiration. He was not the man to lead. But Keble had a decided influence on a younger man, Richard Hurrell Froude, "the most lovable, most human" of Tractarians, who was in turn a close companion of Newman. Had not a delicate constitution kept him from the fray and eventually carried him off, in 1835, at the age of thirty, it is not unlikely that his energy, his forthright convictions, his utter contempt for sham and pretense, his abhorrence for the Protestant Reformation, and his naturally Catholic soul would have made him the dominant figure among his more moderate friends, As it was, his influence upon Newman was incalculable. His loss, in 1835, was in some degree compensated by the accession to the Movement of Edward Pusey, whose standing in the University and outside of it gave the little group new prestige.

Pusey's somber asceticism and ponderous learning stood in strong contrast to the carefree buoyancy of Froude. Both desired to restore the primitive splendor of the Church and to shake it free from earthly accretions. But Pusey bears some resemblance to the Jansenists. He is the type of man who, if he had been born a Catholic, might have led a revolt against the Church. He was, in fact, to remain for forty years an obstacle to any understanding between Anglicans and the Holy See.

Froude, had he lived, would almost certainly have preceded Ward, Oakeley, Ambrose St. John, and Newman into the Catholic Fold. He had not the ingrained prejudices of Newman against Rome to overcome. He hated with a holy hatred the anti-Roman features of the Reformation, its rejection of

Other Leaders

---

[4] *Apologia* (Everyman's ed.), p. 41.

Tradition, its contempt for the medieval past, its fawning on the secular power, its scurrilous invective against Catholic devotions. He was outspoken in his devotedness to the Real Presence, to our Lady and the saints; he admired Christian asceticism and voluntary chastity. In all this he and Newman were kindred souls.

The primary interest of most readers in the Oxford Movement lies in the interior struggle, the motivation, the conclusions, and the final choice for or against Rome of the men who directed its course. It is sufficient for many that John Henry Newman and the hundreds of eminent converts who followed him, and still follow him in an unbroken line, owe their conversion to this attempt to de-Protestantize the Church of England. But the circumstances in which the Movement began are no less important. Without the men there would have been no movement; in other conditions the men might have had no motive for action. Moreover, the irreligious and antireligious forces which were threatening the destruction of the Anglican Church were even more hostile though, perhaps, less dangerous to the Catholic Church.

Oxford University

The Oxford Movement was born of a Catholicizing tendency at a university which has never been able to forget its Catholic origins. Like most other universities Oxford was the scene of a great variety of manifestations of religious opinion. But it was nearer to Rome in doctrine, discipline, and worship than it cared frankly to admit. On the eve of the Oxford Movement, however, it seemed to have slumped with the rest of the Anglican Church to a low level of religious indifference.

The Establishment, much as High Church Anglicans disliked to admit it, was a distinctly Protestant thing. Officially, it was "The Protestant Religion by Law Established." Edward VI and Elizabeth had with the aid of Reformers from the Continent turned the "middle-of-the-road" schismatic, if not heretical, Church of their father into a definitely national, State-controlled body, and nearly three centuries of anti-Roman propaganda had left little of the original Catholic heritage intact. In the first quarter of the nineteenth century the situation was desperate. The Methodist revival had spent itself. The Anglican clergy looked to Oxford for leadership, and Oxford itself was going Liberal. Liberalism, it is true, meant thought and discussion, but it was poison for the supernatural. Two men set the tone at Oxford, Dr. Whately and Thomas Arnold. They emancipated the Church from the State; they also cut theology adrift from divine revelation. Their Rationalism was stimulating, but it inevitably produced a reaction.

Besides this Liberalism, which to the leaders of the Oxford Movement meant "the tendencies of modern thought to destroy the basis of revealed religion, and ultimately all that can be called religion at all," there was cause for anxiety in a general lack of agreement on points of doctrine, not to say ignorance of what the Anglican body really held.[5] Newman and his friends struggled heroically to clarify for themselves and others a doctrinal system which, after all, anyone was free to accept, to modify, or to reject. The combating of Liberalism Newman considered his lifework.

Erastianism was still another danger to the Anglican Church. Long before the Swiss theologian had given his name to this system of State supremacy in ecclesiastical affairs, Henry VIII had made himself virtually pope. Another step was taken when Elizabeth became "supreme governor." But the situation was aggravated since Parliament had assumed the prerogative of making and unmaking kings. And when the Whigs took over the government, Church and Bible were subordinated to the final authority of the State. The resentment of sincere souls at this degradation of the spiritual power needed only an occasion to break out in protest.

Erastianism

A rapid succession of events threw consternation into the Anglican camp. Catholic Emancipation in 1829, or more correctly the abolishing of the Test and Corporation Acts in 1828 admitted Dissenters to active participation in the sovereign state. The National Church, which had felt fairly secure so long as government officials had to belong to it, was now faced

---

[5] One section, the Low Church, tends to emphasize the Protestant character of Anglicanism. This group is evangelical. The Liberals, Rationalists, Latitudinarians, who disregard dogma, are the Broad Church. The High Church, with its subdivisions, Anglo-Catholic and Ritualist, admit Catholic influence, especially in public worship.

with the unpleasant prospect of subjection to a Parliament made up largely of Dissenters and Catholics. Moreover, the new spirit of tolerance which had wiped the infamous Penal Laws from the statute books was the outgrowth of religious indifference, which further imperiled the Establishment. Then came the Reform Bill of 1832. The same year the Whigs won a victory in Tory Oxford by the election of Peel. It was a triumph for the Whigs, aided by Dissenters and Indifferentists, and a hard blow to the Tories in whom the Establishment had always found its support. Vague fears were almost immediately substantiated by the introduction of a Bill to suppress ten Anglican bishoprics in Ireland. It mattered not that the privileged but decrepit Church of Ireland had no employment for these sinecures. The significance of the move lay in the threat to the pampered security of the Establishment in both England and Ireland. And so, the meaner motive of safeguarding material interests combined with the nobler sentiment of those who perceived the menace of Rationalism and Liberalism. The most striking result was Keble's sermon on the National Apostasy, and the launching of the Oxford Movement.

Keble's "call to arms" found a party ready for energetic action. Newman and Froude had just returned from their long **"Tracts for** trip abroad. Newman, anti-Liberal and still unshaken in his **the Times"** anti-Roman convictions, came back conscious that he "had a work to do in England," and he set about it at once. The first of the Tracts for the Times appeared on September 9, 1833. *Tract 90,* also from the pen of Newman, was to conclude the series eight years later. The Tracts were uneven in quality and varied in character. On the whole the Tracts, especially those written by Newman, were, according to Dean Church, "clear, brief, stern appeals to conscience and reason, sparing of words, utterly without rhetoric, intensive in purpose." The problem of distribution was met by sending them in parcel lots to propagandists in all parts of England. The first two Tracts reveal the spirit of the movement: its appeal to ecclesiastical authority based on Apostolical succession in the Church against the Erastian sycophancy of those who leaned on the State for support and the Liberalism of those who rejected Revelation.

The year 1835 marks a turning point. Pusey published his treatise on baptism, and the Tracts became more theological. The leaders turned more and more to Patristic studies and to making translations from the Fathers of the Church. At this time also Newman was working hard to construct a doctrinal basis for his *Via Media*. The Anglican Church, lying somewhere in the middle ground between Protestantism and Rome, he thought to link up with primitive Apostolic traditions. Four years of intense study brought him to the conclusion that Rome was still pretty much what she had always been, and that the earlier analogues of the sects which disagreed with her were to be found in the Oriental heretics and schismatics. The *coup de grace* was dealt the *Via Media* by Wiseman in an article on the Donatists in the *Dublin Review*. Newman, who knew his history,[6] refused to see any parallel between the fanatic Donatists and the Anglican community. But Wiseman had quoted St. Augustine's *Securus judicat orbis terrarum*, and the argument kept ringing in Newman's ears. "By those great words of the ancient Father," he wrote, "the theory of the *Via Media* was absolutely pulverized."

Meantime, the *Remains* of Froude had been edited and published by Keble and Newman in 1837. With their insistence upon authority and sanctity in the Church and their ruthless rejection of half measures they were a new impulse in the direction of Rome. In 1840 Newman was beginning to regret some of the hard things, very hard things, he had written against Rome. Toward the end of 1841 he was on his "deathbed, as regards my membership in the Anglican Church." On November 11 he sent a formal protest to the Archbishop of Canterbury against the project of setting up a bishopric in Jerusalem which should be alternately Anglican and Lutheran. But the real climax of the Movement was reached with the publication in 1841 of *Tract 90*. Newman could still throw his defiance at Rome: "Perpetual war is our only prospect." But he was already convinced that the Council of Trent was more in harmony with the Fathers than was his Anglican Church. He attempted to reconcile the Thirty-Nine Articles with the

---

[6] *Apologia*, 120 f. Döllinger is said to have asserted that Newman knew more about the first three centuries than any man then living.

Council. The result was a storm of indignation. Newman resigned his place at St. Mary's, retired to Littlemore for four years of prayer and study, and eventually, on October 9, 1845, became a Catholic.

Before this event, so heavy with happy consequences for the Church, the Oxford Movement had suffered a split.

Converts

William George Ward, most aggressive fighter of them all, had led the way to Rome; a second group had taken the opposite road toward Liberalism; while Pusey and Keble maintained their shifting, but still comfortable position, as leaders of High Church Anglicanism. This party had displayed unmistakable signs of religious earnestness up to a point. Many of them drew nearer to Rome in doctrine and in devotional practices. Their great disillusionment was to come when Leo XIII, on September 15, 1896, in spite of his friendly attitude toward England, was forced by historical evidence to declare Anglican ordinations invalid.

What the Oxford Movement has meant for the Catholic Church is beyond exact computation. It brought to her a trained army of scholars and writers at a time when she was still a *gens lucifuga* in England, silent and helpless against calumny and contempt. The ordeal of soul-searching, the mental wrestling and the sacrifice of material interests on the part of the convert, prepared him to be a determined and effective champion of his new faith. The movement in its very inception was an apostolate of the pen. It holds a major interest today for the student of literature. Only those who, if there be any such, can accurately gauge the impact of Catholic thought on the English world of letters, and the importance of the English language around the globe, are fitted to pronounce on the results of the Oxford Movement. Converts are entering the Church at the rate of over ten thousand a year. Proportionately few of them are Oxford scholars, but they and the whole Catholic body are better able to meet the modern world in a spirit of calm and unabashed confidence because they know, and all the world knows, that the Church can still appeal to an elite among the intellectual classes. But besides these men of "words," there were also men of "deeds," of whom Cardinal Manning is

DANIEL O'CONNELL

The "Uncrowned King of Ireland" (1775–1847)

JOHN HENRY CARDINAL NEWMAN

One of the greatest spiritual forces of the century
(1801–1890)

NICHOLAS CARDINAL WISEMAN
First Archbishop of Westminster after the Restoration
(1802–1865)

HENRY EDWARD CARDINAL MANNING
Successor of Wiseman in the See of Westminster
and ardent worker for social reform (1808–1892)

typical. In his own day he was a more imposing figure than Cardinal Newman. His giant figure still looms large in the second half of the nineteenth century. But for most students of the Catholic past Newman occupies a place alone.

On September 29, 1850, Pius IX re-established the Catholic hierarchy in England. During the long penal era the English Church had been administered as a mission under four Vicars. Catholic Emancipation opened the way for expansion. The Oxford Movement brought an influx of converts. Natural increase and immigration chiefly from Ireland added to the Catholic population. In 1850 there were nearly a million Catholics, where a hundred years earlier there had been, perhaps, sixty thousand. Between 1840 and 1850 the Catholic population had more than doubled and the number of priests had mounted 50 per cent. Attempts had been made in 1783 and again in 1815 to restore the hierarchy. In 1840 the number of Vicars was raised to eight. In 1848 the revolution in Rome had prevented the restoration. By the Brief of 1850 a Metropolitan with twelve suffragan bishops was appointed. Wiseman was made Archbishop of Westminster, and Cardinal.

Restoration of the Hierarchy

This would seem to be all very natural and proper, but it stirred up a tempest in England. Leaders in public life who should have known better, and probably did know better, aroused the latent bigotry of the less enlightened masses by their panicky protests. The *London Times* led the way. Lord John Russell was even less excusable. The Anglican bishops were very likely laboring under the resentment they felt at having lost so many converts to Rome. The outcome of the excitement was the Ecclesiastical Titles Bill of Prime Minister Russell, which stood as a sad and futile reminder of a lingering fanaticism until Gladstone had it removed from the statute books twenty years later.

The Tempest

On the other hand, the restoration of normal Catholic life to England was a new incentive to expansion and intensive growth. But the explosion of public feeling also served a purpose. Wiseman had been warned that it was unsafe for him to return to England. He hastened to London and published his *Appeal to the English People,* the common-sense tone of which made most respectable Englishmen feel ashamed of the late outburst. The converts from Anglicanism who came into the Church at this time were influenced in other ways, but in the case of Henry Edward Manning, after Newman the outstanding figure among the Oxford converts, opposition to the hierarchy seems to have been a positive help in his slow progress toward Rome.

Most of the Catholic history of England in the past century will be found in the biographies of three or four great Cardinals: Nicholas Wiseman, John Henry Newman, Henry Edward Manning and, to complete the story, Herbert Vaughan. Pioneer work had been done by bishops like John Milner, who closed his energetic career in 1826; while the scholarship of John Lingard, especially his monumental *History of England* which, between 1819 and 1830, uncovered a clear picture of the English past, removed the excuse for blind prejudice as well as the literary distortions which were its polluted source. Besides this there was, of course, the whole galaxy of writers, Oxford converts for the most part, from William George Ward, Faber, Dalgairns, and Allies down to the Chestertons and Knoxes of the twentieth century. But the new era after Emancipation is filled with events and movements that revolved around the Cardinal Archbishops of Westminster, and with thought currents that centered in Newman.

Cardinal
Wiseman
Before he became Metropolitan in the restored hierarchy, Nicholas Wiseman, as scholar, writer, lecturer, and friend of prospective or actual converts, had been a power for good. The brilliant men who abandoned the halls of Oxford for the persecuted, impoverished, mission Church in England saw in him an intellectual equal whose erudition and keenness of mind they could admire. They found in him also a sympathetic friend whose understanding of their problems smoothed the roughness of the way for them. The quiet scholar among his books in Rome made a deep impression upon the elite among his countrymen who came to visit him. When he turned to apostolic work in England his pen became the best defense of the Catholic position. As head of the English hierarchy he was criticized by the "Old Catholics" for his excessive favoritism to converts. He was, in some degree at least, responsible for unpleasant controversies which perturbed the peace of

e Church in England and prevented its more rapid growth. ut his mistakes were due to difficult circumstances rather an to any autocratic strain in Wiseman himself. It was ite natural that many should resent his apparently hasty omotion of Manning; yet it might be maintained that anning was his greatest gift to England.

The lives of Manning and Newman ran very nearly parallel, ough the two Cardinals were entirely unlike in mental equip- ent, in character, and in the type of service they gave to ligion and the welfare of souls. Both were Oxford converts ho had spent their lives in the Anglican Church. Both had eld aloof from Rome until their honest convictions forced em to sacrifice promising careers for peace of soul. Newman as the scholar, the thinker, the writer; his were the specu- tive mind, the finer feelings, the delicate literary touch. anning was the man of action, the eminently practical omoter of works for the betterment of social conditions, the terprising administrator of a great diocese, the counsellor people who had to meet the difficulties of daily life. New- an diagnosed the mental ills of the nineteenth century. anning threw his tremendous energy into the solution of its onomic, social, political, and moral problems.

Manning and Newman

Manning, like Newman, the son of a London banker, was orn in 1808. Six years younger than Newman, he was rdained according to Anglican ritual in 1832, married in 1833, nd spent his life in the Church of England as Rector of avington. He followed the Tractarian Movement at a istance, but remained a zealous Anglican until his faith was aken in 1847 by the government's appointment of the heretical" Doctor Hampden to the Bishopric of Hereford, nd shattered in 1850 by the promotion to an Anglican enefice of Doctor Gorham, who had openly repudiated aptismal regeneration. Received into the Church by the esuit, Father Brownhill, April 6, 1851, he was ordained to e priesthood by Cardinal Wiseman barely two months later. e went to Rome for a year of study, and on his return evoted himself to intense and increasingly influential labors. e heard confessions, instructed prospective converts and erformed other ministerial duties. Always in conjunction with

Wiseman, he founded the Oblates of St. Charles in 1857. Hi
appointment the same year as Provost of Westminster cause
some ill feeling among those who disliked Wiseman's eviden
preference for converts. On the death of Wiseman in 186!
Pius IX passed over the names of candidates submitted b
the Chapter of Westminster, and, quite significantly, appointe
Manning to the vacant post. By an exercise of papal initiativ
he gave to the papacy one of its most ardent supporters. Bu
he also gave to England a great Metropolitan.

The new archbishop was a pastor of souls conscious of hi
obligations to his people. During twenty-seven years no cor
sideration of age, health, or personal convenience was allowe
to stand in the way of duty. Never sparing himself, he pei
formed the ordinary functions of his office, convinced that i
this he did his most solid and enduring work. But his plac
in history is due rather to his relations with the leaders c
political thought on the one hand, and to the oppressed labo
ing classes on the other. The Church needed a representativ
who could move with dignity and distinction on the highe
social level, but she had even greater need of a prelate wh
would accredit her with the stirring masses. Manning ha
an influence for good with men like Gladstone, but his inte
est in the supremely important question of labor and it
rights made his name a power in Rome, in France, i
Belgium, and in America. He actively endorsed Cardin
Gibbons in his effort to make Rome appreciate social cond
tions in America on the occasion of the "Knights of Labor
discussions in 1887. His letter to the Congress of Liège, i
1890, was "a trumpet call to charge. It roused the majorit
to enthusiasm while it angered those who were more conser
ative than Catholic." The energy with which he champione
the Dock Strikers of London in 1889, won the gratitude of th
men and the hearty approval of social reformers throughou
the world.

In his many-sided activity Cardinal Manning was remark
able. But there was a singleness of purpose running throug
the whole of his life. His mistakes even, were the result c
a masterful character ruthlessly pursuing a definite end. I
the hectic days before the Vatican Council he was on the righ

ide, but excessive zeal for papal infallibility had the effect
f stiffening opposition to the definition. His determination to
uild a complete Catholic school system trebled the number
f grade schools, but met with failure on the college level.
Ie was instrumental in obtaining from Rome four prohibitions
gainst Catholics attending Oxford, but two years after his
eath, in 1894, his successor reversed his policy. He endeavored
o improve the intellectual, social, and religious status of his
lergy, but he did so in a roughshod manner. The important
question of the relations of the Regular Orders to the bishops
e carried to a successful issue, but he was not careful of the
eelings of others in doing so. By the final test of results
roduced, Cardinal Manning was a great religious leader.
Under him the Church in England made rapid progress in
ts internal organization, in numbers,[7] and in its outward
manifestations of vitality. In the estimation of outsiders it
ose with the personal reputation of Manning.

---

[7] The best study of the numerical growth of the Church in England
(including Wales) is that of Herbert Thurston, "Statistical Progress of the
Catholic Church," in *Catholic Emancipation, 1829–1929* (Longmans, 1929),
p. 243–264. Always critical, Father Thurston discounts the exaggerations
f early Catholic enthusiasts and the fears of the panicky No-Popery
lement. In 1840 there were "roughly half a million" Catholics. He accepts
,000,000 as a fair estimate for 1851. At this date 500,000 of the whole
opulation were "born in Ireland." In 1929 "rather over than under three
million souls" could be classified as Catholics. In other words, while the
otal population was little more than doubled, and religion outside the
Church was sinking fast, Catholic numbers were trebled. Statistics for
onverts, usually a mature and earnest type, showed 12,000 conversions
nnually since the World War.

XV

THE POPE AND ITALIAN UNIFICATION

ON FEBRUARY 11, 1929, A LONG AND BEWILDERIN chapter of Italian and of papal history was closed amicabl by the Lateran treaty. The most aggressive of Italian Nationa ists and a pope who was his match in strength of characte reached a common-sense solution of difficulties which ha baffled others over a period of nearly a hundred years. Th Papal States, with a history and with historical rights founde in titles dating back to the Roman Empire, lay athwart th path of the Italian State. There was an apparently irreconci able conflict between popes who were bound to defend th inherited papal position and all the elements, good and ba honest and disreputable, under the banner of a youthf Nationalism.

Nationalism versus Papacy

Extremists existed on both sides. Reactionaries, whose ide were medieval, and whose abstract logic kept them aloof fro the world of political realities refused to give any conside ation to the claims of Italian patriots. On the other han there were radicals who used the blind of "patriotism" promote a diabolic campaign against religion. There wer also moderate men on either side. Pius IX and Leo XIII love Italy, but they had to set their clear duty to the Churc above sentiment. Victor Emmanuel II wanted to live and di as a Catholic, but he was swept on by the Nationalist force which he felt powerless to withstand.

Right and justice were with the popes. The spirit of th times was against them. Their appeal to reason, conscienc higher principles, and eternal truths scarcely awakened a echo in a century that was ruled by emotion. Europe wa Liberal in sympathy. It was even more strongly Nationalis Popular sovereignty, plebiscites, parliaments, and constitu tions were sacred things. The methods and means employe

to secure them were beyond criticism. The admiration of
Europe for the ability, energy, and cunning of Cavour was
in no way lessened by the fact that he was utterly unscrupulous and unethical in his antipapal policies. For him
as for the age in which he displayed his real talents, the
end justified the means. History is still partial to him, but
before any unbiased tribunal the papacy has a good case.

At the beginning of the nineteenth century Italy was "a
geographic expression." The Italian peninsula and the Italian
people had had a glorious history, but there had been no
Italian nation. City states and petty principalities had warred
among themselves, and had been trampled under the heel of
foreign domination. Spain, France, and the German emperors
had made the land a battleground. There had been no political
unity since the days of the Roman Empire. And yet the
elements of a national spirit were present. In fact, for the
study of Nationalism it would be hard to find a laboratory
specimen comparable to Italy. There were memories to feed
the nobler sentiment of patriotism. There was also the galling
presence of a foreign power to generate hatred. There were
the common hopes of a brighter future. Dreamers and practical
men, underground agitators and statesmen, each contributed
to the compound of good and evil which we call Italian
Nationalism.

The armies of Napoleon had spread the inebriating doctrines
of the Revolution. They had swept away institutions which
weighed oppressively upon the divided peoples. They had
introduced better government. Napoleon himself was an
Italian, and his personal triumph quickened the pride in
Italian blood. But the interlude was brief. The Congress of
Vienna soon tore down the Napoleonic decorations and
restored the old scenery. The princelings came back, the pope
was again secure in Rome, and the iron hand of Austria controlled the northern provinces. The dormant spirit of Italy had
been aroused. The flame of patriotism had been enkindled in
the better class of Italians. More important, the seeds of
Jacobin fanaticism had been sown. Secret societies became
nests of conspiracy and intrigue. The ubiquitous Austrian
garrisons stirred a universal deep resentment. Liberals

demanded the abolition of local tyrannies. Nationalists worked for the union of all Italy. Both hated Austria, and set themselves to the task of driving her out. The military predominance of Austria was the supreme obstacle to Nationalist plans. It was also a powerful stimulus to patriotism and to less noble feelings.

Another obstacle was the papal power. Possession sanctioned by centuries of peaceful and unquestioned rule gave the pope a better title to his States than any in Europe. Besides, the popes had a long record of beneficent service. But a new mentality had entered with the French Revolution. The political power of the popes, and of the German Emperors as well, had been regarded as a natural and normal thing. This was no longer so. The leaders of the Revolution had taught Italy along with the rest of Europe to despise prescriptive historical rights. The spiritual prerogatives of the papacy were meaningless to many, while to a whole group of conspirators they were an object of hate and an added reason for attacking the papal States.

Three plans were presented for the unification of Italy. Giuseppe Mazzini, perfervid spokesman of the Jacobin element in the secret societies, agitated for a radical republic. Vicenzo Gioberti, priest and brilliant professor, with more regard for vested rights and for historical fact, urged a federation of Italian states. Camillo Benso Cavour, with a statesman's sense of the possible and a Liberal's disregard for justice, worked with a singleness of purpose for the extension of the monarchical rule of Sardinia over the whole of Italy. The Rousseauvian eloquence of a dreamer like Mazzini could enflame the fighting spirit of the Carbonari, of Young Italy, and of the motley legion of Garibaldi, but in the order of practical politics Mazzini's only achievement was the ephemeral orgy of the Roman Republic of 1849. Gioberti, also, was foredoomed to failure. His *Primato morale e civile degli Italiani,* buttressed by the writings of Count Balbo and Massimo d'Azeglio, exposed the futility of revolutions and conspiracies, and proclaimed the natural aptitude of the papacy to realize the hopes of national unity, but, even aside from the bitterness of anticlerical opposition to this dream,

Three Plans

the Father of Christendom simply could not accept the leadership of a party. Clearly, the future lay with the practical men who followed Cavour.

Cavour had all the personal qualities, good and bad, of a successful statesman. Circumstances were in his favor, or at least capable of being molded to his ends. He knew how to exploit the weakness of both conservatives and radicals. The Jacobinism of Mazzini had been discredited, and his *Italia farà da sì* had proved impractical. Conscience and a clear sense of duty forbade Pius IX to fight against Austria. On the other hand, Piedmont was prepared to assume the leadership of Nationalists and Liberals throughout the Peninsula. It had a king who was a soldier and who was trusted by patriots everywhere. It had a constitution in keeping with the times and a reputation for economic progress. It had a well-organized and disciplined army. Cavour had the means of co-operating effectively with revolutionists in the other Italian States and, more important, of controlling them when the time for control should arrive. But in the program of Cavour Italy was not to solve Italy's problems. The Foreigner was to be driven out with foreign aid. The military might of Austria was too much for any possible combination of Italians. The obvious solution lay in French intervention. And Cavour set himself to the task of bringing Napoleon III into the conflict.

Cavour sent his Sardinian troops, for no justifiable reason, to fight on the stronger side in the Crimean War. By this criminal act he won the gratitude of Napoleon III and a voice at the peace congress. In 1858 Napoleon, the one-time Carbonaro, was scared into a disposition for action by the Orsini bomb. From then on Cavour could play upon his fears, his inherited dislike of Austria, and his greed. In 1859 Napoleon, the dupe of Cavour, drove the Austrians out of Lombardy. Napoleon's sudden halt, before the work Cavour had mapped for him was fully done, retarded the process, but the most essential step had been taken. When Cavour died two years later Garibaldi's "Red Shirts" had conquered the Two Sicilies; the army of Victor Emmanuel and local plebiscites had secured Parma, Modena, Tuscany, and the Romagna; Victor Emmanuel himself had been proclaimed King of Italy.

Camillo
Cavour

Prussia's victory over Austria in 1866 gave Venezia to the new kingdom, and the Franco-German War of 1870 opened the way for an easy conquest of Rome. The House of Savoy had "annexed" the whole of Italy, and complete success had crowned the plans of Cavour. The dream of *Italia unita* was realized. But Catholic Italians and Italian patriots were faced with the anomalous situation of conflicting and apparently irreconcilable claims on the part of a State at war with the Church whose collaboration it needed, and on the part of the Church which had to defend its violated sovereignty against a State whose friendship was, humanly speaking, necessary for the proper functioning of the spiritual power. Cavour would in all likelihood have found a way out of the impasse. But men of smaller political stature were powerless to remedy the evils accompanying the legacy he left to Italy.

PIUS IX

XVI

PIUS IX: THE IMMACULATE CONCEPTION

ON DECEMBER 8, 1854, THE IMMACULATE CONCEPTION
of the Mother of God was defined. Ten years later, on December 8, 1864, the *Syllabus of Errors* was published. On the same date, five years later, the Vatican Council was opened. This similarity of dates may be regarded as merely a coincidence. It is, in fact, an index to the childlike piety of Pius IX. And the piety of a great pope is by no means a negligible factor in the history of his times. In view of the calumnies heaped upon him it is important to grasp the fact that behind the smiling strength of Pio Nono there was a sense of power generated by an inner life of prayer. The dust of controversy that filled the air about him, the mud that was thrown, metaphorically, by those who hated the Church and the supernatural, left his white cassock unstained. But this was merely an outward symbol of a soul unperturbed amid the apparent triumphs of the "mystery of iniquity." Pius IX loved the Immaculate Queen of Heaven, and he wanted the world to know it. He looked to her for help and protection, and in turn he did what he could to honor her.

But the Bull *Ineffabilis Deus* was something more than a gesture of tender affection toward our Lady. It has its place in the history of Catholic devotions, and devout souls have been grateful to the pope who defined the sinlessness of the Mother of God. But contemporary enemies of the Church, who let it pass unnoticed while they raged and fumed at the *Syllabus* and the dogma of papal infallibility, failed to perceive that the definition of the Immaculate Conception implied two very unpalatable truths. Historians have since noted, quite correctly, that Pius IX asserted his own infallibility in no uncertain terms when he excluded from the Church of Christ all who should henceforth presume to reject his definition. But

Original Sin

171

what historians have for the most part overlooked is the equally obvious teaching of the pope on sin and the fall of man.

The age that still clung optimistically to the old Rousseauvian heresy of man's natural perfection should have been a bit more sensitive to the implied insult to its self-righteousness. This is not the place to dilate upon the inconsistency of an age that claimed near divinity for tainted nature, but had no eye for the solitary glory of its fairest flower. The nineteenth century laughed at the very idea of sin. Pius IX threw the whole weight of his authority into an implicit declaration that sin was a legacy humanity could not escape. The nineteenth century thought the pope was hopelessly out of step with an advancing world. Pius IX declared, again implicitly, that from his definition of truth there was no appeal, and that the world would have to catch up with him.

The inner nexus between the definition of the Immaculate Conception and the *Syllabus* of 1864 may not appear to the surface observer. But it is there, nonetheless, and it should have prepared a deluded generation for the shock it felt when its pet delusions were condemned in eighty selected propositions. Likewise, the very wording of the *Ineffabilis Deus* should have made it easy to foresee the probable outcome of the feverish discussion of papal infallibility. What the pope actually did when he defined the Immaculate Conception was not to assert his own superior knowledge of a truth which, after all, could be known only through divine revelation. He states officially and categorically that the truth in question was *de facto* contained in the "deposit of faith." Quite simply, whosoever refused to accept the word of God was guilty of voluntary exclusion from the Church, shipwreck of his faith, and spiritual suicide. The supreme teacher of the faithful had used every human means to ascertain from a review of Tradition and of more or less obscure passages of the Bible just what God had revealed. He might never have arrived at a definable conclusion, but if and when he did declare the meaning of a revealed doctrine, the case was closed for all times. Further embellishments of the doctrine there might be, but the Church never questioned in practice the irreducible minimum.

The
Infallible
Pope

The *Analecta Juris Pontificii*[1] states that Pius IX "promulgated the definition of the Immaculate Conception at the urgent request and with the applause of the whole Catholic world." But there was a world outside the Church which did not applaud, chiefly because the whole idea was meaningless to it. In whatever terminology it might be expressed the supernatural, grace, sin, especially original sin, the Incarnation — each was a concept foreign to the spirit of the time. But Pius IX gave little thought to a passing mood, though it might require a century or more to die. After a careful combing of historical records to discover the mind of the Church in her manner of praying, after a judicious weighing of Scriptural texts and their interpretation by the Fathers, his collaborators prepared what amounted to a monumental treatise. The substance of decree, however, is condensed into a single paragraph:

". . . To the honor of the Holy and Undivided Trinity, to the glory and adornment of the Virgin Mother of God, for the exaltation of the Catholic faith and the increase of the Christian religion, by the authority of our Lord Jesus Christ, of the blessed Apostles, Peter and Paul, and Our own, We declare, pronounce and define that the doctrine which holds the most blessed Virgin Mary was, by the singular favor and privilege of Almighty God in view of the merits of Jesus Christ, the Savior of the human race, preserved free from all stain of original sin from the first instant of her conception, is a doctrine revealed by God and therefore to be firmly and constantly believed by all the faithful. Wherefore should any presume to dissent in their heart from Our definition, which may God avert, let them know and realize that they are condemned by their own judgment, that they have suffered shipwreck of the faith, and have cut themselves off from the unity of the Church. . . ."

For centuries the Church had been chanting in her ample Marian liturgy a very striking passage: "all heresies throughout the whole world thou alone hast crushed." An acceptance of the *Ineffabilis Deus* in all its implications would have gone far to destroy error and to restore the lost faith of the middle nineteenth century.

---

[1] Cf. Denzinger-Bannwart, *Enchiridion Symbolorum*, 1641.

The definition of the Immaculate Conception deserves even more space than can be given to it here, not only because it is scarcely mentioned in histories of the period, but because the ignorance, incredulity, or contempt manifested toward it is an excellent gauge of nineteenth-century mentality. It has also been taken as indicative of a new policy in papal circles. Pius IX had made a sincere effort to co-operate with the promoters of Italian liberty and national life. He had found the champions of "the people" a deluded, if not utterly degraded lot, fanatical in the pursuit of revolutionary ideals, but utterly unprincipled in their choice of methods and means.[2] He would still have much to suffer at their hands, but his sad experience showed that the way to beneficent collaboration was hopelessly closed. *Il papa liberale* was sick and disgusted with Liberalism. Henceforth, in matters of State and government, he was a conservative. But his conservatism did not mean inactivity. The time and energy saved from external things was employed in what is after all the proper sphere of the Father of Christendom. To speak of his failure as a statesman might lead to misunderstanding. Still, there is every probability that, if Pius IX had found conditions such as to warrant any hope of successful statecraft, he might not have turned so wholeheartedly to spiritual things. It was, in fact, during his forced exile at Gaëta, in 1849, that he first sounded the opinions of the bishops on the subject of defining the Immaculate Conception. And this dogma was a step in the direction of another dogma, that of papal infallibility.

---

[2] Fernand Mourret, *Histoire générale*, VIII, p. 341 ff.

XVII

PIUS IX: THE SYLLABUS

IF THE DOGMATIC TEACHING OF 1854 CREATED LITTLE stir, it was not so with the Syllabus of 1864. The world might ignore what it regarded as a pretty piece of household piety within the Catholic Church. It was not likely to be interested in what it was incapable of understanding. But when its idols were attacked directly, when the pseudo-science and the pseudo-philosophy of its darling authors were held up to censure, it burst into violent eruption. Pius IX had shown himself no lover of peace at any price. He might have enjoyed tranquillity, he might have purchased popularity, personal well-being, and prestige by merely falling in line with the radical element in Italy. He might have closed his eyes and his ears to the wild vagaries of popular writers or watched the disintegration of society unperturbed. He might have overlooked the errors of Catholic thinkers who tried to effect a compromise between philosophy and faith, or between Liberalism and the Church. But that would have been disloyalty to duty and treason to Christ. Pius IX raised his voice, and when eighty propositions culled from thirty-two documents were published in the *Syllabus* of 1864 the cumulative effect was something very much like an anathema against modern "civilization."

Anathema of Modern Errors

And yet the *Syllabus* contained nothing new. It was compiled and sent to the bishops throughout the world in order that they might be able to take in at a glance "all the errors and pernicious doctrines" proscribed and condemned by the reigning pope. If, as was probably the case, many of the encyclicals, allocutions, and apostolic letters of the past eighteen years had not reached the clergy of distant parts, or if, as was more probable, they had been mislaid or for-

The Reason for the Syllabus

175

gotten, here was the gist of the most dangerous doctrines reduced to the compass of a few pages. As a practical device the *Syllabus* had obvious advantages. Where not one in a hundred among the clergy would make his own digest of papal utterances or, perhaps, even read them, there was reason to hope that the majority of those who needed definite ideas on modern trends would become familiar with this condensed résumé.

Among the anticlericals there was a widespread acquaintance with the *Syllabus* in circles into which no other papal document had penetrated. It was well, of course, that the world should be aware of the uncomplimentary opinion the pope had of it, though, unfortunately, this brief summary of propositions wrenched from their context was open to misinterpretation. And it was precisely the tendency to misinterpret the *Syllabus* which makes the historian hesitate to emphasize its real importance.

Next to the content of the *Syllabus* the first point to clarify is its authority or binding power. One of the keenest students of the Church in the nineteenth century,[1] distinguishes between the *factum dogmaticum* and the *factum historicum,* and insists that the *Syllabus* was an emergency measure intended to meet the attacks of the moment. It was an authentic statement of the attitude of the supreme teaching and governing authority in Christendom, and as such called for implicit obedience on the part of all Catholics. But from the fact that each proposition was accompanied by a reference to the source from which it was taken (a fact which many pseudo-scholars ignored) it is argued rightly that it was not the intention of the congregation of Cardinals who compiled it, nor of the Holy Father, to add anything to the original documents. It does not even partake of the authority, whatever that may be, of the encyclical, *Quanta Cura,* to which it was attached quite accidentally, to facilitate distribution. Nor is it in any sense an *ex cathedra* pronouncement, much as this bogey perturbed later opponents of papal infallibility. All this leaves untouched the very real, but adventitious force which

---

[1] Albert Ehrhard, *Der Katholizismus und das zwanzigste Jahrhundert,* p. 261.

the *Syllabus* received from its immediate and universal acceptance by the whole Church. Theologians and historians may still apply the principles and methods of scholarly criticism to each of the eighty propositions of the *Syllabus*, but its primary purpose was served when a thousand bishops throughout Christendom were provided with a definite and practical, if negative, guide to the errors, blatant or latent, of the time. More positive teaching was to come from the Vatican Council and the encyclicals of the next four popes.

It is noteworthy that the origin of the *Syllabus* has been traced to Joachim Pecci, or at least to the provincial council of Spoleto of 1849, in which the future Leo XIII was the guiding spirit. After some preliminary work by Cardinal Fornari, in 1852, the idea was given form by the commission which had been set up to prepare the Bull on the Immaculate Conception. In 1860 Bishop Gerbet of Perpignan issued an "Instruction" containing eighty-five repudiated propositions. Two years later the bishops assembled in Rome for the canonization of the Japanese martyrs approved sixty-one theses. Finally, in 1864, a congregation of Cardinals formulated the *Syllabus* as it now stands. It was, to say the least, no hasty catalogue. Rather it bore the marks of Roman leisure and thoroughness in its composition.

For its content the reader is best referred to the *Syllabus* itself. To attempt a more succinct digest would be futile. Attention may, however, be called to the manner in which the various items are classified under headings, a bare list of which affords an excellent survey of the diseased "isms" of the nineteenth century. Seven items are grouped under Pantheism, Naturalism, and radical Rationalism; seven more under moderate Rationalism; four under Indifferentism and Latitudinarianism. A cross reference is then inserted to earlier condemnations of Socialism, Communism, Secret Societies, Bible Societies, and Clerico-liberal Societies, which are laconically labeled: "pests." The last four propositions are reserved for contemporary Liberalism. The rest of the long list has five subdivisions the longest of which have to do with erroneous teachings about the Church and her rights, and about the State and its relations with the Church. Nine counts are

Its Content

registered against false ethics, both natural and Christian; ten against attacks upon Christian marriage; and two against attacks upon the Roman Pontiff. A covering letter of the Cardinal Secretary Antonelli explains the purpose of the *Syllabus*, and calls the attention of the bishops to whom it is directed to the encyclical, *Quanto Cura*, which accompanies it.

The enemies of Pius IX questioned the clearness of his views, and rejected, naturally, his diagnosis of the ills of society. But neither then nor now could anyone accuse the pope or his curia of lack of courage. Those who governed the Church had no desire to stir up trouble, but they were conscious of a solemn obligation to warn Catholics of the poison in the atmosphere they breathed, and they were careless of the consequences to themselves. It is far easier at the present time to recognize that there is something wrong about every condemned proposition in the Syllabus, and to say so. The age of disillusionment has badly riddled the pseudo-philosophy of the past century, and we have seen the necessity of printing much of its terminology and most of its shibboleths in quotation marks. But the writers of the time and their gullible readers took words at their face value. They might be indifferent about eternal verities, but they were extremely annoyed when the half truths of the day were not accepted blindly and humbly. In the age of Individualism, of Evolution and Progress, divine revelation and human reason had little chance in conflict with feeling or personal interests. The age had cut loose from its moorings, blotted out the stars of heaven, and preferred to sail before the wind. It gave little thought to the end of its journey or to anything that might lie beyond it. It had learned to ignore the guidance of the Church long ago. The pope was a leader who had been disowned, a guide of wanderers who wanted to stray, a physician of a society that felt itself in perfect health. Because Pius IX was at perpetual war with the thought of his time, because he devoted so much of his energy to removing unsound elements, his successor had a better foundation upon which to erect a solid constructive social philosophy.

A few typical errors condemned by the *Syllabus* invite

comment. The list of propositions to be anathematized begins with an attack upon the Creator which is a very complex muddle of contradictions and absurdities. It ends with an invitation to the pope to come to terms with Progress, Liberalism, and modern civilization. Scattered through it are theses that raise reason above revelation, nature above the supernatural, Philosophy and natural science above theology, the State above the Church. Morals are reduced to a material level. Christian marriage is made a purely civil contract. Alongside a decrepit Gallicanism which would whittle down the monarchical constitution of the Church there is the still vigorous Liberalism, an amorphous compound of several "isms," which would deprive the Church of the right to govern herself, to teach her members, to exist even, and which made man independent of God and proclaimed his "right" to deny the Creator and defy His laws. Mingled with absolutely false statements there are others which are wrong in the sense in which they were originally written, but which with due qualification and explanation might be allowed to stand. An example is that which asserts the desirability of a separation of Church and State. It would be amusing if the whole sad rigmarole could be transferred to some future age and, let us hope, saner generation, and we could be present to hear the forthcoming comments on the mentality of the nineteenth century. If the fragmentary records should fail to make clear that the catalogue was assembled only to be rejected and reprobated, and if it should be held up as a mirror of what was characteristic of the great machine age, men would wonder at the depths of darkness to which the "enlightened" human mind had descended. It is more likely, however, that history will regard the *Syllabus* merely as an excellent summary of passing distempers and fevers the cure of which was considerably aided by a papal condemnation.[2]

Rightly the *Syllabus* begins with Pantheism, a doctrine that logically leads to atheism, and thus to the destruction of the foundations of society. To the illogical, Pantheism may be merely an opiate producing all the pleasant and soothing

---

[2] Cf. Appendix A.

effects of subtle flattery. Practically, it effectually kills all
sense of responsibility. Thus we read:

Apart from the world there is no supreme, all-wise, all-
provident Divine Being. God is identified with nature and
subject consequently to change. Actually, He evolves (*fit*) in
man and in the material universe, for all things are God and
the very substance of God. God and the world are one and
the same reality; so, too, are spirit and matter, necessity and
freedom, truth and error, good and evil, justice and injustice.

Any man in his right mind will at once pronounce all this
the ravings of a freak. Pantheism is, in fact, so out of harmony
with the ordinary experience of everyday life that the man
in the street will find it hard to believe that "thinkers" from
the dawn of recorded human error have fallen into it. Nor
is it merely a laboratory product, a poisoned luxury whose
secrets belong to the few. In diluted doses it is administered
to readers of prose and poetry. For the healthy mental and
moral constitution the danger may be negligible. But by a
generation of practical atheists, people who lived as if there
were no God, people who had reasons for wishing there were
no God, the theoretic justification here offered was eagerly
accepted. It is one thing to enjoy the lilt in the lines of the
poet: "We are all parts of one stupendous whole, whose body
Nature is, and God the soul," and it is quite another thing
for the sovereign individual to set himself up as an irresponsible agent, an evolving divinity, an autonomous being taking
his law from his own inner self, or at least claiming the right
to mold his actions on such principles, however vaguely
formulated. And yet this was a characteristic of the century
which began with Kantian idealism and ended with the crass
materialism of the Marxists.

The
Eightieth
Proposition

The condemnation of the first thesis of the *Syllabus* excited
little or no opposition. Pantheists are slow to seek an argument
in the open, and others would scarcely be interested at all. But
with the eightieth thesis the case was different. In his allocution of March 18, 1861, Pius IX had repudiated the proposition that: "The Roman Pontiff can and should reconcile
himself and come to terms with Progress, Liberalism and
modern civilization." Those who had devoted but a cursory

glance to the more specific condemnations found in this last anathema all the evidence they wanted to prove that the pope was hopelessly out of step with the age in which he lived. Anticlericals felt justified in their relentless war on the Church as the enemy of humanity. The more the Papacy laid itself open to the charge of being an obstacle to progress and freedom, the more it could be made to look like an antiquated relic of the dead past, the brighter grew their own hopes for its eventual annihilation. Nor did they take time to investigate whether or not the condemnation of the pope might have some reasonable explanation. The pope himself had admitted their major contention that he was opposed to the onward march of the age, and that was to them the funeral announcement of the Papacy. But a rapid perusal of the allocution, *Jamdudum cernimus,* would have revealed what kind of "Progress," "Liberalism," and "civilization" it was that the pope refused to accept. Briefly it was the movement which under these specious names had for its purpose the de-Christianization of the world. Pius IX had employed the terminology which he found current at the time, and he condemned, as he could not help condemning, the thing which certainly was not progress in the sense of human improvement, nor liberty in the sense of freedom to do what man ought to do, nor civilization in any except a materialist meaning of the word. It was not his fault if language had been misused. On the other hand, he had resented the implication that the Church had not made her own great contribution to human progress in the true sense, to freedom and to civilization.

Every one of the eighty theses in the *Syllabus* would seem to call for some comment. Every one of the condemnations touched a sore spot somewhere. But if we may single out a thesis which, along with the last, aroused and still arouses the animosity of anticlericals, and causes perplexity even to many who are well disposed toward the papacy, that thesis is the fifty-fifth. Expressly and directly it repudiates separation of Church and State. What it teaches as positive doctrine most readers did not trouble themselves to find out. To be specific, did the *Syllabus* cast anything like an aspersion on

Church and State

the system now prevailing in America and apparently working
to the satisfaction of all? In the Latin version the condemned
thesis is terseness itself. *"Ecclesia a statu, statusque ab
ecclesia sejungendus est."* The nearest equivalent expression
in English would be: "The Church *must* be [or should be]
separated from the State and the State from the Church."
Now, if this thesis needs qualification, and it does, the thesis
as it stands is not true. Moreover, as a doctrine it may be
harmful to society.

But we are not left in the dark as to the correct interpretation of the condemnation. Within six weeks after the
Syllabus appeared, Bishop Dupanloup published a commentary
which effectually removed all misunderstandings. His famous
distinction between *la thèse* and *l'hypothèse* satisfied all well-
meaning objectors and received, moreover, the warm approbation of Pius IX and of six hundred and thirty bishops. It had,
in fact, been anticipated by the ultraconservative *Civiltà
Cattolica* in its issue for October 2, 1863. In an anonymous
article from the pen of a Jesuit editor we find a very sane
discussion of "modern liberties." After insisting upon the
distinction between "thesis" and "hypothesis" the writer
continues:

> These liberties stated as a thesis, that is, as principles of
> universal application to human nature and to the divine plan,
> should be and have been condemned absolutely by the Roman
> Pontiffs, particularly by Pius VI, Pius VII, and Pius IX. But
> in the form of hypothesis, that is, an arrangement suitable to
> the special conditions of this or that nation, they may well be
> legitimate. As such Catholics may love them and defend them.
> When they employ them as effectively as possible in the service
> of religion and justice they do a good and useful work.

Bishop Dupanloup placed the anathemas of the *Syllabus*
in their proper context, showing that they held for the
Christian society which should exist, but that their severity
might be moderated by the unfortunate conditions then
prevalent. In the present state of Europe and the world not
even Boniface VIII would counsel a union of Church and
State, and it is poor history to bring back his ghost to trouble

admirers of the American system.[3] But the fact remains
separation of Church and State is not an ideal condition
fifty-fifth proposition of the *Syllabus* needed qualifi
Stated abstractly and absolutely, it was erroneous. A
pope was right in condemning it, as he was right in cor
ing the whole long list of half truths and downright er

There were Catholics who were more "Catholic th
pope" in their disagreement with the modern world.
were Catholics who accepted the *Syllabus* without qu
ing because it emanated from the central authority
Church. There were millions of Catholics who s
adverted to the points under discussion. But the bes
to the attitude of the whole Church toward the teach
its head is to be found in the Vatican Council. The
had pronounced Pius IX in his dotage. An assembly of
solemnly proclaimed him infallible. The Holy Fath
saddened by the uneasiness and perturbation of mir
few Catholic leaders who feared the worst from his "r
of modern culture." He could regret the disappro
political leaders like Gladstone, Bismarck, and Napoleon
But the ranting of anticlerical Liberals about "the last
challenge of the dying papacy to the modern world" had its
humorous side, and at the same time provided the best
reassurance that the *Syllabus* had struck home. The hard
language of the pope has been criticized. But for the most
part he had merely called things by their proper names.

---

[3] Cf. Wilfrid Parsons, in *Historical Bulletin,* XIV, pp. 30, 31. "Separation
of Church and State." Also Appendix B.

XVIII

PIUS IX: THE VATICAN COUNCIL

Papal
Infallibility
ON JULY 18, 1870, JUST TWO MONTHS BEFORE THE
army of Victor Emmanuel battered its way into Rome, the
Vatican Council in its fourth and final session defined the
dogma of papal infallibility. In the eyes of many this was the
most important act in the history of the Church in the nineteenth century. And yet, paradoxically, it made no change in
the constitution of the Church. It was feared as an attack upon
the freedom of Christendom. Its effect was rather a liberating
from doubt and divided opinions. All sorts of absurd apprehensions were expressed that individuals, nations, and the
Church itself would suffer from the arbitrary rule of the pope.
But tranquillity, security, moderation have been the marks
of papal action ever since.

Intellectual ability, erudition, and political influence were
strong in the alliance of Catholics, Liberals, and nondescripts
which raised the storm of protest against the defining of the
new dogma. What would have happened had the Council been
permitted to pursue its course in peace and calm may be left
to conjecture. But the records show that papal infallibility was
not included explicitly in the original schemata. And certainly
the formidable opposition of statesmen, scholars, and a part of
the clergy may be counted among the factors that brought
about the definition, if they did not make it inevitable. Because the issue was so beclouded the truth burst through all
the more brilliantly. Because human agencies had been so
bitter in the struggle the outcome appeared the more divine.

Altogether aside from the absorbing question of infallibility,
Purpose of
the Council
there were abundant reasons for convoking the twentieth
Ecumenical Council. It was three hundred years since the remarkable assembly of bishops at Trent had completed their
great work, three hundred years of cataclysmic changes in

184

Christendom. During the earlier part of that period the need of a Council was not felt; during the previous century or more it would have been difficult, if not risky, to attempt such a meeting. In the decade preceding 1870 both necessity and opportunity pointed to a general council. The *Syllabus* and the numerous pronouncements of Pius IX had laid bare the ills of a sick society. A council was the obvious way to find a remedy and to apply it. Where the *Syllabus* had only irritated the patient, the combined efforts of bishops from all over the world might restore health and vigorous life.

In stormy times the Fathers of Trent had succeeded beyond human hopes in clarifying disputed points of doctrine and in stiffening the flabby discipline of the Church. At the very outset of the Arian heresy, an attack on Christianity more formidable than the upheaval of the sixteenth century, the Council of Nicea had been the providential means of preparing the Church for the combats and the triumphs of the Age of the Fathers. So, too, while the Council of the Vatican might fail to exorcise the spirit of Materialism and its manifold progeny from the Bourgeois world, it could nevertheless offer every assurance of rehabilitating reason and revelation, and of vindicating the rights of God and the supernatural. At least, as in former crises, Catholics would know where they stood amid the shifting systems and the chaos of opinions around them.

The Vatican Council was officially convoked on June 29, 1869, by the Bull, *Aeterni Patris*. The solemn opening took place on the December 8 of the same year. Its very impressive final session was held on July 18, 1870, and it was officially prorogued on the October 20 following. Whether the idea originated with the pope himself or was suggested by Dupanloup, the champion of the bishops, or by Manning the ardent advocate of greater centralization, may never be known. But at least this much is clear, the Holy Father was not coerced, physically or morally, into taking the step. There were many among the dignitaries in Rome who seemed to have an eye only for the difficulties of the undertaking. The political situation frightened some; others had a foreboding that powerful groups among the Catholics of France and Germany would render harmonious action impossible. But as the event proved, a dodging of difficulties was not the proper procedure. With Pius IX, in this council, as in many before it, one might distinguish three periods: the disorderly and troubled "period of the devil," the muddled period of human endeavor, and the concluding glorious period when the Holy Ghost would enlighten and purify all.[1] It would be cowardly to be terrified by the devil, or discouraged by human perversity or frailty. The work of the Church should go forward with confidence in God's help. For those who can look back over a space of nearly eighty years there can be no doubt that the Council was providential in its timeliness.

Much of the history of the Council, and by no means the least interesting part of it, belongs to the preliminary stage.

Preliminary Stage

Five years before the Fathers assembled, on December 8, 1864, the pope had begun to sound the opinions of the cardinals in Rome. Early in 1865 a commission of five cardinals was appointed to draw up tentative plans. Memorials returned by twenty-one cardinals, and later by thirty-four selected bishops, showed the vast majority in favor of convoking the Council. There were doctrines to be formulated and defined to meet the onslaught of a dozen "isms"; there were problems of ecclesiastical discipline and religious observance; there were the foreign missions and the hope of a reunion on the part of the Oriental schismatics; there was the perennial problem of Church and State; there was a demand for reform of Canon Law and for the better adapting of the Catechism to modern needs. Theologians, a splendid array of talent, were called to Rome to act as consultors on the various commissions.

When finally, on June 29, 1867, the eighteen-hundredth anniversary of the martyrdom of SS. Peter and Paul, the first public announcement was made, it was enthusiastically received by the assembled bishops. Two years were still to elapse before the opening of the Council. During that time an immense amount of preparatory work was done. Never since the days of the Apostles had the work of a Council been marked out with such businesslike thoroughness. There was

---

[1] Mourret, *op. cit.*, p. 518 ff.

ground for the expressed hope of Guizot, the outstanding Protestant of France, that a remedy for the serious ills of society, even the "saving of the world" might issue from the great assembly.

Just where Pio Nono would draw the line between the "period of the devil" and the period of human bungling is hard to say. He had called the Masonic lodges "the synagogue of Satan," and he had reason to believe that the powers of darkness were behind many of their sinister movements. The historian cannot, naturally, control the evidence that is needed to establish the influence of preternatural forces. But the convictions of men who thought they saw the workings of such forces belong to the realm of objective facts. There was, moreover, the Masonic anti-Council of Naples, convoked for December 8, 1869, to offset the influence of the Council of the Vatican. The purpose of this sham Council, namely, to "proclaim the great principles of universal human right," may not have been diabolic in its inspiration. But among the Freemasons who organized it there were men who had given expression to a satanic hatred of God. The best argument with which to exonerate the devil lies in the utterly ridiculous antics of the Naples assembly. With all his experience in human affairs the devil should be too wise to be held responsible for all the three days' fiasco at Naples. Still, Masonry was an undeniable force in the politico-irreligious world immediately before and after 1870. And the Naples meeting does throw some light upon the attitude of Freemasons toward the Vatican Council.

The Anti-Council

There were, however, two very real sources of anxiety during the period preceding the opening of the Council. They were the possibility, and the danger even, of interference by the governments of Europe actuated by the agitation against the Council proceeding from disaffected Catholics. As it turned out, only Russia actually forbade her bishops to attend the Council. The other governments, after some wavering, at length concluded that they would leave the Church free to conduct her own affairs. Austria and Prussia stated explicitly that they would not meddle in spiritual matters, but that any incursion into the rights of the civil power would be resented. France, whose attitude was of vital interest to the Council,

Threatened Intervention

finally resolved, thanks largely to the efforts of Emile Ollivier, to remain neutral.

All this was after "Catholic" Bavaria, prompted by Döllinger, had essayed to lead an attack on the Council. In April, 1869, the government of Bavaria, in an attempt to organize concerted action against the Council, had sent a note to all the courts of Europe, warning them against the danger of erecting the *Syllabus* into a dogmatic decree, and of defining papal infallibility. After the Council had gotten under way there was some danger that England, under the guidance of Gladstone, who was influenced by Lord Acton and by Döllinger, might cause trouble. But Gladstone found himself checkmated by Lord Clarendon, the Foreign Secretary, who was supplied with reliable information by Cardinal Manning through the English agent in Rome. The upshot of the whole scare was that the Council was "left in peace to do God's work."

It would have been extremely unfortunate if the governments of Europe had not remained aloof. They had the power to impede the calm deliberations of the Council and even to prevent its assembling. That they manifested a keen interest in its proceedings is evidence of the importance of religion and of the Church in an age of political realism. Their threat of intervention may have made the fathers of the Council more cautious, and if so, it was a contribution to the task of accurately formulating statements of objective truth, which was after all the purpose of all the discussion. In any case, the attitude of the statesmen and politicians, whose grasp of Christian principles was rather feeble, is fully comprehensible. They had little or no interest in the religious question. But the Council might touch indirectly upon the field of politics, and their political philosophy would not stand close criticism. Still, whatever may have been the influence upon the Council of potentially hostile governments, these were essentially an external danger.

The "Intellectual" Opposition

But the panic and fury of a group of "intellectuals" who carried on a war of pamphlets and books stirred up considerable confusion within the Catholic body. One may, however, hazard the opinion that out of the noise and heat of conflict no little clarity was born. The history of dogmas is a history of defense against attacks upon the faith. In the present instance, because all the resources of historical erudition, amateur theology, bad logic, and passionate eloquence were marshaled for an attack upon the Council it was humanly improbable, if not impossible, that the Council should decree anything rashly or without full consideration of every angle of the problem. Because there were extremists on either side there was every assurance, even humanly speaking, that conclusions arrived at would be proof against any test.

One may distinguish half-a-dozen verbal duels in which, before the Council and outside of it, principles, publications, and individuals were pitted against one another. There were Gallicanism and Ultramontanism; Neo-Ultramontanism and Liberalism; the *Allgemeine Zeitung* and the *Civiltà Cattolica; The Pope and the Council* by Janus, *alias* Döllinger, and the *Anti-Janus* by Hergenröther. There were also Dupanloup and Veuillot, Newman and Manning, whose mutual opposition was rather that of the cautious and moderate against the overzealous and reckless.

Gallicanism, which stood for local autonomy in France, or in any other division of the Catholic Church, was by definition opposed to the idea of papal infallibility, and consequently to the Council which was expected to define the dogma. It has Gallicanism its historical and theoretical variations, and it was, itself, a premature variety of Liberalism. Opposed to it was Ultramontanism, which as an extreme reaction against Gallicanism tended to undue centralization in the Church, but which in its moderate form, in the sense that is, of the Roman doctrine concerning the prerogatives of the pope, was practically synonymous with Catholicism. Before the Council met the Gallican claims, whether of Germans or Frenchmen, of bishops or Catholic princes, were within limits a matter of free debate. These claims had been refuted by Catholic theologians, notably by Bellarmine, but they lingered on until the dogmatic constitution *De Ecclesia Christi* killed them. On the other hand, Neo-Ultramontanism, which rose up in the person of Louis Veuillot to combat a decrepit Gallicanism and a youthful, generous, but rash, Catholic Liberalism, rushed into all manner of excesses, and was the cause of division in the

Catholic camp and of grief to the more sane and less emotional
leaders. Historically, this reaction against the spirit of the
French Revolution is easily explained. But the fact remains
that from de Maistre and Lamennais to W. G. Ward and
Veuillot this movement, of laymen for the most part, tended
to be more "Catholic" than the Catholic Church. And yet, like
many another exaggeration, it served to "redress a balance."
If these new champions of the Church were unsafe guides
toward a constructive program, they were nonetheless most
effective in destroying much that was an obstacle to the
triumph of objective truth.

The storm center in Germany was the small group of "intellectuals" of which Johann Ignaz Döllinger was the virtual
dictator. Döllinger had, like the great unfortunate Lamennais

Döllinger
before him, rendered invaluable services to religion and the
Church. As professor of history, and of theology, he had attracted eager students to the University of Munich, to send
them back powerful defenders of the Catholic cause. Of these
Lord Acton was, perhaps, the most remarkable. Döllinger's
books were rich in historical erudition and in interpretation.
Through his correspondence with scholars he wielded a wide
influence. In particular, the papal primacy had found in him
an ardent and able champion. But as his fame spread and the
consciousness of his own power increased, his hold on the
fundamentals of faith began to slip. To express the change in
terms of pride would sound like moralizing, but the long
course of ecclesiastical history is strewn with shipwrecks
which can be traced to a lack of humility.

In any case, the approach of the Vatican Council found
Döllinger an object of suspicion and distrust in Rome. When
consultors were sought in Germany his name was passed over.
And reasons could have been given for the omission or over-
sight. Döllinger had not been sparing in his criticism of Rome,
of the Papal States, of the Curia. He had been bitter in his
contempt for Scholastic Theology. He had developed something very near to hatred for the Jesuits. As early as 1850 he
had propounded his grandiose dream of a German national
church, not schismatic, it is true, but hardly Catholic in its
domineering self-sufficiency. He was a protagonist, too, for

GIUSEPPE GARIBALDI
Popular hero of Italian Unification
(1807–1882)

AMILLO BENSO CAVOUR
tesman of Italian Unification
(1810–1861)

GIACOMO CARDINAL ANTONELLI
Secretary of State to Pius IX (1806–1876)

THE VATICAN COUNCIL

nvoked June 29, 1869; final session July 18, 1870; it was attended by more Bishops than
y other council in the history of the Church From a Contemporary Engraving — Soibelman Syndicate

JOHANN IGNAZ DÖLLINGER

Brilliant intellectual and historian. Döllinger's invaluable services
to the Church were nullified by his later apostasy (1799–1890)

"public opinion." And as he became more and more infatuated with "liberal" ideas he became a source of anxiety to many of his former friends. The world still admired his immense learning and his undoubted intellectual powers. But not even Döllinger himself could have foretold whither they would lead him. Only by reading history backwards does one get the full significance of his appeal for deference to public opinion at the Munich assembly of 1863. The following year the *Syllabus* sent him into a rage. His exclusion from the deliberations preparatory to the Council was a final "insult." He threw his great weight into a most determined opposition.

On February 6, 1869, the *Civiltà Cattolica* printed a slightly hysterical letter from Paris in which the writer drew a distinction between "liberal Catholics" and Catholics properly so called, pleaded for a minimum of discussion at the coming Council, a dogmatic condemnation of the theses of the *Syllabus*, and a definition of papal infallibility. The writer also expressed a hope that the whole affair would be settled by an "explosion of the Holy Spirit." The Jesuit editors disclaimed personal responsibility for what was after all merely a report on conditions in France. But a bombshell had fallen in the camp where Döllinger ruled. In rapid succession, beginning on March 10, five articles appeared anonymously in the *Allgemeine Zeitung* of Augsburg, under the general caption: *The Council and the Civiltà.* The German Protestants applauded, and all Europe was interested. Other articles followed in the *Allgemeine Zeitung* and in *Augsburger Gazette*.[2] Before the end of the year the original five articles were revised and published in book form under the more appropriate title: *The Pope and the Council.* Döllinger's quarrel was no longer with the *Civiltà.* He was attacking the Papacy directly, and the Papacy had found in Joseph Hergenröther a champion less brilliant, perhaps, than Döllinger, but his equal in learning and his master in theological insight. Döllinger had written under the pseudonym: Janus. Hergenröther called his book: *Anti-Janus.* It was a duel of giants, and Döllinger emerged from it with his reputation badly shaken.

War of Periodicals

---

[2] Dr. Hergenröther, *Anti-Janus*, I and II.

The *Anti-Janus* may have missed a few of the innumerable difficulties raised by Janus. But so much of the attack on the Papacy was shown to be groundless or based on distorted facts and a strained interpretation of dubious sources that Döllinger was discredited for all time, at least among Catholics. But the *Anti-Janus* could not appear until an immense amount of harm had been done. Already "in the streets, merchants, artisans, artists of every sort, soldiers, women, and boys, and especially state-functionaries"[3] were discussing "the doctrines about Council and Pope, the propositions of the Encyclical and the *Syllabus*." Döllinger had protested against the decrees of the Council before he could have known what those decrees would be. He had held up the *Syllabus* to reprobation without caring to understand what was really the meaning of its condemned propositions. For him they were the expression of "the common sentiment and moral sense of every civilized people, and of all the institutions that have grown out of them."[4] To curb the Roman Curia Döllinger appealed "not to bishops, not to theologians, but to the whole educated secular world."[5] And this world was predisposed to sit in judgment upon the pope who had rejected *in globo* its dearest follies. "On the laity, possessing theological culture and religious sentiments" proclaimed the *Allgemeine Zeitung*, "devolves the solution of the ecclesiastical problem of the present time."[6] Döllinger and his misguided associates might, with what sincerity no one can guess, consider themselves crusaders for reform. But the movement they led was, quite simply, a revolt of "modern man" against divinely established authority. One can understand why the human mind, exalted by the triumphs of science, should wish to trim the constitution of the Church to its own measure. Döllinger had the mental equipment of a great heresiarch. But fortunately he stopped short in his course, and left the new sect of "Old Catholics" to carry on without him. The net result of his rebellion was a few apostasies, a state-

---

[3] *Ibid.*, p. 267.
[4] *Ibid.*, p. 27.
[5] *Ibid.*, p. 267.
[6] *Ibid.*, p. 7.

supported sect, and a clarification of the issues he had endeavored to confuse.

In France, where extremes so often clash, much printer's ink was spread over thousands of pages in a lively controversy between two fairly well defined parties. In contrast to the Janus-Anti-Janus debate, both parties were wrong, though neither went so far wrong as did the "intellectual" group in Germany. To be more specific, each party was opposed to the excesses of the other, but not to the Primacy of Rome nor to the divine constitution of the Church.[7] Hard blows were dealt and received, but it was a battle of principles rather than of personalities, and both sides were predisposed to accept the decision of the future Council. In this age of inflated individualism there was a readiness to submit. And submission to truth is the most essential condition for successful religious controversy.

Louis Veuillot and his Neo-Ultramontanism have been mentioned. The exaggerations of this noisy, but not unlovable journalist, whose enthusiasm ran away with his judgment, irritated and frightened men no less devoted to the Church than himself. But they were exaggerations in the right direction, and the good they effected outweighed the harm. Opposed to Veuillot was the towering figure of Dupanloup, and, in the sphere of politics, Montalembert. These "Liberals" had a double fear. The bishop saw the danger of an absolute monarchy in the Church; the statesman wished to avert a needless conflict between the papacy and the better elements in the modern State.[8] They hoped that papal infallibility would not be defined. But should an admittedly infallible council, a council headed by the pope, or the pope supported by the assent of a council, declare the pope alone to be infallible they would accept the definition. The voice of the coming council would be the voice of the Church, and the voice of the Church would be

Louis Veuillot

---

[7] A peculiar position is taken by Msgr. Maret, *Du Concile générale et de la paix religieuse*. Maret combats an infallibility, "personal and separate." Cf. Mourret, *op. cit.*, pp. 534–537.

[8] Montalembert was opposed to "erecting an idol in the Vatican," cf. Butler, *The Vatican Council*, p. 289. Asked what he would do in case the Council defined the dogma, his reply was: *"Eh, bien, tout simplement je croirai."*

the voice of God. The council they agreed had a great work
to do. By combating atheistic materialism, by restoring the
rights of reason as well as of revelation, by defending justice
in social relations, it would mark an important date in the history of the century. These very moderate views and hopes were
given expression in a lengthy article in the Paris *Correspond-
ant* of October 10, 1869. The article as a whole was denounced
by Veuillot and the Ultramontane party, but it reflects honor
on the moderate group who, with all their loyalty to the
Church, were determined to check a stampede of the extremists
in favor of papal infallibility.

The domestic quarrel in Germany had afforded considerable
satisfaction to the Protestants. In France there was little to
delight a non-Catholic or an anticlerical beyond the fact that
Catholics disagreed among themselves and expressed their
disagreement in forceful language. Dupanloup was almost
bitter in denouncing Louis Veuillot and the *Univers,* and also
the *Civiltà,* the *Tablet,* and the *Dublin Review.* On the other
hand, the *Univers,* had resorted to the ultramodern "straw
vote" as a means of ascertaining the *sensus communis* of the
faithful, and Dupanloup was himself denounced by amateur
theologians of the market place and the drawing room. Two
years later Pius IX was to comment on the controversy in his
own characteristic way, when he remarked that of the two
warring parties in France "one lacked charity and the other
lacked humility." But a censure of Veuillot's imprudence
would have reflected upon too many devoted bishops who had
sided with him, and Dupanloup's record of service to the
papacy had won for him the unbounded confidence of the pope.

On December 8, 1869, the first solemn session of the Vatican
Council was held in the north transept of St. Peter's. Of the
1,050 who had been invited to participate in the deliberations
723 were present, later arrivals brought the number up to 774.
These included besides the forty-nine cardinals, patriarchs,
archbishops, bishops, abbots, and generals of religious orders.
Never before had so many bishops gathered for a council;[9]

**The
Assembly**

---

[9] The number of delegates at the second and fourth Councils of Lateran
and the second Council of Lyons was higher. But not all the delegates
were bishops. Cf. Mourret, *op. cit.,* p. 540, note.

never had they come in such numbers even from the farthest
mission lands; never had a council been so well prepared for
its work. The Vatican Council was unique in this, too, that
Catholic princes were virtually ignored. They might attend the
solemn general sessions; but their influence was reduced to a
minimum. The Schismatic bishops of the Oriental rites, on the
other hand, were cordially invited to participate in the Council, and Pius IX even went so far as to undertake to pay all
their expenses. But the invitation was coldly received, especially in the higher ranks of the Oriental clergy, and one of
the hopes of the Council, namely, the return of the Orientals
to Catholic unity, was blasted.

To all Protestant Christians the pope sent an appeal couched
in general terms. As "separated brethren" they were exhorted
to profit by the occasion to do their part toward a restoration
of unity. This appeal met with a varied reception. In France
there was an attitude of mixed sympathy and antipathy. The
German Lutherans assumed a tone of high indignation, and
rejected the pretensions of Rome in the name of patriotism
and "Protestant civilization." The case of England was
peculiar. Negotiations were carried on chiefly by the Bol-
landist, Victor de Buck, under the direction of Bishop Dupanloup. But after a period of rising and falling hopes the attempt
to reach the Anglican clergy floundered completely on the
rocklike obstinacy of the "infallible" Dr. Pusey. The aloofness
of various groups of Greek Schismatics and of Protestants
facilitated, no doubt, the settling of internal problems in the
Church; but for the great task of dealing with the materialist,
rationalist, secularist mentality of the nineteenth century the
Catholic Church was left to fight alone.

During the feverish months that preceded the opening of the
Council it was quite clear that the Catholic Church was a
monarchy. Many pretended to fear that it might become an
absolute monarchy, an autocracy. When the seven hundred
bishops from all over the world, many of them dynamic personalities,[10] gathered in Rome the aristocratic element in ec-

Constitution
of the
Church

---

[10] Butler, *op. cit.*, gives a sympathetic portrait of the leading bishops at
the Council. He refers the reader to Ollivier, *L'Eglise et l'état au concile
du Vatican.*

clesiastical government was for a time to the fore. The nineteenth century boasted its liberal institutions, its representative, parliamentary, constitutional democracy. But the Church
could learn little from the modern age. She had in fact been
the *alma mater* of Europe, and the best institutions of Europe
had developed under her guidance. She had ever been a complete society, a "perfect society" in the sense of possessing
all the means to realize the corporate ends for which she was
founded. She was a divine-right monarchy, but the power,
temporal or spiritual, of her head was not an arbitrary power.
The pope might, naturally, abuse his high prerogatives, as
might any other constitutional ruler. But the bishops also
claimed to hold their position by right divine, and no pope
could dispense with their co-operation in his government, any
more than a human head can function apart from a human
body.

All metaphors aside, it is well, however, to bear in mind that
this divine institution was operated by human agents. Moreover, the Church was not a lifeless architectural monument,
nor was it a machine whose wheels revolved with mechanical
precision. It was a living organism subject to disease and
functional disorders, but possessing and conscious of possessing internal vitality and powers of recuperation, procreation,
and indefinite harmonious growth. The Church had seen the
rise and fall of states and empires. Her life was independent
of them, though the mental, moral, and emotional life of her
individual members was influenced by the political, social, and
economic conditions in which it was cast. Every bishop at the
Vatican Council was fully aware of his relations to a peculiar
world around him. He was also aware of his place in a body
that was not identified with the passing forms of any age.

The Two Constitutions Out of the Vatican Council came two great "constitutions":[11] the *Constitutio dogmatica de fide catholica,* adopted
unanimously on April 24, 1870, and the *Constitutio dogmatica
de Ecclesia Christi,* which was the final act of the Council. As
reproduced in the widely used *Enchiridion Symbolorum* they

---

[11] Manning's English translation is printed along with the Latin text
of the two constitutions in Butler, *op. cit.*

cover some eighteen octavo pages, which may be further boiled down to the twenty-two canons, or short paragraphs containing the essence of what was decreed, with the definitive *anathema sit*. For the immense mass of petitions, reports, speeches, and other documents which are here condensed to so brief a compass the reader is referred to the six thousand folio pages of Mansi,[12] to be further supplemented by a formidable array of pertinent material in the *Collectio Lacensis*. One may debate the relative importance of the two constitutions. In the preliminary schemata provision was made for the discussion of modern errors and their bearing on the truths of revelation and reason. There was no such explicit preparation for the decree on the Church herself. But the storm that raged around the question of papal infallibility made this issue so supremely important that for the historian there is a danger that he may fail to see anything else. It will be best, therefore, to dispose of this topic first, though for the Church's reaction to specifically nineteenth-century deviations from religion, reason, and common sense the canons on God, revelation, faith, and reason have more to offer.

From the very beginning of the Council two parties stood out, the Infallibilists and the anti-Infallibilists. The latter embraced those who rejected the doctrine itself, those who were opposed to its definition at that time, and a so-called "Third Party," which was chiefly intent upon watering down any official pronouncement of the subject. Opposed to the doctrine were Hefele, Rauscher, Strossmeyer, and Schwarzenberg, all powerful men, but carrying little weight in the Council for lack of supporting numbers. In the "Third Party" were Bonnechose, Lavigerie, and Guibert. They put little spirit into their program, however, and their influence was negligible. The real battle was between the Inopportunists, aided, of course, by the extreme anti-Infallibilists, and the Infallibilists. To avoid the jolting effect of this terminology it will be better to designate the two parties as Majority and Minority. In par-

The Parties

---

[12] *Sacrorum Conciliorum nova et amplissima collectio.* Five folios (XIL-LIII) are devoted to the Vatican Council. Likewise Volume VII of the *Collectio Lacencis* contains 1,942 pages on the Council.

liamentary parlance the Minority may even be called the
Opposition.

The leader of Majority was Deschamps of Belgium; the
"whip" of the party was Manning of England. Their following
was well distributed over the globe. Spain, Portugal, Italy, and
the Mission lands were almost solidly behind them, while
Cullen, Martin, Pie, Mermillod, and Spalding were the most
prominent representatives, each of his respective country. In
the Opposition, besides the Germans and Austrians of the
extreme "left," the leaders were Ketteler, MacHale, Mathieu,
Dupanloup, and Darboy. These had the advantage of repre-
senting the interests of the episcopacy in an assembly of
bishops, each presumably jealous of his authority. Their position was in harmony with the liberal views around them, but
it would hardly have aided their cause to appeal to the Time-
spirit, the *Zeitgeist*, in a group of bishops, assembled precisely
for the purpose of combating that spirit. Their real strength
lay in the fact that they were in possession of the field, as it
were. The Majority had to prove positively and beyond all
cavil that the new dogma was a part of the deposit of faith
and that it should be formally defined. If the Opposition, with
all the resources of scholarship at their command, could cast
doubt on the arguments adduced, if they could present insoluble difficulties from history, if they could establish the imprudence or, in their own words, the inopportuneness of the
dogma, it would be, humanly speaking, impossible for the
Council to go on with the definition. On the other hand, the
Majority had the advantage of being, in the face of modern
ideas to the contrary, really the progressive party. They were a
majority from the beginning. They were conscious that the
Catholic people were overwhelmingly in favor of the dogma.
They knew that the Holy Father was with them. And with
an aggressiveness that comes from a sense of being in the
right they swept away the specious arguments of the
Opposition.

But the Opposition did not yield without a struggle. And
from a purely human point of view it was fortunate that they
fought to the end. There had been protests and petitions
against what looked like "steam-roller" tactics on the part of

the Majority-controlled presiding officers. But if there were evidence of unfair discrimination, or rather of unintentional mass pressure by the Majority, this could be used as an argument to strengthen the Opposition. However, a Council that endured seven weeks of free discussion was surely anything but high-handed in its methods. From May 13 to July 2 fourteen general congregations listened to 164 speeches for and against the new dogma, and when on July 4, in accordance with predetermined rules, the debate was closed, no one could reasonably claim that liberty had been unduly restricted.

Most objections to papal infallibility would fall of their own weight if objectors would read the conciliar decree. The final formula was the result of long discussion, and when it was **The Decree** given to the world it was not the monstrosity against which so much futile declaiming has been heard. In the words of the Council:

> The eternal Shepherd and Bishop of our souls, in order to perpetuate the life-giving work of the Redemption, determined to establish His Church, in which as in the temple of the living God those who believe should be united in a common bond of faith and love.

In St. Peter, as the Gospel teaches us, the Redeemer set up the primacy, and provided that it should be carried on to the end of time by Peter's successors, the Roman Pontiffs. With the primacy goes the supreme teaching office of the Vicar of Christ. Thus the Council concludes:

> Wherefore, faithfully adhering to the tradition handed down from the beginning, for the glory of God our Savior, for the exaltation of the Catholic Religion, and the salvation of Christian peoples, with the approbation of the Sacred Council, we teach and we define the divinely revealed dogma that: when the Roman Pontiff speaks *ex cathedra,* that is, when in the discharge of his office as Doctor and Pastor of all Christians, in virtue of his supreme Apostolic authority, he defines a doctrine concerning faith or morals to be held by the whole Church, he enjoys, by the divine assistance promised him in Blessed Peter, that infallibility with which the divine Redeemer willed that His Church should be endowed for the purpose of defining doctrines concerning faith or morals.

Such is the dogma in all its simplicity. There is nothing here to perturb statesmen with a theological bent like Mr. Gladstone; there is nothing to justify the fears of scholars like Dr. Döllinger. Logically, Gladstone could reject the dogma because he rejected the premises. Döllinger, who accepted the premises, is an example of a limited human mind entangled in too much erudition.

When the first vote was taken, on July 13, the strength of the Opposition had sunk from a hundred and forty to eighty-eight. In the final count of July 18 only two had remained to vote against the definition. The figures are interesting. On July 13, there were 601 present. Of these 451 voted *placet;* 88, *non placet;* and 62 *placet juxta modum.* But the Council wanted a unanimous decision. Those whose convictions were still unshaken resorted to the simple expedient of absenting themselves from the final session. With permission most of them departed from Rome with the result that when the votes were counted for the last time there were only two members out of a total of 535 who had voted *non placet.* One of these was Bishop Fitzgerald of Little Rock, Arkansas, the other, Bishop Riccio of Cajazzo. These two provided what was, perhaps, the most touching scene of the whole Council. Stalwart to the end, while there was even the shadow of a doubt, Bishop Fitzgerald came forward, knelt at the feet of Pius IX, and said simply: "Holy Father, now I believe." Bishop Riccio followed with his *Credo.* A tempest was raging out of doors. It was a fitting ending of the Vatican Council.

But the submission of the American bishop was symbolic. The world at large, the Catholic world, accepted papal infallibility enthusiastically. That had been a foregone conclusion for months past. Many had regarded the dogma as inevitable from the beginning. But it was really the Opposition that made it so.[13] Now that the Church has spoken, the case was closed for all time. A few of the Minority, however, held back on the plea that the Council was not yet over.[14] Strossmeyer hesitated until December, 1872, while the Irish op-

General
Acceptance

---

[13] *"Quod inopportunum dixerunt necessarium fecerunt."*

[14] The Council has not yet been formally dissolved. There was talk of reopening ten years ago.

ponents of the dogma, MacHale and Moriarty, made their
first move in 1875. For some there was an interior struggle,
but it ended in peace of soul. For the greater number it was as
simple as an elementary syllogism. They had sat as judges
in a doubtful case. They had followed their conscience and
their reasoned convictions. But the infallible Church in an
infallible Council had defined the infallibility of her visible
head. If the Church could not be wrong, men of pronounced
views like Hefele, Schwarzenberg, and Kenrick could be right
only if they accepted her decision. Inopportunists like Dupanloup had believed the doctrine all the while they resisted its
definition. For them there was no interior struggle. The same
is true of men outside the Council like Newman.

But the saddest example of all is Döllinger. His followers
went completely astray, and ended in the State-supported
schism of the "Old Catholics." Döllinger refused to go with
them to the logical conclusion of his own shortsighted principles. He had stated that "as a Christian, a theologian, and a
historian" he could not accept the dogma, and he clung stub-
bornly to a pitiable isolation until his death in 1890. Pre-
scinding from his peculiar reading of history, it is obvious
that his theology was woefully inadequate and his Christianity
was not that of a Catholic. It would be rash for a human
tribunal to pronounce on the subjective state of his mind, but
objectively he remains one of history's shipwrecks. In strong
contrast to his warped attitude is that of the "unbeliever,"
Ollivier, who saw in those who admitted defeat men of
"honor and good sense," men who "have reasoned well" in
putting the faith established by Jesus Christ above an erroneous conscience.

The dogma of papal infallibility is in the minds of many
the sole achievement of the Vatican Council. It loomed so
large in the acrid discussions before, during, and after the
Council, inside and outside the Vatican; it carried so much
of intrinsic human interest; its genesis can be traced in such
detailed and voluminous records; its consequences have been
considered so awful; it was so timed in its final adoption, that
historians, and writers dependent upon them, have been prone
to see nothing else. But the doctrine is contained in a single

chapter of one of the two condensed "constitutions" of the Council. It is, so to speak, but the crowning conclusion of the constitution on the papal primacy. It exalts the supreme teaching office of the pope, and throws around it, in certain restricted circumstances, the charisma of inerrancy for the greater security of all believers.

But the Holy Father is also the supreme ruler of the faithful, and the Council, after much debate, defined the extent
The Primacy and character of his jurisdiction. He is not a mere honorary president, a mere overseer; he possesses the plenitude of episcopal power; he is the universal bishop with "ordinary and immediate" power over every church, pastor, and individual Christian. And this by the unanimous formal decree of six hundred bishops who were fully convinced that they, too, were by right divine successors of the Apostles. Nor does this erect an absolute, arbitrary autocracy in the Vatican. Essentially, there was not, and could not be, any change in the papacy. How groundless were the fears of papal "despotism" is clear enough from a comparison of the course of history before and after the Council.

Several projects or schemata on reform and discipline, on reunion of the Churches, on the Church and her relations with the civil power lie buried in the records of the Council, possibly to be reconsidered if ever the still undissolved Council resumes its work. It is a patent fact, however, that the successors of Pius IX have been able, thanks perhaps to their increased prestige, to discharge effectively much of the unfinished business of the assembly. There remains for rapid consideration one of the two completed constitutions, the first in the order of time, and for the student of the nineteenth century, perhaps, the most important. Its title, in the light of later developments, is significant. Even before the decrees on the primacy and infallibility this constitution is labeled, not from the "Council approved by the pope," but from "Pius, Bishop, Servant of the Servants of God."

The dogmatic constitution on the Catholic Faith was
The Catholic adopted by a unanimous vote on April 24, 1870. Its purpose
Faith is not so much to condemn after the manner of the *Syllabus*, modern Naturalism, Pantheism, Materialism, and Atheism, as

it is to teach the positive doctrines to which these errors are opposed. The constitution is not a theological treatise, though in its original form as presented by its author, Franzelin, it was severely criticized as such by the bishops. That the bishops took the matter seriously is evident from the number of amendments, some five hundred in all,[15] which were proposed and, amid scenes marked by intense excitement, debated until the assembly grew weary. The non-Latin bishops especially wanted no censure of Protestants; while others insisted upon tracing characteristic modern evils to Protestantism and its ultra-individualistic principle of private judgment. Spaniards showed a penchant for theorizing, while Americans and Englishmen pleaded for statements of truth that could be applied in the world of human beings. In its final revision the constitution is an excellent commentary on the downward process by which humanity, in the person of its most vociferous leaders, turned its back upon the Church four hundred years ago and then successively upon Christ, God, and rational human nature itself, until now "the deepest foundations of human society" are in peril. The danger to the Church was not an external one only. Her members, says the Council, "have strayed from the path of true piety" and the Catholic spirit has been weakened in them. "Confusing nature and grace, human science and divine faith, they deprave the true sense of dogmas . . . and endanger the integrity and sincerity of the faith."

So far has society sunk into the abyss of Naturalism, with its logically contiguous sloughs of Pantheism, Materialism, and Atheism, that the old elementary truths about God and His attributes must be stressed. The Council is here diagnosing the diseases of an age. Were it merely a question of individual lapses, the bishops would never have labored so hard in the preparation of their solemn anathemas. It is a sad index to modern "Progress" that a return to the first page of the penny catechism should be deemed necessary. In the long past the Church had had to meet denials of the Trinity, the Incarnation, the Sacraments. The "Reason" of man had refused to

Modern
"Isms"

---

[15] Cf. Butler, *op. cit.*, I, pp. 269, 276, 277.

accept each and all of these. In the nineteenth century reason itself had abdicated, and by a strange irony the Church, so often attacked in the name of reason, now rose to the defense of reason. "If any man shall say that the one true God, our Creator and Lord, cannot be certainly known by the natural light of human reason; let him be anathema." But reason has its limitations, even in the natural order; and in the supernatural order it is wholly inadequate. Hence, the Council recalls to the secularist age that divine Revelation has been given to supplement man's natural efforts. Against the Materialist it defends the spiritual nature of man; against the Atheist it confesses an infinite God, "infinite in intellect and will and all perfection . . . protecting and ruling all things by His Providence"; against the Pantheist it insists upon the essential distinction between God and created things.

In anticipation, as it were, of the foggy sentimentality of later Modernists the Council teaches that faith is not a "blind act of the mind" (and much less a mere "funny feeling"). It is an assent of the intellect moved by the will, but elevated and enlightened by divine grace. It is not based on the evidence of scientific knowledge; but on thoroughly rational grounds it accepts the truth of what God has revealed. Miracles are the sufficient guaranty that God has spoken, and among these the reasonable man must recognize the moral miracle of the Church herself. Natural reason and divine faith may differ as sources of knowledge, but between them a real conflict is impossible. The dogmas of the Church may not be understood, and the guesses of Science may be set down as facts. But the same God is author of both nature and the supernatural, and He cannot contradict Himself. The Church encourages scientific investigation, which may, and should, lead to God. But the "deposit of faith" remains unchanged through the ages. Thus spoke the Vatican Council, clearly and definitely, while the nineteenth century was still blissfully unconscious of its own distorted vision.

LEO XIII

XIX

LEO XIII:

GERMANY AND THE KULTURKAMPF*

THE PERIOD IMMEDIATELY FOLLOWING THE VATICAN Council has been called the "era of Kulturkampfs."[1] It is also known as the "era of the benevolent Bourgeoisie," the period in which Liberalism, Nationalism, and the whole Revolutionary heritage reached maturity. The two concepts are by no means mutually exclusive or contradictory, just as there is no difficulty in reconciling the picture of material prosperity, of triumphant science, industry, business, and finance with the ominous approach of the Great War. The "benevolent Bourgeoisie" made, in fact, a model army for a "crusade to save civilization." It is understood, of course, that the struggle could, and actually did, take place only in lands where the Catholic Church was, with whatever degree of sincerity, considered a "danger to the State," or more precisely to the prevailing theory of the State. This excludes the English-speaking world, and confines our attention to the Latin countries of Europe with their languid, lamblike majority of Catholics and, more particularly, to the new German Empire with its aggressive anti-Catholic majority of National-Liberals.

The name, *Kulturkampf*, centers our thought on Germany where it was first used in 1873 by the scientist Virchow, and

The Struggle for Civilization

---

* The best available source for contemporary comment on the Kulturkampf, and at the same time one of the most potent factors in the Catholic defense, is the Jesuit *Stimmen aus Maria-Laach*. This review was launched in 1865, became a monthly in 1871, was forced into exile in December, 1872, and returned to Germany after the World War. In 1915, Volume 88 appeared as *Stimmen der Zeit*. All during the struggle with Bismarck it kept up a vigorous fight. Down to the end of the century and after there is scarcely a volume that does not contain a scholarly contribution to the Catholic cause.

[1] Albert Ehrhard, *Der Katholizismus und das zwanzigste Jahrhundert*, p. 287.

where the movement it calls to mind ran its brutal course during the 1870's. It was primarily a Prussian thing, with imitations in Bavaria, Baden, and several other smaller states. Its great protagonist, Bismarck, wanted to make it international, and by a strange bit of irony, when he was about to admit defeat and failure at home, he saw his program adopted in its most essential features by Germany's great rival to the west. The anticlerical ramp of Gambetta and his friends down, one might say, to Herriot is, in its inspiration, personnel, and objectives, a French edition of the German Kulturkampf. And this idea may be carried further. Italian unification and the consequent "Roman Question" can be without much straining of logic fitted into the same category. The Germans called their attempt at State absolutism, supported by anticlerical Liberals, a Kulturkampf. The French and Italians had no single word to express their "struggle for civilization." In all three movements, however, the absolute State, Liberal-Protestant in Germany, Liberal-Atheist in France, and merely Liberal in Italy, sought to crush the liberties of the Catholic Church. Each movement was typical of the nineteenth century.

The name, *Kulturkampf*, like a thousand other misused terms, betrays a philosophy of life, a mentality. *Kultur* should mean truth, order, justice, the elevating of man to a higher level of perfection. The fight for this *Kultur* should be directed toward the conquest of error, injustice, and all that is vicious in man's animal nature. Unless the Catholic Church is synonymous with savagery and barbarism, as in the minds of a few of Bismarck's followers it probably was, then we have here one of the best examples of a catchword which was employed to express the loose thinking and the false philosophy of the nineteenth century, and which still stands in the history books to reveal strange mental processes. Of course, on the supposition that the Church was what her enemies, some of them, liked to think she was, her destruction might be a service to civilization. But it really does not raise one's opinion of the nineteenth century when its ignorance, blindness, and hate are made to rest on an untenable hypothesis, which in turn was rendered secure by a refusal to consider any modification of its hypothesis in the direction of fact.

Before Bismarck's Empire was a year old his Kulturkampf was under way. On July 8, 1871, the Catholic section of the Prussian Ministry of Worship, which dated from 1841, was abolished and the destiny of the Church was entirely in Protestant hands. This was followed by a series of legislative acts, the first of which, on December 10 of the same year, was the "Pulpit law." Freiherr Johann von Lutz, president of the Bavarian ministry, had suggested that the clergy be muzzled. Accordingly penalties were laid upon any criticism of the Reich and its constitution. Shortly after this, on May 2, 1872, the appointment of Cardinal von Hohenlohe as ambassador to the Vatican was rejected by the Vatican. The cry went up that the Jesuits were to blame, and they together with "affiliated orders"[2] were suppressed as a body and their movements placed under police supervision. Meanwhile, trouble was brewing in the Polish section of Prussia. Archbishop Ledochowski of Gnesen-Posen had refused to obey government orders to have all religion taught in German. When the government dismissed his teachers he set up private schools. These were closed, and the Archbishop was arrested and later banished. A school-inspection law was passed on March 11, which effectually crippled Catholic education. Pius IX, meanwhile, was condemning the high-handed measures of the government, and encouraging the Catholics to resistance.

A crucial move was the appointment of Adalbert Falk as Minister of Worship. During eight years of persecution until his dismissal in 1879, as Bismarck's mouthpiece or his evil genius, he enjoyed an unenviable popularity and power. The "May laws," or "Falk laws" were his work.[3] The first of these, in May, 1873, brought the training and placement of the

The German Attack

The May Laws

---

[2] These were the Redemptorists, the Congregation of the Holy Ghost, the Vincentians, and the Religious of the Sacred Heart, none of which religious bodies was connected with the Jesuits. The decree, extended to the whole Empire on July 4, 1872, was equivalent to expulsion for the Jesuits. The "affiliated Orders" were banished in May, 1873.

[3] This incoherent jumble of "laws" has been compared to the French "Civil Constitution of the Clergy." Its Liberalist framers wanted to make the bishops independent of the pope, the clergy independent of their bishops, the people independent of the clergy, and the whole Church dependent upon the State.

clergy under the control of the government. Candidates for ecclesiastical livings had to be graduates of the gymnasium, spend three years in theological studies at a German university, and pass a state-board examination, for the most part in non-theological subjects. State inspectors controlled all seminaries and houses of ecclesiastical students. Only Germans could occupy positions of responsibility, and the authority of Rome was diminished. The administration of the Church was brought as completely as possible under the State. Every effort was made to break the authority of the bishops over their clergy. But the results of tyranny were disappointing. Bismarck was visibly failing to divide the Catholics. In fact, he was forcing them into more compact unity.

Again in May, 1874, new laws were promulgated for the purpose of tightening the hold of the government. First a law for the expulsion of recalcitrant priests, then another to overcome passive resistance on the part of bishops. Theoretically, the Church should have been on her knees. But the victory of the government reached only as far as its police power. It could not touch the soul, the conscience, of its victims. They suffered, but in suffering was renewal of strength. The persecution became more bitter, more violent, and more petty. The Prussian embassy to the Vatican was withdrawn in 1874. New laws enforcing civil marriage were passed. Exemption for the clergy from military service was abolished. All religious congregations, except those engaged in care of the sick, were suppressed. Church property was put under the control of laymen. The clergy were deprived of means of livelihood.

Catholic
Vitality

It was only forty years since the Church had weathered a similar tempest. Catholics had been much weaker then. Now, they had not merely the example of their fathers and grandfathers to spur them on, and to give them hope, but they had the increased vitality of a generation that took religion seriously, and enjoyed comparative liberty in its practice. They had organization, leadership, an efficient press, improved

---

[4] Cf. "Verfassungsurkunde für den Preussischen Staat, v. 31. Jan. 1850," in Mirbt, *Quellen,* pp. 444, 445. Article 12 guarantees freedom of religion, and makes civil rights independent of religious affiliation. Article 15 reads: "The Evangelical and the Roman Catholic, as well as every other religious

tactics, and a closer union with Rome. They were fully conscious of the righteousness of their cause. They could appeal to the constitution against the government, though the constitutional guarantees of 1850 had been modified,[4] and to the spirit of liberty against the Liberals.

Windthorst had said: "close our churches and we will worship at home; take our priests and we will pray alone." The most vital phase of the struggle was hidden in the souls of men determined to be loyal to conscience, to resist tyranny, and to defend spiritual rights even at a tremendous sacrifice of material goods. But in the pages of history the great fighting force on the side of the Church was the Center Party under its brilliant and able leaders, headed by the incomparable Ludwig von Windthorst. The Center Party was not a religious organization; it was a political party battling for civil rights on constitutional grounds. But neither was the Catholic cause merely a religious one; they, too, fought for the rights of a political minority. Had there been no Kulturkampf, the Center would still have had a role to play. It was, in fact to continue as a great stabilizer of the Empire after the Kulturkampf had become a memory. But it strengthened its sinews, increased its membership, and secured its position during the decade of struggle when its name became identified with the fighting and persecuted Catholics.

The Center was organized, or reorganized, immediately after the founding of the Empire. Its leaders were Mallinckrodt and Windthorst, the two Reichenspergers, Frankenstein and Lieber. Its strength lay in its unity of purpose, the harmonious action of its leaders, the confidence and stanch support of the Catholic body, and its close contact with the pope and the bishops of Germany. A compact phalanx of nearly a hundred wideawake members,[5] under a clever debater whose barbs could

Windthorst

The Center Party

---

society, orders and controls it affairs independently, and retains the possession and enjoyment of institutions, foundations and funds devoted to worship, education and social welfare." Article 16 granted free communication with higher superiors. Article 18 abolished State interference with ecclesiastical appointments. By a "law" of June 18, 1875, articles 15, 16, and 18 were suppressed.

[5] In the November elections of 1873 the Center increased its membership in the Prussian Landtag from 50 to 90, and in the Reichstag from 63 to 91.

penetrate the clumsy armor of Bismarck almost at will, stood
in marked contrast to the motley group of allies whom the
Iron Chancellor had mustered on no more solid principle than
hatred of Rome. These champions of political as well as religious rights went down repeatedly under the weight of numbers, but they never lost heart. They checked every move of
Bismarck and he was never allowed to forget their presence.

The dwarfish figure of Windthorst, with his huge head and
his bandy legs, looked pitiably insignificant in opposition to
the colossus who could browbeat his adversaries into submission. But Bismarck was ever the blustering Goliath foiled by
an agile David. Bismarck's threat to put his puny enemy into
his vest pocket, and Windthorst's quick rejoinder that he
would then have more brains in his pocket than under his hat,
may be a groundless anecdote, but it helps to characterize the
two men and their manner of debate. Windthorst was a parliamentary tactician, a master of dialectic, a debater who
could ask discomfiting questions, who could interrupt with
impunity because there were few who dared to interrupt him.
With natural right and justice, with history and the constitution on his side, such a man was a power.

"The Kulturkampf began in frivolity, was carried through
with brutality and ended ingloriously."[6] So concludes a recent

Bismarck's
Motives

German historian of the Church. About the reasons, the motives behind the Kulturkampf, there is some obscurity. The
main lines are clear enough. Bismarck had crushed internal
and external opposition to found his mighty Empire. He would
brush aside any obstacle to its unity and strength. The National-Liberal party, which should have withstood the absolute
State, forgot its principles, as it conveniently could do on
occasion, to fight the Catholic Church. But it is not so clear
how much is to be attributed to incidental factors, to Protestant convictions, to Freemasonry, to Papal Infallibility and
the "Old Catholics," to Polish activities, or to the political
program of the Center Party.

---

[6] Ludwig Andreas Veit, *Die Kirche im Zeitalter des Individualismus,* 2,
p. 285.

[7] Cf. Georges Goyau, *Bismarck et l'Eglise,* I, 1–26.

[8] Fernand Mourret, *Histoire générale,* VIII, 599.

Bismarck was a religious-minded man, in his own way,[7] and he regarded the *Kleindeutsch* victory over Austria and the North German victory over France as a triumph of Protestantism. Falk was a Freemason,[8] and so also was the Emperor. The Vatican Council and its definition of Infallibility aroused much resentment in the Fatherland. The religion of the Catholic Poles made it more difficult to make good Prussians of them. The Center Party stood for States' rights in an Empire that Bismarck was determined to centralize. In the pope, the Poles, and the Center Party Bismarck saw potential, if not actual obstruction to his dreams of absolutism. One looks in vain for light in the writings of the Iron Chancellor. His memoires and his recorded statements in formal speeches or in private conversation present a variety of contradictory views which effectually conceal his real mind. He wrote and he talked for effect. Even von Ketteler, who knew him well, found him and his policies an enigma. He was not a sectarian fanatic, yet he talked about destroying the Latin nations by overthrowing Catholicism. He denied that he had any desire to Protestantize the Empire, but toward Papal Infallibility he felt the resentment of a man who did not understand what it meant. He knew that his National-Liberal majority hated the Church, but he merely used them without being influenced by them. For him the State was the sole reality.

"God" was the God of Bismarck's Prussian State, and the enemies of Prussia or of Bismarck were the enemies of God. In politico-religious matters he was ruthlessly intolerant. Toward religion apart from politics he was indifferent, skeptical, contemptuous. His own conscience never stood in the way of his plans, and he could not comprehend why the conscience of anybody else should. He was a *Realpolitiker* to whom the power of ideas was meaningless. His great battalions could crash through the defenses of a nation. He anticipated no serious difficulty from a defenseless minority. Bismarck, in a word, was an egotist, blinded by success. In his full-blown pride he stands as a symbol of the nineteenth century, exulting in its material bigness, puny in things of the soul. But he had some good qualities, even as the great bloated century had its good qualities. When his Kulturkampf failed he showed that

Character of Bismarck

he was still a statesman by stopping it. By his taming of the hostile Reichstag, his smashing of the French Empire and his building of the German Empire he merited a place among Carlyle's "heroes." But surely all this helps to gauge the vitality of the Church which he could not subdue.

The Kulturkampf in its origin, violent course, and sorry anticlimax was the work of one man. But that man had willing allies to do his dirty work for him. The German Liberals, having discovered the futility of fighting the man of "blood and iron," became as members of the new National-Liberal Party his strongest support. But they still retained their old anticlerical animosity. They resented the measure of fair dealing which the Catholics received in the Constitution of 1849. Above all they were perturbed by the evident progress the Church was making in Prussian Germany. These feelings were shared by the Conservative Protestants. Both groups could look back on a period when the German Church had been enervated by its own internal decay and beaten to the ground politically and economically by the wholesale Secularization of 1803. But Catholics were stirring out of their cultural and social inferiority. In Germany the new life generated by the Cologne Affair and the display of Catholic consciousness in the Munich School; in Rome the publication of the *Syllabus* and the alarming decrees of the Vatican Council had been so many sources of mounting apprehension.[9] Moreover, Liberalism could not stand criticism, and Catholic writers were merciless in exposing its inconsistencies.[10] The Liberal had, to be sure, his intangible first principles. They were bad principles, but once they were granted, or rather assumed, his most elementary logic made him the mortal enemy of the Catholic Church. The fact that he had become a National-Liberal did not detract from his perverted sense of responsibility. And the further fact that the hidden hand of Freemasonry was pulling the strings gave an added impetus to his crusading spirit. The combination of such allies with Bismarck's abso-

---

[9] Cf. Martin Spahn, *s.v.* "Kulturkampf," in *Catholic Encyclopedia.*

[10] E.g., Buss, Kolping, Jörg, Ketteler; and earlier, Schlegel, Baader, Görres.

lute State rendered the situation more perilous for the Catholics, and the outcome more glorious.

When Leo XIII succeeded Pius IX in 1878 the Kulturkampf was seven years old. The Church had been crippled in the pulpit, in her primary schools, in the training of her clergy. Nine bishoprics were vacant; nearly two thousand priests had been subjected to fine; young clerics had been made liable to military service; nearly seven hundred thousand of the faithful were robbed of pastoral care; the "Old Catholics" were a recognized sect in close alliance with the State; civil marriage had been made obligatory; the revenues of the Church had been stopped. The omnipotent State had completed its vicious work. But the rather ignoble hate and fear which had motivated the persecution were subsiding. The danger to the political unity of the Empire, if it had ever existed, was past. The champions of Protestant predominance had awakened to the fact that the Liberal attack on the Church was, in reality, an attack on all religion. Bismarck, who had never been impressed by the ravings of the Liberal Intelligentsia and who had no interest in any political theories except his own, was tired of his "struggle for civilization." Besides, he was terrified by the real menace of a rising Socialism. Finally, he had the foresight to discern the advantages to the State that might, and actually did, result from the friendly support of the Center Party. He was ready for a way out of the impasse. He was ready even for his *Gang nach Canossa*. And the new pope was just the man to smooth the path for him and to enable him to save his face.

Less than twenty-four hours after his elevation to the papal throne Leo had written a kindly letter to the Emperor. Shortly after this Bismarck had an informal conversation with the Nuncio Massella. The obnoxious Minister Falk was dismissed and his work gradually undone. A sort of diplomatic hide-and-seek game went on until the last remnants of the mass of Kulturkampf legislation were swept away with the exception of the anti-Jesuit laws, the supervision of Catholic schools, and the government approval of appointments to parishes. The process was a slow one, but it was virtually complete in 1887,

Leo XIII and the Kulturkampf

End of the Kulturkampf

when the May Laws were satisfactorily modified. It was only in 1891, however, that the government subventions to the clergy, which had been withheld since 1875, were again granted. By this time Bismarck himself was in retirement. If he had been slow to acknowledge in a practical way his first great failure and to rectify his mistakes, he had nonetheless "gone to Canossa." And his reputation as a statesman had not suffered on the way.

The Center Party emerged from the conflict and its dénouement with an established place in the Imperial government. But the Party had been asked to make a hard sacrifice for the general welfare of the Church. Windthorst and his followers were by no means ready to lay down their arms when Leo XIII began negotiations with Bismarck. They did not see eye to eye with the pope, who had the larger interests of Christendom in mind, while they wanted to keep up the fight on constitutional grounds. They were alert enough to see that the wily Chancellor was scheming to use the intervention of Rome for his own ends. After their heroic struggle it was hard to stand aside while others made the peace. It was harder to submit to pressure on the part of the pope in nonreligious matters. They were, after all, a political party with principles and constitutional rights to defend, and with a membership that was not wholly Catholic. A dictatorial solution arranged by Leo and Bismarck and imposed upon them was hardly in accord with their ideas of government. But when Windthorst, the uncrowned king of Catholic Germany, loyal to the Church and to his constituents, yielded to higher authority for the common good he gave unmistakable proof of his own greatness of soul. His self-effacement was an index to the spirit in which religious liberty had been defended.

Other states of the Empire, Baden, Hesse-Darmstadt, and Saxony had their little Kulturkampfs on the Prussian model.[11] Bavaria was infected by the same Liberal-Absolutist ideas, but remained relatively quiet. Württemberg alone among the German kingdoms was untouched. Austria, restless under the Concordat of 1855, showed some inclination to imitate Prussia

---

[11] Ehrhard, *op. cit.*, p. 288 ff.

in 1874. Albert Ehrhard expresses his regrets that, in view of the salutary effects of persecution in Germany, Austria went through no purification process. The debilitating burden of a whole century of Josephism and its own languid brand of Liberalism called for radical treatment. In Hungary during the closing years of the century an aggressive minority of Calvinists, Jews, and Freemasons threatened to rob the Church of all independent action. But it was chiefly the Latin countries, with their nominally Catholic majorities unorganized and passive, and their controlling cliques of anticlerical Liberals, that presented the least impressive picture of Catholicism.

LEO XIII: FRANCE AND *RALLIEMENT*

THE ANTICLERICAL MOVEMENT UNDER THE THIRD Republic in France began about the time the German Kultur-kampf was exhausted and verging toward its end. There are, to be sure, points of similarity between the two attacks upon the Church. But it would be incorrect to maintain that the French persecution was a mere imitation of Bismarck's attempted Caesaropapism. The French needed no German inspiration or example. They had a century of tradition behind them. The Third Republic claimed to be the child of the great Revolution,[1] and in its Jacobin features it bore a close resemblance to its parent. The whole nineteenth century was conditioned and determined largely by the Revolution. But, quite naturally, no section of Europe was so visibly affected as was France, and at no other period were French politics so much under the influence of the Revolution. The hard days upon which the Catholics of France fell were the distant outcome of the religious policies of 1789 and 1793.

One may go a step further. Not only was anticlerical Republicanism a carry-over from the Revolution, but the Royalist attitude of the Catholic body, so unfortunate in its blindness and obstinacy, must be explained, if not condoned, by reference to bitter memories still strong after a hundred years. The horrible picture left by de Maistre was fresh in their minds: an orgy of blood and destruction, blasphemy, murder, rape, robbery. "In the midst of all conceivable crimes . . . seducers and tyrants have founded your *liberty.*" The speech and action

---

[1] This is apparent from the general trend in the historiography of the period. In 1886 the Municipal Council of Paris founded a chair for French Revolution history, and called the historian Aulard to fill it. A new Société de l'histoire de la Révolution Française and a scholarly review, *La Révolution française,* are other indications of active interest.

of their enemies kept alive these prejudices. For the Liberal, the Radical of the Third Republic, it had been a glorious Revolution, and he was determined to guard the heritage it left him. At least, he talked in this strain, and so, very likely came to believe even the inconsistencies and contradictions involved in his Liberalism.

At any rate, the two parties were poles apart in sentiment, in personal interest, in philosophy of life. They represented two distinct and hostile views of man and society, two mutually antagonistic "civilizations." In either case the principles were clear enough, though even the proverbial French logic and clarity of thought could not cut living, emotional, rational beings to a precise pattern. "Religion first," "Politics first," were formulas that anyone could understand. They aptly described a general tendency; they were suitable as party slogans. But in the realm of concrete fact the defender of religion was a politician, and the politician seldom was neutral in religion. Too often it appeared that religion was employed for political purposes, and politicians were more intent upon destroying the Church than upon building up the State. The Catholic side was encumbered by an aristocratic group, Royalist and Gallican by conviction as well as by tradition. *The* Church was *their* Church, as it had been the subservient tool of their ancestors in the Old Regime. The anticlerical camp was Masonic, Jacobin, Rousseauvian. It exalted its omnipotent, omnicompetent State to absurd heights. Under any name, *République, État, Patrie,* they thought only in terms of their own peculiar type of government, of a party State, of a State controlled by gangster methods in the interests of a clique.

In such circumstances it was difficult for Leo XIII to make his voice heard, and the valiant Frenchmen who did hear him had to meet discouraging odds in their fight for order, justice, and liberty. When Leo declared that forms of government were relatively unimportant, Monarchists pointed to the Revolutionary origins of the Republic. When he insisted that all Catholics align themselves under the Constitution to combat iniquitous laws, they still clung to the phantom of kingship and disdainfully sneered at democracy. "Social Catholics"

Royalist
Catholics

might argue the futility of adhering to the fetish of monarchy;
Albert de Mun might plead for the subordination of partisan
politics to the larger interests of religion and humanity; he
might propose an integrated religious-social-political program
which promised liberty and security for the Church, for the
school, for the family, for the laboring classes; and as a reward for his intelligent devotedness to the best interests of
Church and State and people, Catholic votes would bring about
his defeat in the elections of 1893.

The contrast between Catholic division and confusion on
the one hand, and the compact organization and clever
maneuvering of the anticlericals on the other, goes far to
explain the persecution of the Church in "Catholic" France.
Liberal Radicals and Socialists, who would normally have
been at one another's throats, banded together in a solid *bloc*
against the "Clericals." The cause of religion was defended or
let us rather say defeated, by seven discordant typical groups
of Catholics.[2] There were Monarchists, reactionary in politics
and Liberal in economics; there were Monarchists who were
anti-Liberal in both politics and economics; there were *Ralliés*
opposed to economic Liberalism and, in obedience to papal
instructions, neutral in politics, as well as *Ralliés* whose
economic theories were in conflict with needed social legislation; there were Progressists sincerely devoted to the Republic,
who hoped to inject the leaven of tolerance into law and administration; there were Christian Democrats, more democratic
than Christian; there was, finally, the formless inert mass of
the indifferent, too discouraged or too indolent to deserve more
than a passing glance of contempt. In all these diverse and
divergent elements the anticlericals saw, or pretended to see,
only one thing, the enemy, Clericalism. *Le cléricalisme, voila
l'ennemi!* Catholic weakness and discord was the strength of
the close-knit Masonic "government." Not even the genius of
Leo and his appeal to higher motives could bring harmonious
action among them.

Leo seemed never to grow weary of repeating his expressions

---

[2] Parker T. Moon gives substantially this classification for the eighteen-
nineties. *The Labor Problem and the Social Catholic Movement in France,*
p. 225 f.

of affection and esteem for the "eldest daughter of the Church."
His encyclicals, particularly those dealing with political topics,
have a peculiar application to conditions in France. The perennial question of Church and State may arise anywhere. But in
France, where patriots, sincere and insincere, breathed an
atmosphere of hatred and resentment at the political power
of the priests, and where Catholics claimed a monopoly in
patriotism, it was acute to a degree not felt elsewhere. The
Napoleonic Concordat was still in force. But for nearly a century the Concordat meant different things in partisan politics.
To Catholics it was still a guarantee of religious rights in the
home, the school, and religious life generally; to the anticlericals it was chiefly the Organic Articles by which the
Church was subjected to police control. Now, however, the hour
was approaching when the Concordat itself, that is, what was
left of it, would be scrapped after a quarter of a century of
hacking away at Christian marriage, Christian education, and
the personal and property rights of the clergy.

Leo's
Attitude

Roughly the period of conflict coincides with the pontificate
of Leo XIII. It was preceded by nearly a decade of preliminary skirmishing, and followed by a dénouement in the form of
Separation of Church and State in 1905. Out of the disorder
and confusion consequent upon the collapse of Napoleon III
and the wild orgy of the Paris Commune the Conservative,
Monarchist, Catholic group emerged numerically the strongest.
In the National Assembly of 1871, which made peace with
Germany, put down the Commune, elected Marshal McMahon
to the presidency, made a fragmentary constitution, and governed France until 1875, the Royalists held a two-thirds
majority. But they embraced three potentially warring sections, the Legitimists, who supported the Bourbon, "Henry
V," the Orleanists, and the Imperialists. Menaced by the aggressive and growing power of the Republicans of various
hues, their position became so insecure that President
McMahon was forced to resign in 1879. On his election tour
of 1877, in anticipation of the Republican triumph, Leon
Gambetta launched his great campaign for the laicization of
the laws and institutions of France with the battle cry already
cited, that proclaimed in clericalism the country's enemy. This

The Conflict

was a modern equivalent of the *Ecrasez l'infame* of Voltaire, whose centenary, promoted by the Freemasons, but really a fiasco, was celebrated the following year in Paris. It was also a rude salute to Leo XIII, whose pontificate of peace was soon to begin.

Attention centers on the laicizing of the schools. The first object of attack, however, was the hospital. In 1879 the clergy were expelled, and laymen took over the administration of all hospitals and welfare departments. The next move was to suppress military chaplaincies. A project for "liberty of education" was introduced in 1879. Even before this, in 1878, Gambetta had directed the attention of the working classes to the billion-franc assets of the Religious Congregations. The French version of the German Kulturkampf was under way. Its spirit is contained in an address of the Masonic Grand Master to an enthusiastic gathering of the Grand Orient on September 24, 1878:

> Down with Rome, with Ultramontanism, with ignorance, and all their progeny! May they perish forever through the development of education, which leads the way to morality, through the progress of instruction, which leads to the full development of the intellect![3]

The essence of all that was antireligious in Kant, Comte, Renan, and their like had been distilled into a poison by contemporary writers and called "civilization." Of this the Catholic Church was proclaimed the "natural enemy." And Freemasonry, with its century and a half of underground organization, traditions, and technique, was at hand to direct the onslaught on the Church.

As in Germany eight years earlier, the Jesuits were singled out for the first direct attack. It was a costly compliment for it meant the closing of fifty-six French houses, including twenty-eight "colleges."[4] And it was effected not by legislative act, but by administrative decree, based on obsolete

The Jesuits

---

[3] Quoted in Mourret, *Histoire générale*, IX, 55.
[4] L. Marion, *Histoire de l'eglise*, IV, p. 431, note; Veit, *Die Kirche im Zeitalter des Individualismus*, 2, p. 250 (Hergenröther, *Kirchengeschichte*, p. 580) states that 75 Jesuit schools were closed, and that the Religious were driven from 261 houses.

LUDWIG VON WINDTHORST

Leader of the Center Party and antagonist of Bismarck in the
troubled days of the Kulturkampf. His greatness of soul was
clearly shown in his acceptance of the peace arranged by Leo
XIII (1812–1891)

OTTO PRINCE VON BISMARCK

A symbol of the nineteenth century, exulting in material bigness,
puny in things of the soul, and withal having some good qualities
(1815–1898)

From Lenbach's painting, Corcoran Gallery, Washington

"existing laws," dating from the preceding century. On March 29, 1880, two decrees appeared in the *Journal officiel*:[5]

> I. The non-authorized so-called Society of Jesus shall within three months dissolve, and vacate its establishments. . . .
>
> II. All non-authorized congregations and communities are bound to apply for authorization within three months, submitting at the same time their statutes, rules, the number of their members. . . .

Eight thousand men and one hundred thousand women were affected by these two decrees. Bishops, lawyers, and eminent French citizens protested. But the government clique had its own efficient methods for organizing public opinion as well as the machinery needed for the brutal execution of the "law." They lacked, however, the dogged determination and thoroughness of Bismarck. Even in a nation nominally Catholic it might not be prudent to deal too roughly with the religion of the majority.

A primary aim of the anticlericals was an education, universal, compulsory, free, and entirely divested of religion. They discoursed at length on the "neutral school," and the *école unique*. It is to be noted, however, that whereas the privileged public school of America held God and religion at the threshold, theoretically at least; the French imitation was distinctly anti-God and antireligious in practice. `Education`

Rightly seeing in the women of France the real stronghold of religion, the government set out to eradicate "prejudice, superstition, and mere routine" from the schools for girls. This step was taken on June 20, 1880. The next move, on June 16, 1881, was against religious women. Those who remained at their work, with government authorization of course, were not to be considered qualified merely by reason of credentials given them by their own superiors. They submitted, however, to the government examinations with a success that was disappointing to the anticlericals. Then, on March 29, 1882, the government attacked the problem more directly by excluding, absolutely, all religion from the primary schools. Parents, it was stated in Article I of this law, might

---

[5] Cf. Mourret, *op. cit.*, p. 65.

provide for the religious instruction of their children outside the school buildings and after the dismissal of classes. Article II abrogated the legal right granted in 1850 of "inspection, supervision, and direction" on the part of the clergy. Thus was established the "neutral school," the purpose of which was to rob the souls of children of all religious knowledge and inspiration.

The teachers, too, were to be "neutral," as if such a thing were possible in a nation like France! Four years later, the government was still at work on its program of de-Christianizing education in France. The *loi Goblet,* of October 30, 1886, confided education of all degrees to an exclusively lay staff. Expressly, in this new law the wishes of parents and of local municipal authorities were swept aside. The reply of the Catholics (however we may view it) was to erect their own free schools. These *écoles libres,* which stood for a freedom unknown to the "Liberals," were by the pragmatic test of attendance immeasurably ahead of the "neutral" schools, where one was not free to mention the name of God. During the ensuing years the State-supported schools, where the children of well-to-do atheists were taught at the expense of the Catholic population, cared for less than 3 per cent of the number whose parents paid for their education in the "free schools"! Whether the lawmakers were discouraged or merely biding their time, there was no further "progress" for fifteen years. Finally, in 1901, 1902, and 1904, heavy blows were struck, depriving all religious men and women of the right to teach. The obvious way around this difficulty was for the members of religious Orders to don the lay garb, and proceed with their work.

Meantime, vocations to the priesthood occupied the attention of the anticlericals. By withdrawing all exemptions from military service for ecclesiastical students, on July 15, 1889, the number of ordinations was lowered by nearly one third. But the Church which showed itself so pitiably incompetent in resisting government tyranny gave proof of interior vitality by again raising the number of vocations to the normal figure after 1895. Events, however, were moving slowly, but with inexorable sureness, toward the Separation of Church and

State. It is hard for an American of the twentieth century to see why the pope should struggle against this, but for Leo XIII it was the supreme catastrophe. He did not live to witness the final break, but his forebodings governed largely his cautious relations with the French nation.

On February 16, 1892, Leo released his encyclical, *Au milieu des solicitudes*. It was a message of peace, which was the culmination of long efforts to remove dissensions among French Catholics and to arrive at an understanding with their enemies. The way had been prepared by public pronouncements, private conversations, and letters of protest to the highest authorities in France. The doctrine enunciated was not new. It was merely an application to the French situation of teachings contained in previous encyclicals. As a philosopher, the pope knew how to distinguish: Political society was one thing, the form of its government another. Catholics could accept and support the constitution, and still keep up a continual fight for better legislation. Finally, there was the distinction between evil itself and the evildoer. "I fight against ideas condemned by the Church, and the tendencies hostile to her, but I do not make war on men, for each may, by God's will, at some moment become a useful auxiliary."[6] Leo hated Freemasonry as he hated sin, but he could write in the most friendly terms to ministers whom he knew to be Masons. He was a physician who had no desire to kill his patient in his endeavor to cure his disease. And he was served by Nuncios, at least two of them,[7] who were apparently more worried about the ignorance than about the malice of men in government circles. He dealt with France as a father might with domestic dissension. He wanted to put a stop to the de-Christianizing process in Republican France. Paradoxically, to weaken the attack on religion he seemed bent on strengthening the attacking power. What he did was to remove the pretext for anticlerical meas-

The Ralliement

---

[6] Eduardo Soderini, *Leo XIII, Italy and France,* p. 171, note.

[7] Several of Leo's nuncios in Paris were unable to cope with the situation. Msgrs. Czacki and Ferrata were able diplomats, intelligent, witty, fascinating, in the tradition of the great Consalvi. Czacki declared: it was "impossible to realize the ignorance of the Ministers in religious matters." He undertook to teach Gambetta his catechism.

ures because of Catholics who disliked the Republican regime. His policy of 1892 was known as the *Ralliement*.

But the initiative was not altogether from the side of the pope. The five Cardinals of France had united on January 20, 1892, in an appeal to French Catholics to "set a truce to political dissensions, by placing themselves on the Constitutional plane, seeking before all else the defense of their threatened faith."[8] But the most resounding event preliminary to the publication of the encyclical was Cardinal Lavigerie's "Toast of Algiers."

Cardinal Lavigerie

Cardinal Lavigerie, impetuous and imperious according to his Royalist critics, was a great-souled missionary whose brilliant and devoted services to France and the Church entitled him to speak with authority. But when he made his eloquent plea for unity under the Republic he was, and insisted that he was, the "mouthpiece" of the pope.

At a banquet in the Archiepiscopal palace, given to honor the Admirals of the Mediterranean fleet, and attended by the leading military officers and civil officials of Algiers, the Cardinal uttered his prayer to God and his appeal to all Frenchmen for union, the "supreme need in the presence of a still bleeding past and of a threatening future." This was, he assured them, the first desire of the Church and her clergy from the pope down to the parish priests. The will of the people had been clearly stated, the trial of the Republic had been made, it was time to put an end to divisions, it was time to sacrifice all that conscience and honor permit. And to climax the memorable evening the *Marseillaise* was played by the band of the White Fathers, an astounding performance when one recalls the feelings of Royalist Catholics toward the Revolution and their inevitable reaction to this "insult." Cardinal Lavigerie had begged the pope to "strike while the iron was hot"; he had himself succeeded in making it hotter. The answer, after a delay of fifteen months, was the *Ralliement* encyclical.

It was a cause of deepest grief, Leo writes, to "contemplate the depths of the vast conspiracy formed for the annihilation

---

[8] Soderini, *op. cit.*, p. 217.

of Christianity in France." He views the French scene with
grief, bitterness, and apprehension for the future. Yet he finds
some consolation in the renewed zeal of the Catholics and their
increased loyalty to the Holy See. He sees "morals and religion
and even political interests" under attack. His hope for
France lies in the union of all good men for the restoration of
order under God. He recalls the historical role of the Church
in the glorious past of France, which rested on moral greatness, and which neither gold nor military might can save
from decadence and death.

Deprecating the calumny that the Church seeks "political
domination over the State," an ancient and outworn charge
once urged against Jesus Christ before the tribunal of Pilate,
the Pope alludes to

> the vast conspiracy that certain men have formed for the
> annihilation of Christianity in France and the animosity with
> which they pursue their ends, trampling under foot the most
> elementary notions of liberty and justice toward the greater
> part of the nation.

In the threatened rejection of the Concordat he sees nothing
less than a "return to paganism." The enemies of the Church
would separate political legislation from religion. In their
Godless State the Church would be under the common law
until, upon displaying signs of awakening vitality, she would
be put outside the common law. But to the objection that
"the Republic is animated by such anti-Christian sentiments
that honest men, Catholics particularly, could not in conscience accept it," he answers with his distinction between
"constituted power and legislation." The plain duty of Catholics is to rally to the support of the Republic, and under it to
fight for the better laws, for the rights of the Church and of
Jesus Christ.

The *Ralliement* policy of Leo was directed toward breaking the mischievous alliance, in the minds of many the identification, of the Church with the Royalist cause. He wished to
discourage partisan politics in which religion was used for
party ends. His counsel was enthusiastically received by the
best Catholics in France. Obedience to the pope thus became,

as it should be, the determining mark of genuine Catholicism. The bishops, who had been divided up to this time, and the parish priests for the most part submitted at once. Outstanding laymen, Albert de Mun, Étienne Lamy, and Jacques Piou, had been waiting for just such a pronouncement to carry on their work in the political arena. But the die-hard aristocrats, Monarchists from long family tradition and blinded, it may be, by personal ambitions or hatred of democracy, still held to the hopeless cause of Royalism. They had "served" the Church so long, chiefly by occupying practically all the higher positions in the hierarchy, that they could not help resenting the newer democratic tendencies. They felt, moreover, that the Church which had for centuries depended on their generous benefactions should still continue to serve their class interests. This was a fundamental cause of the failure of the *Ralliement*. Another was at hand in the notorious Dreyfus Affair.

Anti-Semitism in France did not rest on a pure figment of the imagination. There were ample reasons for Catholic suspicion of Jewish machinations in the persistent attacks of Freemasons, Socialists, and other radicals upon the Church and upon France. But the anti-Dreyfus[9] campaign inaugurated by Edouard Drumont (a severe critic, incidentally of Leo XIII, Albert de Mun, and others) was conducted with a fanaticism which provided a welcome opportunity to the ever watchful anticlericals. Although the Catholic attitude throughout the whole sorry affair had been generally correct, it was easy to capitalize the excesses of Drumont and a section of the Catholic Press to create a diversion against "Clericalism." In 1898 the Prime Minister, Jules Méline, could sneer at this "convenient maneuver" which made it unnecessary for the Radicals to have a positive program. "If clericalism did not exist," he cynically told them, "you would invent it." At any rate, the Dreyfus affair was a severe blow to the policy of

The Dreyfus Affair

---

[9] In 1894 Alfred Dreyfus, a Jew, was convicted by court martial of selling military secrets to Germany. After a second conviction he was finally vindicated by the Court of Cassation. Thanks to a brilliant publicity campaign, carried on by Anatole France, Emile Zola, and others, the Army, the Monarchists, and the "Church" were discredited, while Radicals and Socialists recovered lost prestige.

Leo XIII, and also to the "New Spirit" which moderate ministers were trying to introduce into French politics.

The elections of 1893 put the Moderates in control of the government. To Leo XIII it must have seemed that France was about to witness a happy ending of her "Kulturkampf," similar to what had happened in Germany. Here, too, the menace of Socialism and disorder had brought wisdom and reflection. Eugène Spuller, speaking for the Casimir-Périer ministry, invited the *Ralliés* to join the forces of order. He declared that the Republic was secure, and that the Church was changing! He called for a "new spirit" of tolerance, for the reconciliation of all Frenchmen, for harmonious co-operation of all good men. But Catholics could not agree to work together, while Socialists and Radicals were determined to prevent "clerical" participation in the government.

The first serious shock to the *esprit nouveau* came in April, 1895, when the arbitrary and exorbitant tax of 1884 on the property of "authorized" Religious Congregations was revised. The declared purpose of the earlier law was to prevent an "increase" of ecclesiastical wealth. In 1895 the purpose was to cripple and ultimately to destroy educational and charitable institutions under religious direction. But this was only a preliminary step in a more vigorous onslaught upon the Church by the Republican *Bloc*. The "laws" against religious education which had been on the statute books for two decades had been only partially effective. The government did not dare, for example, to enforce its unpopular decrees of expulsion against the teaching congregations of women. Besides, there were constitutional guarantees of individual liberty which enabled Catholics to find the means, often at great material sacrifice, to maintain their educational activities, with the result that in 1901 there were nearly twenty thousand establishments of religious congregations, authorized and unauthorized, employing nearly 160,000 members. Their wealth, by a juggling of figures, was estimated at a billion francs. Against this situation, so disappointing to antireligious Radicals, the Law of Associations of July 1, 1901, was directed. The "Law" required new authorizations, which placed Catholic institutions entirely under arbitrary government control, and liquidated, largely

Anticlerical Triumph

for the benefit of the politicians, the "billion francs" which the Congregations were presumed to possess.

The climax was reached two years after the death of Leo XIII in the "Law of Separation of the Churches and the State," which abolished the Concordat of 1801. Its immediate effect was to make the Church poor, but free. The Church suffered severely, in a material way, but gained in moral power and vitality; the State, now formally secularized, freed itself from obligations which it owed in compensation for wholesale confiscations in the past. It was a one-sided move planned by the apostate monk and active Mason, Émile Combes, prepared by a series of petty bickerings and the breaking of diplomatic relations with the Vatican in 1904, and completed by vote of the Chamber and the Senate in 1905. Apart from the injustice involved and intended, it struck at Canon Law and the constitution of the Church by an attempt to put all Church property into lay hands. The pitiful device of the *Associations cultuelles* designed to administer ecclesiastical funds and buildings, was rejected by Pius X. The government was afraid to execute its own "laws," and in the end the Church carried on against external persecution, but with increasing interior energy.

XXI

LEO XIII: ITALY AND THE ROMAN QUESTION

BY A STRANGE CONTRAST THE ITALIAN POPE WHO
sought a *modus vivendi* with the anticlericals of France was
consistently intransigent in his dealings with the Italian State.[1]
He continued the policy of Pius IX, rejecting the "Law of
Guarantees" and upholding the *"Non expedit"* policy. The
reason for this is not to be sought in Leo, but in the radicals
who made the settlement of the "Roman Question" impossible.
Only the lapse of time and a new spirit in the Italian Government could bring peace between the usurper in the Quirinal
and the Prisoner of the Vatican.

Leo's attitude was not due to any lack of patriotism. He
showed by word and act that he possessed a fervent love for
his country and an honest pride in her past. Nor is there
anything to prove that he was moved by personal ambition
or feelings of resentment toward the party which had deprived
his predecessor of the Papal States. He was conscious of responsibility for a great trust committed to him. He knew that
the Temporal Power of the Papacy was founded as that of no
other European dynasty, in historical fact. He felt, moreover,
that Divine Providence had erected the political sovereignty
of the Vicar of Christ as a necessary safeguard for the free
and independent discharge of spiritual functions. To the eye
of a shrewd statesman like Bismarck there seemed to be no
solution that might warrant the apparently hopeless battling
of Leo against the obvious trend of European politics. "Either
the pope," he said at the height of the struggle, "will yield to
the Italian State, and become merely the King's Chaplain, or
the state of antagonism will persist, and he will gradually find

---

[1] Josef Schmidlin, *Papstgeschichte der neuesten Zeit,* has chapter headings
which are significant: "Unbreakable Friendship with France"; "Uncompromising Bearing toward Italy."

himself abandoned by the few who remain attached to him."[2]
But another close observer remarks quite correctly: "At the
time of his death the Pope saw the Papacy in possession of an
authority and prestige such as for centuries it had not known."[3]

The Roman Question has been settled to the satisfaction of
all concerned. One may wonder why this had not been done
earlier.[4] The simplest answer is, perhaps, that there was no
Mussolini on one side and no Pius XI on the other. But the
time element must also be considered. Fifty years ago, few
supporters of the pope would be ready to admit that the loss
of the Papal States might be a blessing. Those who recognized
the defects and deficiencies of the civil government of the
Papal States insisted that the remedy lay in reform, and not
in wholesale robbery. The popes had a long record of service,
and it was hard to give way before an upstart government
which offered no convincing proof of ability to do better. In
fact, inefficiency and incapacity seemed to be the hallmarks of
the Italian State. Finally, there was a consideration of capital
importance which, however, could have had little weight at
the time. It might have been argued that the administration
of the Papal States, above all an efficient administration,
would be a drain on the energy of any pope, and a distraction
from the more proper work of guiding the spiritual destinies
of the universal Church. In the light of present conditions this
can hardly be questioned. But Leo XIII had not the experience
of his successors and their freedom of action to make the case
clear. As he read his history, the prestige of the Papacy had
been always linked with its political influence, and its political
influence depended upon the pope's historical position among
the princes of Europe. The enemies of religion and of the
Papacy were even more deeply convinced of this.

Leo could distinguish the essential from the accidental, the
eternal divine element in the Kingdom of Christ from its
ephemeral human trappings. Those who saw in the Church

---

[2] Eduardo Soderini, *Leo XIII, Italy and France,* p. 120.
[3] *Ibid.*
[4] According to Soderini, *op. cit.,* p. 65, Leo would have been satisfied
with less than the entire Papal States, but he did not consider the
Leonine City, even with a corridor to the sea, sufficient.

merely a man-made institution had confidently expected its fall ever since the collapse of the Old Regime and the rise of democratic Nationalism. In realist politics might was right among princes. Certainly might was right in the secret counsels of ministers. The material power of the Papacy was gone forever. It could not compete with the great secular states. From the vantage point of the present day it is easy to discern in the forced shedding of temporal possessions a condition prerequisite to the rise of spiritual and moral prestige. But Pius IX and Leo XIII had to protest against the bullying injustice of which they were the victims. And their protests served a high purpose. They were a positive factor in building up the increased moral prestige of the spiritual power, and they kept the anticlericals definitely and conspicuously in the wrong.

The Roman Question was founded in a struggle for territorial sovereignty. But Italy also, like Germany and France, had its "struggle for civilization," its Kulturkampf. The nearly parallel movement in the three countries can be traced not so much in the great leaders as in the animus of their supporters. Cavour, of course, could stand comparison with Bismarck. In the pontificate of Leo XIII the best statesman that Italy could boast was Crispi. But the Radicals of the Peninsula were blood brothers of the Radicals elsewhere. For them the secular and the supernatural, religion and patriotism, Church and State were in irreconcilable deadly conflict. By the mouth of Grand Master Adriano Lemmi, Freemasonry launched one of its numerous declarations of war in 1892. He proclaimed the Law of Guarantees an act of permanent treason to Italy, and the Vatican the center of a web of conspiracies against humanity. But, he cried,

Italy's Kulturkampf

> Rome with its name and its fateful power . . . will be the scene of the final struggle. There shall we invoke the genius of ancient greatness, for, having shattered by the revolution the bonds uniting the sword to the pastoral staff, we have armed two worlds and two princes one against the other. The Quirinal and the Vatican face each other. We must settle the ancient conflict between the prince and the Pontiff, between the State and the Church. We do not wish to leave the task

to posterity; secular right must assert itself at once against ecclesiastical usurpations.[5]

This was an echo of Leo's quotation of St. Augustine's "Two cities." His exhortation to "tear away the mask of Freemasonry" and to open the eyes of deluded members who aligned themselves with it through fear or through hope of material advancement was prompted by knowledge of a situation which Masons themselves did not attempt to hide.

A part, at least, of the sorry role of Bismarck's Falk fell to Giuseppe Zanardelli, author of the Penal Code of 1888.[6] This faithful henchman of the Lodges decreed drastic penalties for anyone, meaning the clergy, who attempted to "subject the State or a portion of it to foreign domination, or to destroy its unity." Another article was aimed at the priest who in the pulpit or the confessional "by the abusive use of moral force resulting from his ministry should incite to contempt for the institutions and laws of the State . . . or disturb the peace of the family." Still another article placed the regulation, that is to say, the prevention, of public worship under the control of the government. This was one of the most tangible moves in the campaign to destroy "the head of the priests and his vile slaves . . . to scatter the stones of the Vatican to build with them the temple of an emancipated Nation." Next came, in this same year of Masonic dictatorship, a Public Safety Act which placed all religious gatherings, including collections for pious purposes, under more strict police surveillance. The crowning achievement was, as usual, the suppression of religious instruction in the primary schools. To make legislation effective Thirty-Third Degree Brother Crispi was to be provided with secure majorities in Masonic-controlled elections. Once again, the Church had to suffer, and be hammered into renewed strength by the ordeal.

The foregoing may be taken as indicative of the spirit which animated the anticlerical movements toward the end of the century. They represent one phase of the opposition to the Papacy and the Catholic Church. As an example of moderate legislation the "Law of Guarantees" of May 13, 1871, stands

Anticlerical Legislation

Law of Guarantees

[5] *Ibid.*, p. 103.
[6] *Ibid.*, p. 75.

at the very beginning of the national regime in Rome. On the surface it looks like a satisfactory and even generous provision for the needs of the pope. He was accorded the prerogatives of sovereignty, his person was declared inviolable, and he was to receive an annual revenue of $645,000.[7] Pius IX and Leo XIII rejected it as a mere act of Parliament, a unilateral obligation, revocable at will, which really guaranteed nothing. And a whole series of events followed its promulgation to confirm the distrust of the popes, and to prove that the government, whether it had the power or not, was unwilling to protect the Holy See from the criminal element in Rome and the machinations of sectarian ministers.

The pope was kept busy protesting, futilely it might seem, against outrages which fall, roughly, into two categories. There were insults, premeditated or spontaneous, and there were high-handed sequestrations of ecclesiastical property. To the first class belong the wanton attack of hoodlums, abetted by the police and inspired most likely by some higher power, upon the funeral cortège of Pius IX on the night of July 12–13, 1881; Masonic demonstrations against the Law of Guarantees on August 7, of the same year; the noisy antipapal celebration of the sixth centenary of the Sicilian Vespers on March 31, 1882; the glorification of Giordano Bruno as a "martyr" of papal tyranny by the erection of a statue in the Campo di Fiori on June 9, 1888, amid a concourse of atheist, Socialist, Masonic delegations from foreign countries; and continuously the unbridled license of the anticlerical press. A pope far less sensitive than Leo XIII would have suffered under these gratuitous indignities, but on the whole whatever injury they did the Holy See was small in comparison with the smirch they left upon Italian "patriots."

Insulting the Pope

But property rights were no more sacred than sentiment and honor. The revolutionary government began early with the old revolutionary practice of suppressing religious houses and confiscating their "wealth."[8] In September, 1879, it was in

Ecclesiastical Property

[7] By the Financial Agreement of February 11, 1929, Italy granted the pope an indemnity of 750,000,000 lire, plus 1,000,000,000 lire in government bonds.

[8] Cf. Fernand Mourret, *Histoire générale de l'Eglise,* IX, p. 32 f.

possession of the property of some fifty-six hundred convents. But the biggest single stroke was dealt at the Propaganda. This great Congregation with its world-wide mission activities owned considerable revenue-producing property, largely the result of contributions from Catholics in other lands for the promotion of foreign mission labors, had to submit to a process of "conversion." By the arbitrary act of a liquidating board the Propaganda was reduced in 1881 to the position of a minor whose property is cared for by the State. The 5 per cent government obligations which it received for the auction price of its real estate placed it in a precarious situation. When protests were unavailing arrangements were made to distribute future funds in foreign countries.

Another tyrannical act, motivated by a desire to ruin the great social work of the Church as well as by the greed of politicians, was the virtual suppression of pious benevolent foundations to the number of nearly twenty-five thousand, with a gross capital of two billion lire. The "law" which authorized this robbery provided for government administration of the funds, which meant in practice laying them open to official graft; for their conversion to other purposes; and for the exclusion of the clergy from any voice in their direction. Nine years later, in 1898, some four thousand Catholic associations of various kinds were suppressed with consequent material losses for the poor who were their chief beneficiaries. In view of the pope's persistent and generous efforts to build up social Catholicism this was a cruel blow. But it was all part of the anticlerical struggle for "civilization." About this time, however, the rise of Socialism was having a sobering effect on the government, and most moderate statesmen saw the need of dampening the anticlerical excesses.

One naturally asks, what were Italian Catholics doing all this time, while the irreligious element hounded the Church? The masses were, as is usually the case, quite passive, victims of an aggressive minority which controlled the machinery of government. But there were Catholic leaders who chafed under forced inaction. The *Non expedit* of Pius IX was still the papal policy.[9] This attitude had been first assumed in Piedmont in 1858. It was further recommended up to 1895, when Leo XIII changed it to a *Non licet*. Leo encouraged Catholic participation in municipal administration, but his intransigent aloofness from the National government, which he refused to recognize, entailed a complete abstention of Catholics from parliamentary elections. *Ni eletti, ni ellettori,* was the Catholic slogan. Although this gave the Radicals very much their own way in national affairs, still the pope, after considering and reconsidering every angle of the situation, refused to allow Catholic participation in the government. Against this policy there were critics, the most vociferous of whom was Padre Curci, once an ardent defender of Pius IX. Curci, after the manner of the Catholic Liberals of France, demanded that the Papacy reconcile itself with modern conditions. But the fact that there were critics on the other side who thought that the pope had gone altogether too far in his condescension to human errors proves at least that Leo XIII must have kept somewhere near the middle of the road. He did, in fact, show a willingness to make every concession on points of detail,[10] but he was adamant in his refusal to approve either the spoliation of the Papal States or the satanic attempt to destroy all religion.

---

[9] Soderini, *op. cit.,* p. 6, note.
[10] Schmidlin, *op. cit.,* II, p. 414. During an extended period in 1881–1882 Leo carried on negotiations with the Emperor, Franz Josef, looking to a possible refuge in Austrian territory.

THE GREAT ENCYCLICALS

XXII

THE GREAT ENCYCLICALS: INTELLECTUAL AND POLITICAL

DURING THE PONTIFICATE OF LEO THERE WAS NO solemn assembly of the universal Church in a general Council, nor was there need of any. The Pope had been declared infallible, and he was fully conscious of his right to speak for the Church. If there was an occasional echo of the panicky protests against papal autocracy or of apprehensions of arbitrary and capricious mishandling of the supreme teaching prerogative, it was negligible. Leo could use hard words in his defense of truth and justice, but never was there a general outcry that he had anathematized civilization and the modern world. If he felt himself the Vicar of Christ, if he allowed no appeal from his formal pronouncements on all the great religious questions of the day, he spoke not as a dictator browbeating his subjects into submission, but always as a father, warning, guiding, and teaching his children. Even this attitude the world might resent, but for the most part sincere men outside the Church conceded to him his role of Great White Father. As a working hypothesis, at least, the Pope's conception of his office must be accepted by anyone who would understand this chapter in the history of the Church.

The Supreme Teacher

It is not important to determine, if this were possible, how much of Leo's influence upon his times and upon our own is to be attributed to his personal qualities, nor how much to his position as supreme pontiff. As a teacher, apart from his official capacity, he could speak with the authority of a student of modern conditions who had applied his naturally keen and alert mind to reading and meditation. He had taken a lively interest in political, social, and economic affairs throughout the world, but he never permitted his knowledge to remain

Leo's Preparation

241

merely theoretical. As Archbishop of Perugia,[1] he had been an extremely active and watchful shepherd of his people. His first care was the intellectual and spiritual training of this clergy. But the workaday struggle of the lower classes occupied his thoughts. In them he saw in miniature the brutalizing effect of absorption in material things. He was far from the great industrial centers of Europe, but the chief problems of humanity were on his doorstep. To the extent of his slender purse he gathered the best publications, and from their contents he drew the data upon which to build in a practical way his ambitious plans for the re-Christianization of the world. When he became pope he had only to continue in the path he had laid out as bishop.

Leo had seen in the production of wealth the supreme end of a perverted civilization. He had seen in the rejection of God, of Christ, of the Church, the fundamental cause of all the evils from which society suffered. He saw the dignity of man outraged as a member of the family and as an individual. He raised his voice against long hours of labor, against the drudgery and slavery of women and children in the factory, against the breakup of the home and its attendant vice and corruption. In his pastoral letters[2] he set forth the teachings which were later to be broadcast to all Christendom in his great encyclicals. From history he drew the firm conviction that the Church and civilization were closely identified, that the Church was the mother of a modern civilization which had gone wrong. He castigated current errors in the writings of an apostate Renan, an anarchist Proudhon, and a whole array of atheists. He defended the temporal power of the pope, the prerogatives of the Church, the divinity of Christ, the primacy of God against those who carried on a campaign of violence and hate. He demanded the freedom of the Church to promote

---

[1] Fernand Mourret, *op. cit.*, IX, pp. 9, 10.

[2] During his thirty-two years as Bishop of Perugia the future pope wrote Lenten pastorals, many of which were learned treatises on questions of the day. Magnetism, Marriage, Current Errors, Renan's *Life of Jesus*, the Church and the Nineteenth Century, the Temporal Power, the Church and Civilization. Most of his later encyclicals are here found in germ. The last named especially foreshadows his policy as pope (French translation, Paris, 1878).

civilization and progress, and to combat incredulity, heresy, and all the disorders in society. He had little to learn and nothing to change when he was raised to a higher throne with the whole expanse of humanity at his feet.

The teachings of Leo XIII might well be grouped and classified under half-a-dozen headings: philosophical, political, economic, social, moral, and religious. But taken in their chronological sequence, they form a complete and well-rounded historical whole, which it is needless to rearrange. Within two short months after his elevation to the papacy appeared his encyclical *Inscrutabili*, a treatise of a general character on "the evils affecting modern society, their causes and remedies." These evils, these diseases, he enumerated:

The First
Encyclical

> Widespread subversion of the primary truths upon which as on its foundation human society is based. . . . Obstinacy of mind that will not brook any authority, however lawful. . . . Endless sources of disagreement, whence arise civil strife, ruthless war and bloodshed. . . . Contempt of law, which moulds characters and is the shield of righteousness. . . . Insatiable craving for things perishable, with complete forgetfulness of things eternal leading to desperate madness and wholesale suicide. . . . Reckless mismanagement, waste and misappropriation of public funds. . . . The shamelessness of those who, full of treachery, pretend to be champions of country, of freedom and every kind of right. . . . In fine, the deadly plague which affects society in its inmost recesses, allowing it no respite and foreboding ever fresh disturbances and final disaster.[3]

The source of these maladies he saw in the repudiation of a Church founded to rule society in God's name, but crippled and brought into contempt by anticlerical laws, insidious calumny, interference, robbery, and secularization of life, and on the other hand in the free propagation of error, the reign of greed and concupiscence, the impunity of criminals, and the persecution of the best citizens. Civilization, he declared, was a fiction of the brain if it rests not on truth, the unchanging

---

[3] April 21, 1878. The best available collection of the Encyclicals in English is *The Great Encyclicals of Leo XIII*, edited by Rev. John J. Wynne, S.J.

laws of morality, justice, love, and mutual service. But his final word was not so much a plea for the Church as an offer of aid to princes and rulers. The Church had saved civilization before. She was there to do it again.

Quod Apostolici

Following closely upon the *Inscrutabili*, came a more specific condemnation of

> a sect of men who under the motley and all but barbarous terms and titles of Socialists, Communists and Nihilists are spread abroad throughout the world and, linked together in baneful alliance, no longer look for strong support in secret meetings held in darksome places, but standing forth boldly and openly in the light of day, strive to carry their purpose of uprooting the foundations of civilized society.[4]

The pope then rises to the defense of the "right of private property sanctioned by the law of nature." Later, in a more famous encyclical, Leo was to be an ardent champion of the laboring class. But in the menace of Marxism he sensed, what we after more that half a century can see so clearly, the beginning of the most formidable attack of all time on Christianity.

Scholastic Philosophy

In his *Aeterni Patris*[5] the most modern pope of the nineteenth century urged a return to a medieval philosopher of the thirteenth century. But was there anything paradoxical in this? Leo XIII had taken for his province all truth; St. Thomas Aquinas before him had done likewise. Leo's writings present a fairly full synthesis of solutions for all the intellectual problems that agitated his contemporaries. He sought unity, perspective, balance, harmony, completeness. He found all this ready to hand in the *summa* of sound philosophy, the *philosophia perennis,* of the Master of the Schools. He wished to build his social program on a basis of solid metaphysics. In the nebulous chaos of modern thought, amid the labyrinthine windings of pseudo-philosophers he had to set the feet of his people again on the sure road to reality.

The doubting and the distinctions, and still more the "certainties" of Descartes had led humanity astray. A whole troop

---

[4] *Quod Apostolici,* December 28, 1878.
[5] August 4, 1879.

of powerful, but erratic thinkers down to Kant and Hegel and beyond had increased the confusion. Catholics, too, had joined in the general revolt against a sane Scholasticism which few of them had ever taken the time to study. In a frantic effort to meet the attack on religion they abandoned the ramparts and occupied the perilous ground halfway between orthodoxy and error. And the Church was forced to disown them.[6] Leo had no inclination to pursue pseudo-philosophy into all its devious byways, or to attempt to refute the fallacies latent in all the forty-odd "isms" of the century. It was a more pleasant and a more practical thing to recover the main highway of truth and to follow it. Nor was he a reactionary. He had no quarrel with the real conquests of science. He was not opposed to new discoveries and inventions. He encouraged research and experiment. He was definitely on the side of progress. Everything that tended to better the material conditions of life received his blessing. But he was no admirer of mere motion, of feverish activity without direction. He felt that the modern world needed above all a safe guide after so much aimless wandering, and he found him in St. Thomas.

In a reinvigorated Scholasticism Leo had a system that would harmonize reason and faith, sacred and profane learning, philosophy and theology, sense and intellect, prayer and action, the real and the ideal, the experience of the past and new discoveries.[7] If the system was ancient, it still had potentially the rugged strength of youth. Into its making had gone the best Greek thought, the treasures of the revealed Word of God, the wisdom of the Fathers of the Church. If it was "the logical and formally complete expression of a philosophy which stands in eternal opposition to the search for knowledge based on man's unaided reason,"[8] it was at the same time the highest product of reason enlightened by faith.

Characteristically, Leo begins his encyclical with a search for the source of the "troubles that vex public and private life" and he comes to the obvious conclusion that

---

[6] Cf. Condemned opinions of Lamennais, Hermes, Bautain, Bonnetty, Günther, Frohschammer, in Denzinger-Bannwart, *Enchiridion Symbolorum*. Also errors of Rosmini-Serbati, repudiated in 1855, condemned in 1887.

[7] Fernand Mourret, *op. cit.*, IX, p. 360 ff.

[8] René Fulop-Miller, *Leo XIII and His Times*, p. 175.

a fruitful cause of the evils which now afflict us, as well as those which threaten us lies in this: that false conclusions concerning divine and human things, which originated in the schools of philosophy, have crept into all the orders of the State, and have been accepted by the common consent of the masses.

It is in the very nature of man, he continues, to follow his reason. Hence "if his intellect sins, his will soon follows, and thus looseness of intellectual opinion" filters down into human actions and perverts them. And yet he refuses to admit a conflict between reason and revelation. With St. Augustine, the "powerful genius" who combated all the errors of his age, he sees in reason and science an aid and a defense of faith, while he holds up faith as the necessary safeguard of reason in the "human mind exposed to error."

There is a certain irony in the fact that the pope, like the Vatican Council before him, stood forth as a defender of reason in a world in which Rationalism was abdicating in despair.

> After incomparable triumphs, writes a clever observer outside the Church, after a long period of domination over the minds of men, after the era of natural science, of the Enlightenment, of critical philosophy, of materialism and of technical science, the suicidal impulse of reason seems to have chosen our century for the end of its present reign.[9]

The death of Rationalism, to quote further from the same admirer of Leo XIII, is similar to its abdication two thousand years ago:

> What took place in the Academy of Athens is now being enacted in the chairs of European and American universities, in observatories and in laboratories, and from continent to continent we hear many voices which ask again the question of Pilate.[10]

Pilate had asked: "What is truth?" But he did not wait for the answer. His generation had wandered far from Aristotle and Plato. The generation of Leo, also, despaired of an answer

---

[9] *Ibid.*, p. 179.
[10] *Ibid.*

to its doubts. In its relativism, subjectivism, and positivism it had thrown over the old metaphysical certainties, and loved passionately only values perceived by the senses. The Enlightenment had believed in the "infallibility of reason, unlimited progress and almighty science." The old shibboleths were still in use, but Rationalists were no longer so sure of themselves. Reason, raised to dizzy heights, had crashed to earth. But the pope was there to assert its just claims.

Human reason, he taught, can demonstrate that God *is*. It can show us an infinite Creator excelling in all perfections, in wisdom, in justice and truth. It can prepare the way for a rational act of faith. Applied to the deposit of divine revelation, it can build a system of theology marvelous in its unity, coherence, and completeness. This work had been done by the Fathers of the Church and the great Scholastics. But St. Thomas, following in the footsteps of illustrious teachers, "had inherited the intellect of all."[11] Their doctrines he had,

> like the scattered members *of a body*, gathered and cemented together, arranged in wonderful order, and so augmented with important additions that he is rightly regarded as the special bulwark of the Catholic faith. . . . Richly endowed with human and divine science, like the sun he warmed the world with the ardor of his virtues and illumined it with the splendor of his teachings.[12]

His method, his principles, his clarity, elegance and felicity of expression made him the master teacher of his age and of all ages. No part of philosophy had eluded his all-embracing mind. At his feet moderns might sit to learn what it was humanly possible to learn about liberty, authority and law, about the duties and rights of princes and their subjects. And so, in a world where a few valiant Scholastics were meeting with contempt, Leo XIII inaugurated the great neo-Thomistic revival with its lofty inspiration and its common-sense conception of reality.

When Leo urged a return to the philosophy of St. Thomas he intended, no doubt, to promote thereby the mental health

---

[11] *Aeterni Patris.*
[12] *Ibid.*

of his clergy. He wished to provide them with the best kind of immunity from the moral infection around them. But sound principles, clearness of vision, and intellectual acumen were to be an equipment for vigorous action. Leo had a great social program, which he could not hope to see realized in his own lifetime. Even if his hopes for an intellectually strong clergy should be fulfilled, this would be only the starting point for a reconquest of the world for Christ. A sane philosophy must be not merely a safeguard for its possessor; it must be a stimulus to action, and an incentive to attack and to remove the evils rampant in society. If the world wondered when a modern pope went back to a medieval saint for guidance in the realm of thought, it had reason to be further astounded when he presumed to apply medieval thought to social action. But it requires little imagination to picture St. Thomas himself dictating a whole series of encyclicals which Leo published on the family, the State, and the laboring class, as well as on the Sacred Scriptures, the Holy Eucharist, the Holy Ghost, and other specifically religious topics. St. Thomas philosophized on the totality of things. In his writings Leo found everything he needed except a direct application of his thought to nineteenth-century problems. Leo had not the full measure of genius of the greatest of the Scholastics, but he had all that was needed to apply a ready-made system, and his exalted position gave his teaching an added weight.

The Family

Society is an aggregation of families, and its health depends on the homes from which its members come. In his *Quod Apostolici* Leo had indicted Socialism as a menace to family life. A year later, in February, 1880, his fourth great encyclical, *Arcanum Divinae*,[13] presented a complete treatise on Christian marriage. He dealt at length with its nature, its origin, its history, and the perils to which it was exposed in the moral chaos about him. An institution established by God, rooted in nature, elevated by Christ to the order of grace, and confided to His Church was denatured by man-made laws, threatened by the civil power and degraded by a licentious Liberalism. This attack on the foundations of social well-being was an

---

[13] February 10, 1880.

index, though the encyclical did not say so explicitly, to the character of the secularized nineteenth century.

Leo's vision of an ordered universe under God was clearly before his mind. His appeal was to the will of God manifested by divine revelation and by human reason. But he could, also, draw a sad picture of the results of fighting against nature. He pointed to pagan degradation. He recalled the magnificent work of the Church in protecting the child, ennobling the wife with a new dignity and imposing a salutary restraint on the passions of men. Wife and child were subject to the headship of father and husband, but they were not his slaves. Equality of rights and duties raised the family life to a level above caprice and brute force.[14] Polygamy and promiscuity had been banned from Christian society. The pestilence of divorce was a present crime against nature and divine law. But the lay state with its satanic maxims and its revolt against the sovereignty of God was taxed with a major responsibility for the progressive lowering of a sacrament to a mere civil contract. Christ had made matrimony a holy thing on His own independent authority. He had not been a "delegate of Pontius Pilate or the Roman Empire." Only by a like absurdity could His Church be dictated to by the modern State. To a society imperiled by elemental passions and by its own folly Leo offered the good offices of religion and the Church. The State had its rights in civil affairs, but the Church had a solemn duty to protect morals, and indirectly to promote the happiness of all citizens. Against a false Liberalism the pope demanded liberty to uphold the law of nature and of God.

For the instruction of a society in which "Democracy," theoretical and practical, was strong but unsound Leo XIII wrote his *Diuturnum Illud*.[15] It was an exhortation to "give to Caesar the things that are Caesar's"; it was also a warning to "obey God rather than men." It was a recognition of the right of any people to choose its form of government, but a repudiation of the Rousseauvian fallacy that society origin-

Democracy

---

[14] Leo quotes liberally from Holy Scripture and the Fathers. He cites St. Jerome: ". . . with us that which is unlawful for women is unlawful for men also, and the same restraint is imposed on equal conditions."

[15] June 29, 1881.

ated in a social pact, or that the power and authority of rulers derived from any source short of the Divine Author of society. The religious turmoil of the sixteenth century had been the fatal breeding ground of a spirit of rebellion, and the "new philosophy" of the Enlightenment had issued logically in the modern pests of Communism, Socialism, and Nihilism. The Church, on the other hand, had throughout her long history tendered her aid and guidance to the civil power. Princes had no cause for suspicion of her motives, nor should nations be jealous of her. In affairs of the temporal order she would not interfere; in the middle field where political and religious interests crossed she desired only concord and harmony. The whole encyclical reveals a peace-loving pope ready to accept what was good in modern democracy, but uncompromising in his demand for justice and right order.

Ten popes have anathematized Freemasonry. And their serious charges of assassination, blasphemy, sacrilege, and Freemasonry treason, of revolution against lawful government and of deliberate war on God, Christ, and the Church have never been revoked. Against this supersect which gave to the most vicious elements in nineteenth-century Liberalism "its forms, its organization and international solidarity" Leo XIII wrote one of his major encyclicals, the *Humanum Genus*.[16] His condemnation falls on all secret societies, "which though differing in name, in ceremonial, in form and origin, are nevertheless bound together by community of purpose." He sees the forces of evil "struggling with united vehemence, led on or assisted by that strongly organized and widespread association called the Freemasons." The Kingdom of Satan[17] has come out boldly and openly to attack the Kingdom of God. It is the old conflict described by St. Augustine: "Two loves formed two cities: the love of self, reaching even to the contempt of God, an earthly city; and the love of God, reaching to the contempt of self, a heavenly one." Leo takes for granted this most fundamental fact in any intelligible philosophy of history. His

---

[16] April 20, 1884.

[17] Pius IX had called Freemasonry the "Synagogue of Satan." Rev. E. Cahill, *Free-Masonry and the Anti-Christian Movement*, Chapter VI, has a number of excerpts from papal condemnations.

concern, however, was not with the problems that agitated the genius of Augustine in the fifth century, but with the specter that was haunting Europe in his own day. Nor was this a childish apprehension born of ignorance and credulity. Catholics have, perhaps, exaggerated the role played by secret societies, and Masons may have misled the gullible.[18] But the popes, from Clement XII down to the present day, had too much at stake to allow groundless and imaginary fears to upset their judgment when they penned documents for the universal Church. And the sources of information at their disposal would seem, even humanly speaking, to reassure the most critical. It is one of the implications, at least, of papal infallibility that the popes of two centuries, each confirming and amplifying the teachings of his predecessors, could not be wrong.

Freemasonry has been studied from widely divergent angles. Its story has been written by its own adepts and by those who hated and feared it. Pius IX called it "the Synagogue of Satan," which sums up, along with its anti-Christian Jewish ingredients, the more or less equivalent expressions: counter-church, synthesis of all heresies, mobilization of the powers of evil, and social atheism.[19] Masonry, on the other hand, proclaims ideals that have an almost irresistible appeal to the modern mind. But after all due allowance is made for the sincerity of individual members of the craft, even in the cryptic and guarded language of its best apologists or panegyrists there is virtually nothing that cannot be reduced to pure Naturalism. And this "scientifically elaborated paganism"   Naturalism
would alone be reason sufficient for all the papal warnings to Catholics who might feel drawn to membership. Naturalism, too, is as good a term as any to characterize the spirit of the nineteenth century which created the peculiar problem with which the Church and the popes had to deal.

[18] The "revelations" of the notorious Leo Taxil (Gabrièle Pages-Jogand) were a huge hoax which showed, however, what Catholics were ready to believe about Freemasons. The fact that he was clever enough to expose the credulity of Catholics, and the fact that his supposed accomplice, Diana Vaughan, never existed, does not affect the papal condemnation of the sect. The affair caused considerable excitement during the four years preceding its termination in April, 1897.

[19] Cf. *Dictionnaire apologétique de la foi.*

Had there been no attempt, as there obviously was, to destroy religion, had there been no attack, overt or insidious, against the Church, had the manifestations of irreligion been confined to a benevolent or contemptuous indifference, the danger to souls must have aroused the vigilance of the supreme Pastor. But Naturalism was not a negative thing. It was an aggressive movement to root out the supernatural and all reference to a future life. Divine revelation and the divinely instituted sacraments were objects of ridicule, when they were not pursued with diabolic hatred. Abundant documents prove that Naturalism, as professed by Masonic spokesmen, tended directly and of set purpose to the destruction of the Church, of Christianity, of the very idea of the supernatural. There were, of course, enemies of religion who were not Masons, as there were many deluded members of the sect who had no personal hatred for religion. But the identification of Freemasonry, in the broad sense given the term by Leo, with mysteriously co-ordinated anti-Catholic forces, was close enough to warrant the specific accusations of the *Humanum Genus*.

In the encyclical the Naturalism of Masonry is charged explicitly with attempting to overthrow religious and political order, admitting no dogma and no authority in religion, laicizing the schools and making education irreligious, lowering marriage to the level of a commercial contract rescindible at will, and excluding God from society and public life. As a secret oath-bound organization it reduces its members to a kind of slavery. It sponsors public temptation in the licentious press and on the stage. Its Realism in art is a source of corruption. Its pursuit of pleasure and comfort begets softness and effeminacy. Its exaggerated belief in the perfection of nature and the autonomy of reason is absurd. Masonry was decidedly on the side of the "natural," and for this reason, if for no other the Church had an ungrateful task in opposing it.

But there is one point which, after half a century, assumes a peculiar interest in the light of present-day experiences. Leo speaks of "the overthrow of society deliberately planned by Socialists and Communists, abetted by the Freemasons."

Could the pope have had any intimation of a great Capitalist government like our own supporting and fostering a Bolshevist regime beyond the Rio Grande? Could he have foreseen the anomaly of a Capitalist press favoring the cause of the "Reds" in Spain? His hypothesis, which was surely something more than a hypothesis, does explain several enigmas. But the important thing to grasp is that fifty years ago the pope, with no material force to rely upon, openly challenged a powerful international organization, made it responsible for most of the ills of society, and called upon the bishops of the world to unmask its intrigues. That he never came to regret his strong words is attested by his return to the topic less than a year before his death in an Apostolic Letter of March 19, 1902, in which he writes:

> Embracing almost every nation in its immense grasp it unites itself with other sects of which it is the real inspiration and the hidden motive power. It first attacks and then retains its associates by the bait of worldly advantage which it secures for them. It bends governments to its will sometimes by promises, sometimes by threats. It has found its way into every class of society, and forms an invisible and irresponsible power, an independent government, as it were, within the body corporate of the lawful state.[20]

In his *Immortale Dei*[21] Leo XIII set forth the doctrine of the Church on the relations between Church and State. As a philosopher he looked into the nature of the two societies, each sovereign in its own sphere, and saw that there was no essential conflict. He reviewed the history of the Christian era, and found that the Church had collaborated with the civil authorities over a long period with beneficent results for society. Then he turned to the world about him and was pained to discover the modern State, the child of Rationalism and Naturalism, at enmity with the Church, intent upon "sterilizing Christianity, and installing the supremacy of man to the exclusion of God."

The State and the Church

The Catholic Church, imperishable handiwork of an all-

---

[20] Quoted by Cahill, *op. cit.*, Preface.
[21] November 1, 1885.

merciful God has for its purpose the saving of souls and the attaining of happiness in heaven. And yet in the temporal order so manifold and great were her services to humanity that the chief end of her existence might seem to be the procuring of earthly well-being.[22]

In the pursuit of her primary purpose she has not interfered with the State. In the benefits she brought to society in general she has been a positive aid to it.

Leo rejected as a calumny the charge that the Church was opposed to progress. He recalled that the charge had been made before, and had been answered for all time by St. Augustine. Only by spurning the dictates of reason, to say nothing of revelation, could humanity succumb to the age-old errors. But looking more closely at the nineteenth century he beheld absurd exaggerations of modern "liberties" and of "popular sovereignty." Insofar as these were groundless assumptions or an inevitable source of disorder he had to repudiate them. Likewise, he pronounced indifference in religion, another fallacy of the century, the equivalent of atheism. His aim was to bring the State into conformity with the original designs of the Creator. If this were realized the two societies, each independent, the one in spiritual the other in purely temporal affairs, could co-operate harmoniously in matters of mixed character. The State was a natural society intended by the Author of nature, and deriving its limited powers from Him. Let it stay within those limits, and no matter what peculiar form its constitution might take, it would find the Church a willing and helpful ally. With this, Leo rested his case at the bar of revelation, reason, and history.

Libertas Praestantissimum   "Liberty," says Leo XIII in the opening words of an important encyclical,[23] "is God's most precious gift to man." It is an endowment of man's rational nature which raises him above brute creation, and makes him responsible for his actions. But the physical liberty which enables man to act freely to the full extent of his physical powers must not be identified or confused with the moral liberty by which he

[22] *Immortale Dei.*
[23] *Libertas Praestantissimum,* June 20, 1888.

FRANCESCO CRISPI

One of the moving figures in the Unification of Italy and the
most competent Italian statesman during the reign of Leo XIII
(1819–1901)

is a free agent only within the limits of the moral law. In other words, man *can* do what he ought not to do. His progress and his perfection depend upon the right use of freedom. And this right use means that will must wait on reason, and that reason must be subject to the law of God. These elementary distinctions were part of a very necessary lesson which the pope thought it worth his while to teach. For it is but another strange anomaly of nineteenth-century history that the age which has gone farthest in the study of physical laws became steadily less sensible to the moral law; that unprecedented progress in confining and controlling the blind forces of nature was paralleled by an unprecedented lack of moral restraint. "Amid an ordered universe man's spirit only dared rebel." Speculatively and practically, by thinkers and nonthinkers it was considered proper for man to bend nature to his will and to ignore the will of his Creator. But, the pope insisted, this pretended autonomy was rooted in a defect of human nature. Man was liable to mistake the apparent good for the real on which he could turn his back. God's most precious gift could be perverted to man's ruin.

Liberty, along with Equality and Fraternity, had been the great slogan of the French Revolution. In Liberty's name crimes had been committed; Equality had had a history red with injustice and violation of rights; Fraternity had degenerated into the mania of Nationalism. It was the purpose of Leo XIII to lead the world back to saner ideas of liberty. And in this, as in almost everything else, he turned to the philosophy which presented a view of life divinely ordered and functioning according to a rational plan. Brushing aside inadequate man-made theories of authority, right, and natural law, he pointed to the origin of all these in God. There was a Natural Law because there was an Eternal Law, and there was Eternal Law because there was a plan and a purpose in the Divine Mind which the Divine Will imposed upon His created universe. To this high source must be referred all authority and obligation, all rights and duties. Human laws may be formulated by society, but their ultimate basis, their binding force, is in God. Liberals, of course, never went so far back for the foundations of their liberty, or for its limitations.

Liberalism

They, as well as all other Rationalists or Naturalists, lived in a world of their own creation. And their system would not stand this kind of criticism.

Of liberty in the only reasonable sense of the word, of liberty as he defined it, the pope insisted that the Church was a friend and protector. But with the Liberalism which emancipated the individual or the community from every higher law the Church could never agree. She could not admit that society derived its powers ultimately from itself, or that the human reason was the determining factor in questions of right and wrong. She could not admit that the majority was always right, or that Liberals were free to set up an absolute State and to walk on the liberties of those who disagreed with them. Once again, the Church in the person of her supreme pontiff undertook the defense of a human endowment which modern excesses had badly discredited. In the Vatican Council she had defended reason and defined its powers. Now, she defended free will in the physical order, and at the same time declared the limits beyond which it might not go in the moral order.

But Leo could also be specific in his treatment of modern "liberties." Liberals had claimed freedom of worship, of conscience, of speech, of the press, of teaching. In the full consciousness that he was the authorized interpreter of the moral law, and that the order of the universe required that the physical freedom of man be kept within bounds set by nature and reason as well as by the teaching of revelation, he took up these "liberties" one by one, and boldly pointed out the fallacy in each of them. There was here no question of repression, of coercion on the part of Church or State or any other human agency. The pope was merely making clear to Catholics and non-Catholics how untenable were some of the ideas to which the century clung most tenaciously.

Liberty of Worship

If man is a creature dependent upon his Creator, then surely his first duty is to acknowledge that dependence, and to give expression to it in a way acceptable to the Creator. But the bewildering multiplicity of sects proliferating from the religious upheaval of the sixteenth century and its principle of "private judgment" left millions of people without any uniform or definite manner of worshiping God, while the downward trend of the Rationalist-Liberalist "Enlightenment" was toward not worshiping Him at all. What the sincere religious-minded individual who had been born into this confusion might do could be left to the justice and mercy of a higher tribunal. But the teachings which during a century and more had loudly proclaimed the forms of religion a matter of indifference were justly flayed by the pope. Nor was the State more free than the individual. Reason proved that there is a God. The same reason proved that He should be recognized by His rational creatures both privately and publicly. History proved that God had spoken. And it was man's duty to understand His message. Whatever false freedom individuals or institutions might claim was the unfortunate result of defective knowledge. But liberty of worship, erected into a principle of universal application, was in the common-sense philosophy of Leo XIII absurd.

Liberty of speech, of the press, of teaching could, of course, be rightly understood. It belonged to the very nature of man to communicate his thought to his fellow man. But when Liberals placed truth and error on an equal footing, when self-styled intellectuals demanded the irresponsible privilege of propagating any and every wild idea, the pope knew that it was his duty and the duty of right-minded men generally to protect the helpless victims of literary poison. In an age of chaotic subjectivism it was necessary to keep before the minds of men the objective reality of right, justice, and truth. An attack upon these was an attack upon the foundations of social life which no theory of Liberalism could justify. Nor would the pope concede that the Church in thus bridling liberty of expression was thereby impeding the progress of learning, of technical science, or of civilization. The Church had ever favored the forward advance of humanity. But disregard for law and order, for reason and divine authority, was not rational liberty. And as a last bit of perversity Leo pointed to the inconsistency of Liberals demanding license for every brand of opinion, and at the same time hampering the Church

Liberty of Thought

in the exercise of her teaching office. They had emancipated the individual from God and the Church; they were handing him over (Was the vision of Leo prophetic?) to the caprice of the omnipotent State.

On the fiftieth anniversary of his ordination to the priesthood Leo published an encyclical[24] which was, in keeping with the occasion, rather general in character. The tone is more intimate, more fatherly, than that of the greater encyclicals. In its English version it bears the title: "The right ordering of Christian life." "Public and private morals," he tells the faithful, "differ vastly from the precepts of the Gospel." There is an inordinate quest of wealth, comfort, and luxury, and a patronizing contempt for the poor. The stage, books, periodicals, even the fine arts "are made to minister to depraved passions." Education is irreligious and materialistic. In such conditions Christians must profess their faith fearlessly; they must fight and they must pray. The Church, like Christ her Founder, has overcome the world before. She is not frightened by present problems.

Christian Duties

Similar to the foregoing is the encyclical issued a year later,[25] "On the chief duties of Christians as citizens." Progress in material wealth and power the pope admits, but he is filled with "serious alarm for the future." The State has become the last end of man, and civil rulers forget their duties toward God. There is danger that "force alone will remain to preserve public tranquillity and order." But force without religion is feeble; it begets slavery and the germs of future disaster. The Church has had to suffer from the encroachments of the State and the arrogance of "science." And yet there was no reason for antagonism between Church and State. Each was sovereign in its own sphere, and the Church was ready to co-operate with any form of government. Catholics should realize that "supernatural love of the Church and natural love of country proceed from the same eternal principle," which is God. In the mind of the Christian public authority was a hallowed thing, a likeness and symbol of divine authority.

---

[24] *Exeunte jam Anno,* December 25, 1888; title of English version: "The Right Ordering of Christian Life."

[25] *Sapientiae Christianae,* January 10, 1890.

However, constitution makers must have due regard for the moral and religious nature of man. For Catholics, on the other hand, it is a duty to resist, a crime to obey iniquitous laws. They should not recoil before an aggressive enemy, nor should they submit to injustice in silence. Excessive prudence and excessive zeal alike were wrong. Let them follow the lead of their bishops in the fight against evil.

XXIII

THE GREAT ENCYCLICALS: SOCIAL

Rerum
Novarum

THE RERUM NOVARUM WAS A CONDEMNATION OF Socialism, and for two or three decades comfortable Bourgeois-minded Catholics saw in it nothing else. The *Rerum Novarum* was also a condemnation of the "civilization" that had produced Socialism, and as such it was epochal in its importance. But the great encyclical was not mere negative criticism; it was positive in its constructive program. If it defended property, it also set limits to the use of property. If it laid bare the sores of society, it did so to heal them. It pleaded the cause of the worker, but at the same time reminded him of his duties to others. It read a lesson in social obligations to the rich, but upheld their legitimate rights. There was in it no straddling of issues after the manner of a politician, careful not to offend or antagonize. It was the voice of the supreme teacher, proclaiming the moral law in a world that had come to know only the argument of physical force. If one were to reduce its message to a single word, that word would be: justice.[1] In perfect consistency with the whole tenor of his pontificate Leo XIII had gone back again to the *philosophia perennis* for a cure of modern ills. *Pax, ordo, justitia* had been the high ideals of a saner age. To Leo they were eternal values that he was determined to restore to a civilization that had forgotten them.

---

[1] Cf. Léon Grégoire (Georges Goyau), *Le Pape, les catholiques et la question sociale,* for one of the earliest and best discussions of social justice in connection with the encyclical. M. Goyau has been a prolific writer on religious historical topics during nearly half a century. He is always stimulating. The most up-to-date treatment of the *Rerum Novarum* and the *Quadragesimo Anno* will be found in Joseph Husslein's *The Christian Social Manifesto* (Milwaukee, 1931) and Oswald von Nell-Breuning's *Reorganization of Social Economy* (translated by Bernard W. Dempsey, Milwaukee, 1936).

The encyclical deserves attention here because it was an attempt to solve a great social problem, and as such it mirrors some of the most vital aspects of the century. It marked a giant step forward toward an alliance of the pope with the workers, of the Church with the common people, and so was heavy with consequences for the future. It is an important arch in the great edifice reared in grandiose fashion by Leo XIII. It has enjoyed a steadily increasing influence in the Catholic and non-Catholic world, and finally, it has received an official commentary in the *Quadragesimo Anno* of Pius XI.

"The spirit of revolutionary change," had agitated the nations of the world throughout the nineteenth century. But it was no longer predominantly political. Economics, once the servant of politics, as politics had been the servant of religion, was occupying more and more of the public stage. Kings and parliaments and forms of government were giving way before the struggle of the classes. Karl Marx had exaggerated a half truth when he reduced all history to a seesaw between the "haves" and the "have nots." But there was enough plausibility in his materialism to win destitute and suffering millions to his banner. The Bourgeois Capitalist had abused a recognized right until there seemed to not a few to be ample justification for "expropriating the expropriators." Catholic thinking, too, was confused. There was need for a solution, or at least a declaration of the mind of the Church. When Leo spoke on May 15, 1891, it was in the form of his best known encyclical, a document which is better understood now than it was forty years ago. It was not the emotional appeal of a party leader, as was, for example, the *Communist Manifesto*. It was a reasoned statement of objective fact, a demand of justice for the mistreated worker, and an arraignment of lawless wealth which flouted the moral order. The sane, balanced judgment of the pope and his calm, clear expression naturally could cause little excitement. Only those few who had the sincerity and the energy to make a study of the *Rerum Novarum* would see in it the revolution that it was.

Liberals had been maintaining that there was no social

problem, while Socialists were clamoring with greater
vehemence that there was nothing else to talk about or to
fight for. Gambetta had said explicitly in 1872: "There is
no remedy for social ills, for the simple reason that there is
no social question."[2] The only peril that humanity had to
worry about was Clericalism. Leo XIII countered with the
obvious fact that a gulf yawned between the omnipotence of
Capitalism and the obvious weakness of the working class.
In this he agreed with the disciples of Marx. But against
Marx and materialist Liberals he insisted that the only solution lay with the Church and religion. He saw plainly that
the Liberal State had no case against a rising Socialism.
Liberals proclaimed unlimited liberty of thought and speech.
The Marxist, therefore, was free to propagate his ideas. The
Liberals stood for the infallibility and the absolute dominance
of the majority. Marxists knew that numbers were on their
side. It was merely a matter of time and indoctrination. The
masses, potentially omnipotent, would become conscious of
their power, and in a world where "might made right" they
would rule. As the Third Estate had supplanted the old
aristocracy, so, too, the Fourth Estate with equal right (or
might) would sweep aside the new privileged parasites.

    The position of the pope was a difficult one. He could
not take sides. But thanks to the genius of Leo the Church
would not be found tied to a falling caste, as it had been
locally tied to the Old Regime. The Church had little in
common with the Bourgeois world, though a few "conservative" Catholics and most Socialist radicals thought she
had. But if the Bourgeois Liberal was an anticlerical, the
Marxist was an out-and-out atheist. The pope could make no
choice between them. He rejected both. Kings had during
long centuries supported the Church and enslaved her. They
had treated the clergy as government functionaries, as a sort
of spiritual police force. The French Revolution broke the
chains of gilded slavery, and the Church was virtually com-
pelled by the contemptuous treatment she received in the
nineteenth century to shake herself free from the State, and
to develop her own innate powers. Providentially, she was

---

[2] Cited by Goyau, *op. cit.*, p. 272, note.

equipped for the battle of the classes. Leo could still offer his aid to rulers and statesmen. He could still plead with the rich in the name of religion. But the future lay with the yet inarticulate masses, and the pope, like his great predecessors whose power was in their alliance with the common people, was prepared, whether he adverted fully to his new opportunity or not, to become the great moral force in the revolutionary era that was just dawning.

Aside from Leo's all-embracing philosophy and his personal alertness to social conditions, three great factors are discernible in the preliminary and immediate preparation of the *Rerum Novarum*. In America the Knights of Labor, a powerful organization, 750,000 strong, under a Catholic president, had been condemned in 1886 by the Archbishop of Quebec. Cardinal Gibbons, backed by the American episcopate carried the case to Rome. The men were convinced of the justice of their cause, and so was Cardinal Gibbons. It was a perplexing problem for authorities in Rome, but the pontiff of nearly eighty years had the viewpoint of a youth of twenty. And the Knights were left to fight their battle for justice without fear of censure by the Church. In London, two years later, a quarter of a million dock hands were staging a mammoth strike. Amid the general despair of mediators Cardinal Manning took up the cause of the strikers, and after some negotiation brought about a happy solution. All this was far away in a predominantly Protestant land. But for the pope it was an experiment in social Christianity, and he was in active sympathy with Manning and the working class. Meantime two pilgrimages of French workingmen had knocked at the gates of the Vatican. The first, in 1887, numbered 1,400, besides several hundred priests and sympathetic industrialists. The second, in 1889, was an army of four thousand (according to one account, ten thousand). The Archbishop of Rheims, Cardinal Langénieux, a great social theorist, Albert de Mun, and a model employer, Léon Harmel, were the leading spirits in this unprecedented march on Rome. For the pope it was the announcement of a new age. At the moment, the impression of fatherly interest which he made upon the men was important. There was none of the pompous ceremony to

The Laboring Classes

which fidgeting ambassadors of princes had to submit. The workingmen felt that the pope was their friend, and they went back to their work with increased loyalty to the Church. But the successor of the Leo who had crowned Charlemagne was also impressed by this informal embassy of the power that would rule the society of the future. The time had come for him to pronounce the judgment of the Church on the great question of Capital and Labor.

Forerunners of Leo

But if Leo XIII was so visibly affected by the stirrings of labor in America, England, and France, it was largely because his delicate mind was attuned to catch whatever concerned the mission of the Church in the new age. It must not be thought, however, that Leo stood alone. Other Catholic thinkers had been in closer personal contact with social conditions than he; other Catholic workers had made a more profound study of social theory.[3] In 1887 a clever French journalist wrote: "The day that brings to the throne of Peter a pope animated by the sentiments of Cardinal Gibbons or Cardinal Manning will see the Church take her place as the most formidable power the world has known."[4] But besides the Cardinals of America and England, there were Mermillod in Switzerland and Langénieux in France. In Germany the "great precursor," Bishop von Ketteler, was the equal of any of them. And marching with, and sometimes ahead of, the social leaders among the prelates were the elite among laymen and the lower clergy: Ozanam, de Mun, Decurtins, Kolping, Hitze, Vogelsang, and a host of others.[5] Half a century before Leo's classic encyclical Villeneuve-Bargemont[6]

---

[3] René Fülöp-Miller, *Leo XIII and Our Times*, gives the incorrect impression that Leo inaugurated and carried through his renovation of Catholic thought and action single-handed.

[4] M. de Vogüe, quoted by Goyau, *op. cit.*, p. 276.

[5] The great clearing house for Catholic social thought was the Fribourg Union. The Union was launched in 1885 by a group of scholars to discuss labor problems, wages, credit, agriculture, and industry, and to work for international legislation.

[6] For a striking parallel between the social programs of Leo XIII and Villeneuve-Bargemont see Sister M. Ignatius Ring, *Villeneuve-Bargemont; Precursor of Modern Social Catholicism*, XXVI. See also Parker Thomas Moon, *The Labor Problem and the Social Catholic Movement in France*, pp. 163–165; a Comparative Table, in which parallel ideas of Albert de Mun are shown to anticipate Leo XIII.

was working out theoretically and practically the principles contained in it.

Leo had a philosophy of his own, and facts were brought to him from all over the world. But he was in no sense a lone pioneer. When in 1881 he set up a commission to study economic conditions he found able theologians at his elbow. When he looked abroad he beheld study clubs and congresses and effective organizations in which, as in a great laboratory, the ideas he was to broadcast to the Catholic and non-Catholic world, had been discussed and tried in actual application to life. Behind him, too, lay a whole century of social reformers,[7] radical and conservative, Liberal and anti-Liberal. He could learn from the experiences of Bismarck; he could not help learning a terrifying lesson from the colossal perversion of Marxism. An open mind was essential to Leo's mission. That he had an open mind is evident from his readiness to consult others. An infallible pope need not be an original thinker. He could well afford to leave to others the glory of daring to say the first word. When he spoke there must be an air of finality about what he said.

The reception accorded the *Rerum Novarum* in restricted circles showed that the pope had spoken well. The slowness with which the world at large reacted showed that he had spoken ahead of his time and before the world was ready to listen. "Quite novel to worldly ears," the teaching of Leo

Forty Years Later

was looked upon with suspicion by some, even among Catholics, and gave offense to others. For it boldly attacked and overthrew the idols of Liberalism, swept aside inveterate prejudices, and was so far and so unexpectedly in advance of its time, that the slow of heart ridiculed the study of the new social philosophy, and the timid feared to scale its lofty heights. Nor were there wanting those who, while professing their admiration for this message of light, regarded it as a utopian ideal, desirable rather than attainable in practice.[8]

---

[7] Two excellent source books are Donald O. Wagner, *Social Reformers,* and Emil Ritter, *Katholisch-konservatives Erbgut,* both published in 1934. Wagner gives lengthy selections from thirty-odd writers — from Adam Smith to John Dewey. Ritter limits his field to twelve Catholic Germans — from Friedrich Schlegel to Franz Hitze.

[8] *Quadragesimo Anno.*

Thus writes the most august and the most authentic commentator on the *Rerum Novarum,* who forty years after its publication confirms it without reserve. And Pius XI assures us that this "remarkable document," the way for which was prepared by previous encyclicals of Leo,

> stood out in this, that it laid down for all mankind unerring rules for the right solution of the difficult problem of human solidarity, called the Social Question, at the very time when such guidance was most opportune and necessary.

Leo's great successor emphasizes the timeliness of the encyclical. He continues with a brief survey of the situation met by Leo: new economic conditions widening the cleavage between the satisfied and prosperous few and the discontented, desperate masses; charity, a poor makeshift, offered as a remedy for legalized injustice; the consequent threat of disruption of the whole social fabric and the more reasonable demand for reform of a system evidently out of harmony with the designs of the Creator; the confusions and uncertainties of reformers; the courageous and effective action of the pope.

During the forty years between the *Rerum Novarum* and the *Quadragesimo Anno* issues had been clarified considerably. It was easy for Pius XI to apply his fuller knowledge to the problem, but the remarkable thing is that he built upon the foundation as Leo XIII had left it, without alteration or criticism. Both pontiffs saw that there was a social question which Liberalism had created and which the Liberal State could not solve; they knew that Socialism was a cure infinitely more fatal than the disease; they probed the deeper centers of infection in the social body and demanded their eradication by a return to more wholesome moral and religious life. As historical documents, available to all who can read the languages of Europe, they are indispensable to students of the Church and her relations with modern civilization.

XXIV

THE GREAT ENCYCLICALS: SPIRITUAL

IN THE ENCYCLICALS WHICH FILLED OUT THE TWENTY-five years of Leo's pontificate one may distinguish two periods. Somewhat arbitrarily the first may be said to end with the *Rerum Novarum*. In this period Leo was predominantly the political and social philosopher. Speaking always as supreme pastor, his appeal was to reason. In the second period, while still remaining the disciple of St. Thomas and the *Philosophia perennis*, his chief concern is with religious, one might almost say pious, topics. Ten years after the *Rerum Novarum*, however, we have his Apostolic Letter on "Christian Democracy."[1]

Amid alarming discussions of economic issues, prompted by "bad philosophical and ethical teaching . . . fomented by professional agitators," the pope turned his attention to a name: Christian Democracy. But the important distinctions he made and his further elaboration of ideas contained in former letters gave to the *Graves de communi* the character of a farewell message. "Christian Socialism" was rejected as a contradiction in terms; so, too, "Social Democracy" as a synonym for Socialism, with its earthly outlook, its class war, and its attack on property. Christian Democracy, however, was built on nobler foundations.

Christian Democracy

> Philologically and philosophically it implies popular government, yet in its present application it is to be so employed that, removing from all political significance, it is to mean nothing else than a benevolent and Christian movement in behalf of the people.

Christian Democracy must free itself from party politics and problems of administration, and while striving to improve the

---

[1] January 18, 1901.

lot of the working class, devote itself to the welfare of society as a whole.

The Social Question, Leo maintained, was a moral and religious as well as an economic one. The toilers must be taught that they are "not animals but men, not heathens but Christians." For without moral restraint misery would continue "in spite of shorter hours and larger wages." In a "brotherly way" Catholic leaders must induce the workers "to keep aloof from seditious acts and seditious men; to guard inviolate the rights of others; to show the proper respect to superiors; to perform willingly the work in which they are employed; not to grow weary of the restraints of family life." *Graves de communi* really adds little to previous encyclicals. It has, however, its own place as the last among the numerous antidotes to Socialism administered by Leo XIII.

On November 18, 1893, Leo XIII sent forth one of his longest encyclicals, the *Providentissimus Deus*, which defined the doctrine of the Church on the "Study of Holy Scripture." His earlier writings on political, social, and economic problems were a mirror of the age in which they were written. They were the authentic voice of the Church condemning Naturalism, Materialism, and Secularism, and offering religion and the moral law as a corrective of the evils arising from them. The *Providentissimus Deus*, apparently so different in character, was also a reflection of the spirit of the times. It was likewise a necessary preparation for a later appeal to the truths of Revelation, and for their application to an erring society.

After recalling the Reformers and their reliance on the Bible, privately interpreted, as the sole source and rule of faith, he turns (in the words of the encyclical).

> to meet the rationalists, true children and inheritors of the older heretics, who, trusting to their own way of thinking, have rejected even the scraps and remnants of Christian belief which had been handed down to them. They deny that there is any such thing as revelation or inspiration, or Holy Scripture.

In the name of their "newly invented free science . . . which they are perpetually modifying and supplementing" they declare miracles and prophesies to be founded upon myth and

Holy
Scripture

fable. Their blind intolerance regarding the supernatural is "directed chiefly against the ignorant masses," among whom

> they diffuse their deadly poison by means of books, pamphlets and newspapers! . . . they are in possession of numerous schools, taken by violence from the Church, in which, by ridicule and scurrilous jesting, they pervert the credulous and unformed minds of the young to the contempt of Holy Scripture.

Against Rationalists, pseudo-scientists, and "Higher Critics" Leo asserts the absolute inerrancy of the inspired Word of God, and he calls upon Catholic scholars to pursue with greater energy the study of Scripture in seminaries, academies, and private research. Leo was anticipating the battle against Modernism. But he was no Fundamentalist. Whatever God actually said through the medium of the inspired writer was infallibly true. But obviously not every amateur exegete, whatever his standing in the laboratory, sewing circle, or village grocery store, could presume to possess infallibility in interpreting the meaning of texts that had been penned by men and in idioms with which he was totally unfamiliar. As for self-sufficient professional students of the Bible, their closed minds precluded anything like the attainment of objective truth.

The Church, and the Church alone, could speak with finality. Under her guidance scholars might labor to extend the rich domain of Biblical learning. They would find that philosophy and history and the natural sciences were not in conflict with the Word of God. The hypotheses of scientists and the misreadings of *a priorist* critics might create difficulties. But within the limits of established fact truth was truth whether it came from the laborious effort of the human intellect working on natural phenomena or from divine revelation. Furthermore, although the proper function of faith was to communicate knowledge beyond the reach of created reason, the Word of God was actually an aid to a better and clearer understanding of truths which the sluggish and erring mind of man might not otherwise know. With Revelation to guide him the philosopher or the scientist could with increased security penetrate the mysteries of nature as well as of supernature.

The Index of Forbidden Books is always a delicate topic. The religious indifferentist is bewildered by it and often irritated; the Liberal is positively exasperated; the half-educated Catholic or the Catholic infected by the Liberal atmosphere in which he moves is generally embarrassed when conversation turns upon the subject. But the blindest fanatic or the most unsympathetic observer will, at least, credit the Church with courage and determination when she challenges the modern mind by affixing the label of poison on much of its mental and moral food. Leo XIII knew that he was doing an unpopular act when, on January 25, 1897, he published his constitution, *Officiorum ac Munerum,* on the "Prohibition and Censorship of Books." But it was the "chief duty" of the supreme teacher he declared:

> to watch over the integrity of Christian faith and morals . . . especially in these days when men's minds and characters are so unrestrained that almost every doctrine which Jesus Christ, the Savior of mankind, has committed to the custody of His Church, for the welfare of the human race, is daily called into question and doubt. In this warfare, many and varied are the stratagems and hurtful devices of the enemy; but the most perilous of all is the uncurbed freedom of writing and publishing noxious literature.

Accordingly, in response to petitions from French and German bishops and in keeping with the policy of the Church since the sixteenth-century abuses of printing, he set about a revision and reaffirmation of the rules laid down by Pius IV. This he found imperative in view of the "contempt of religion and manifold allurements to sin" arising from changed circumstances in which popular custom and the connivance of civil laws encouraged the wildest license. Unapproved editions of Holy Scripture, heretical and obscene writings, books and periodicals promoting newfangled devotions or tending to the corruption of morals generally, were forbidden to Catholics. In his ten pages of specific items were included also the rules to be observed in censoring all publications of religious character, along with sanctions for disobedience. Those who might be tempted to contrast the conciliating Leo with the intransigent Pius could here find one more proof that the unchanging

Church was still herself. The revised Index is, in fact, in perfect harmony with the whole orderly structure erected by Leo XIII.

During the jubilee that marked the close of the nineteenth century Leo XIII began his encyclical on Christ our Redeemer with a reflection of the reawakening of spiritual life, the revival of piety and faith, and the general growth in virtue, which he observed around him. From about this time, certainly, we must date a very positive resurgence of interest in the supernatural which bore visible and tangible fruit in every department of the Church's activity. The Church has never been without her elite few in whom her indispensable mark of holiness can be found by the well disposed. But with the dawn of the twentieth century, in which irreligion and immorality scored amazing triumphs, there was an unquestionable broadening and deepening of Catholic life. Among clergy and laity the Eucharistic revival, the Liturgical movement, Catholic influence in literature and the aggressive enthusiasm of Catholic writers, the renewed energy of religious congregations, the recovery of due emphasis and perspective by Catholic educators, Mission crusades at home and abroad, retreats for all classes of people, popular devotions honoring the Sacred Heart and the Kingship of Christ, and increased loyalty to the Holy Father were real manifestations of vitality which the historian may have some difficulty in checking. The essential element in them is not the stuff of historical narrative, as is, for example, a world war or a depression, national rivalry or class hatred, the general letdown of morals or the emancipation of women. But there were unmistakable signs of vigorous Catholic life which not only made the Church a factor in world history since the turn of the century, but also threw considerable light on the struggles of the past hundred years and more. In the passing of reticence, of reverence, and of regard for the Ten Commandments the Catholic population suffered along with the rest of men. But the fact remains that the Church was better prepared spiritually than she had been for many generations past to meet what may prove to be the most terrible onslaught of the powers of darkness in her history.

The Spiritual Revival

There is some danger, perhaps, of exaggeration in attributing to the letters of a nonagenarian pope a renascence of the supernatural which was the result of many factors. It is indeed the fashion to pass over the spiritual encyclicals of Leo XIII as relatively unimportant in comparison with his great pronouncements on political and social questions, or as somewhat colorless and pale beside the greater encyclicals of (we venture to think) greater popes who came after him. But comparisons aside, when Leo XIII, during the closing years of his long life, appealed to the Catholic world for a renewal of devotion to the Holy Ghost, the Sacred Heart of the Redeemer, the Holy Eucharist and the Rosary — a theme to which he constantly returned — he was putting a fitting crown to his work for souls, and at the same time pointing the way for his successors.

The Sacred Heart

In consecrating the human race to the Heart of Christ, and in proclaiming the social kingship of the Saviour of mankind to a world that disregarded the law of God in public affairs he was, it is true, speaking a language that the nineteenth century could scarcely understand, but he was offering the only remedy for its many social ailments. To an unbeliever the rule of Jesus Christ in the home, the school, the factory, in the halls of legislation, and in all public institutions, in a word, wherever members of human society were assembled might seem fantastic. But for one who believed, as Leo did, in the Incarnation, the Redemption, and the real Presence of Christ in the Eucharist this was the means to combat social atheism. It was his duty to broadcast these ideas, whether men felt a corresponding duty to listen to him or not. Leo pleaded consistently for order, justice, and charity. And there would never be order nor justice nor charity in a world estranged from Christ.

The Holy Spirit

But perhaps the hardest doctrine for a materialist age to accept was that contained in the *Divinum Illud*, which Leo published on May 4, 1897. It was an exhortation to know and worship the Holy Spirit. But too many people, like St. Paul's benighted neophytes; "had not so much as heard whether there be a Holy Ghost." The world had moved a long way from the great Trinitarian controversies which shook the Church in the fourth century. And yet, in the philosophy of Leo, all rational creation had for its first and highest purpose the glorification of the Trinity. The Church as well as each individual Christian belonged to the supernatural order precisely by reason of the mysterious indwelling of the Trinity in souls who thus participated in the Divine Nature. The neglect of this truth was surely a tremendous count against the "after-Christians" of the modern world. An understanding of it would have provided an effective antiseptic against Naturalism, Materialism, and Atheism. It would have meant a recognition not only of the spiritual in man, but also of his supernatural destiny and all that this involved. It would have meant a changed attitude toward Christianity and the Church. Christianity would not have been thought merely one of many religions, a more or less original system of doctrines, devotional practices, and irksome disciplinary regulations, emanating remotely from a half-mythical founder who, for all his sublime teachings and magnetic personal qualities, was only one of humanity's great religious leaders. The Church would have been something more than a human organization with a long historical record rich in achievements, but also carrying the burden of all the sin and superstition of nineteen centuries. She would not have been regarded as an anachronism, a medieval, childish thing strangely out of place in the mature age of science and progress.

Out of the patristic tradition Leo had selected for quotation a statement of St. Augustine: "What the soul is in the body, that is the Holy Ghost in Christ's body, the Church." In spite of the frailty and the perversity of her human members, who after all shared the human nature of her unspiritual enemies, the Church was essentially an organism animated by the Spirit of Christ. But since the Spirit of Christ worked necessarily with and through members endowed with free will, bound to material things that weighed them down like a kind of spiritual gravity, and subject to all the emotions which can becloud and distract a limited and fallible intellect, it was inevitable that the chequered history of the Church should be what it was. It was natural, too, though not altogether logical, that those who failed utterly and completely to correspond

The Soul
in the Church

with the promptings of divine grace should be critical of those
who did so falteringly. Leo's treatise on the Holy Ghost and
his exhortation to a better appreciation of supernatural knowledge and love is a historical document to which the unbeliever
may turn for light on much that is dark in human history. It
was directed, however, to believers. And the subsequent resurgence of spiritual thought and activity among Catholics is
evidence sufficient that it was effective.

The foregoing comment on the more spiritual encyclicals
of Leo XIII would seem to be a fitting conclusion for this
chapter, if not on the whole book. These exhortations to renewed piety and to a deeper comprehension of the Kingdom
of God among men were prompted in no small degree by the
Naturalism which was so characteristic of the nineteenth century. While in no sense abandoning the ground of reason and
philosophy, the great pope was conscious of the futility of
human effort in an age that was proud of its titanic achievements and felt little need of anything beyond material bigness,
speed, and comfortable living. One prefers, however, to regard
insistence on revelation and the supernatural in a more positive light. This teaching was not merely a remedy for the ills
of the century; it laid a new foundation and generated new
energy for the great spiritual revival under Leo's successors.
The establishing of sound criteria for the reading of Holy
Scripture, the consecration of the world to the Divine Heart
of Christ, and the promotion of Catholic devotion to the
Eucharist and to the Holy Ghost were constructive, forward-
looking acts, which belong to the story of the twentieth century. But it so happened that the round of events called forth
in the closing year of the nineteenth century a pronouncement
which may serve as a means to draw together in a sort of
synthesis the main features of the period.

On January 22, 1899, Leo XIII wrote a masterly letter to
the Archbishop of Baltimore, Cardinal Gibbons. Its theme was
Americanism "Americanism." Its opening words, and consequently its title,
were *Testem Benevolentiae*. Both are highly suggestive. Leo
had a sincere appreciation of American ideals. He knew how to
prize the energy, the practical sense, the determination to
crash through obstacles and get results of the youthful, if

somewhat boisterous, Republic. He had an understanding for
its peculiar customs and the conditions in which the Church
so marvelously multiplied its numbers and perfected its organization. He cast a tolerant eye on political and economic institutions, as well as on the essentially imperfect but workable
relations of the Church with the Government and with society. He had manifested a lively interest in the Plenary
Council of Baltimore of 1884; in the thorny problem of the
schools, parochial and public; in the founding of the Catholic
University; in the delicate situation created by German immigration; in the Columbian Exposition at Chicago. His
letter of January 6, 1895, *Longique Oceani,* breathed a
fatherly solicitude which is also apparent in the opening words
of his *Testem Benevolentiae.* In the thing called "Americanism" he detected a danger, a disease that might work havoc
in a section of the Church on which he built roseate hopes for
the future.

It is easy to understand the resentment felt in many quarters
at the possible implication in the use of the term: "Americanism." No one will question the importance of the issues in the
controversy. One may sincerely admire the great Paulist,
Father Isaac Thomas Hecker, around whose name the controversy raged; one may have every assurance that the Faith
in the United States is fundamentally strong; one may feel
indignant at the distortion of American Catholic ideas by ill-
informed writers in Europe. He can still be grateful for the
clear and decisive teaching of the Pope. If the scare is a mere
memory, this argues the timeliness of Leo's action, not by any
means the nonexistence of the peril. The Catholic press of the
time[2] is full of the discussion. The energetic support which
Leo found in the American bishops is the best commentary

---

[2] The *Tablet* (London) is as nearly objective as one could wish. It
reflects the attitude of the press generally, and reproduces important letters
of the American bishops to the Holy Father. A more complete reprint
of these letters is found in the *Civiltà Cattolica* (Rome). For French
opinion the *Études* (Paris) is excellent. In America the *Catholic World*
devotes much space to Father Hecker. As far back as April, 1891, *The
American Catholic Quarterly* carries an article, "American Catholicity,"
by Bishop Thomas S. Preston, which raised many of the charges later
resented by American Catholics.

on the situation. It would seem significant that the editors of the *Catholic Encyclopedia,* when they published their first volume in 1907, prudently relegated the topic to Volume XIV, which appeared five years later.

Altogether, aside from the reasonable claim of the Church in America to be free as a body from anything like anti-Roman tendencies (though an anti-European spirit was widely admitted) there is much to justify, or at least explain, the use of the odious term. In the eyes of Europeans, both radical and reactionary, America was the land where the industrial age was scoring its greatest triumphs. It was the land where the good and bad features of Liberalism, Nationalism, and Bourgeois Industrialism were most readily discerned. There the modern shibboleths of Progress and Science were freely accepted without qualification. There the venturesome, the aggressive, the self-assertive won the rewards of success. Why should not the American be absorbed in material things? And how could he have a proper regard for authority, the Christian spirit, the supernatural? Doctrinaire Royalists in France had a low opinion of American Democracy; conservatives generally disliked our modern ways; pious souls thought our religion was entirely on the surface; rigid Catholics were sure we must be half Protestant. Add to this the expressed conviction of Liberals abroad that American Catholics would not long sacrifice their independence to the "dictatorship of the Vatican," and we have a sufficient explanation of the flare-up when a mistranslated *Life of Father Hecker* appeared in Paris, in 1898. The time had come for the Holy Father to act. He spoke in a tone, fatherly but firm. On the part of the American Catholics, clergy and laity, submission was prompt and without reservation. At this distance the thing the Pope condemned seems to have been more prevalent in Europe than in the land from which it took its name. When Pius X alluded to "Americanists," eight years later, in his condemnation of "Modernism," he was certainly speaking to Europeans.

A brief analysis of the *Testem Benevolentiae* will reveal that the Pope was dealing with what he considered a very *Testem* serious problem. He writes "in virtue of his supreme apostolic *Benevolentiae* office, to safeguard the integrity of the faith, and to preserve the faithful" from the danger of error. The fundamental source of wrong opinions, he says, lies in the effort to facilitate conversion to the Catholic Church by adapting discipline and even doctrine to the "grown-up" modern mind, by a relaxation of former severity and an indulgence of new ideas. Against this stands the Vatican Council with its insistence on the unchanging sense and interpretation of dogmas. Individual speculation is out of place, and laxity of doctrine is not the proper approach to conversion. The expansion of civil liberties has no connection with religious truth. Papal infallibility was not defined to permit a wider range of irresponsible teaching. The Church, Leo insists, will always aid in the search for truth; she must also protect fallible men from error.

In dealing with the consequences flowing from this "American" attitude, the Pope then takes up five specific points. Spiritual direction, it had been maintained, was less necessary since in an era of liberty, the Holy Ghost would guide the individual soul. The answer to this was that the Holy Ghost could always be relied upon, but individuals might easily fail to follow His promptings. Moreover, the Divine plan provided for the saving of men through the agency of other men. A second error extolled the natural virtues above the supernatural, on the strange pretext that they were more modern, more manly. A third error emphasized the active virtues to the exclusion of humility, charity, and obedience, which were merely passive virtues. A fourth error rejected religious vows since they cramped the freedom of the individual and were of no utility to society. Finally, new methods were to be adopted in leading non-Catholics to the faith. On each of these points Leo patiently laid down the correct doctrine. He concluded with an appeal for unity and loyalty to the Church. He had uncovered the fallacies of a few well-meaning but misguided Catholics, and the exposure, in the healthy atmosphere of America, was sufficient to end them. Whatever danger there may have been from the side of Nationalism, Liberalism, Democracy, or the still hidden Modernism was effectually dissipated. There was no further talk of the Church in America accommodating itself to the modern world. The characteristic forces of the nineteenth century were powerless, even

in the most modern section of the Church, to lessen its vitality
or to change its course.

On July 20, 1903, a pen and ink sketch of the earth encircled
by a huge band of crepe mutely told the readers of a great
metropolitan newspaper that all nations, classes, and conditions of men were in mourning. The drawing was an eloquent
tribute of a popular American artist to the memory of Leo
XIII. Better, perhaps than the countless editorials and
obituary notices of the time, John T. McCutcheon had caught
and expressed the universal grief of humanity at the passing
of the nonagenarian pontiff who during a full quarter of a
century had devoted his splendid talents, his unflagging energy,
and his fatherly affection to the best interests of high and
low, rich and poor, Catholic and non-Catholic, saint and
sinner. The whole world felt the shock, and yet paradoxically
enough, business and politics and pleasure-seeking went on
undisturbed. The spirit of the dead pope to whom no human
affair was foreign, *nihil humani alienum*, had moved in a
sphere essentially removed from the turmoil of mundane life.

Leo had finished his part of the unending task of the papacy
brilliantly. He had done his day's work, but he had also seen
the future dark with clouds and was conscious of the difficulties he was leaving to his successor. There were unsolved
problems; there were weighty questions the settlement of
which his fine diplomacy had succeeded only in postponing;
there was above all the progressive alienation of the human
intellect from the faith, and the divorce of a practically
atheistic society from God and the supernatural. Leo's place
was taken by a man of prayer, a simple, sincere, and holy
priest, whose aversion for diplomacy, statecraft, and worldly
affairs generally was in strong contrast to his own active
interest in the shifting scene about him. The times seemed
to call loudly for another Leo. Yet at a later date there
would be few to regret that the choice of the Cardinals fell
upon a peasant's son, unlike but not inferior to him. The
democratic character of the Church had made it possible for
a poor man, with no claim to rule beyond his moral worth,
to rise to the highest throne in Christendom.

EPILOGUE

EPILOGUE

THIS BOOK IS FINISHED. ITS DEFECTS, WE HOPE, ARE negative, omissions merely of details which might have been included. Readers of larger volumes by MacCaffrey, Mourret, Schmidlin, or Veit will recall innumerable facts that could have been mentioned. But we trust a fuller display of erudition will not be deemed essential to an introductory interpretation of the nineteenth century. An amassing of factual data would indeed have been relatively easy. It is still possible to write another and, no doubt, a better book. Certainly, there is room for a popular story of the Church in the twentieth century. Such a book should arouse a new curiosity about the period here covered. For the author at least, the long approach of a hundred years has been a study of problems of vital interest which grew out of the nineteenth century, and which now crowd upon the attention of all of us.

The Great War and its aftermath; the changes, rapid, fundamental, and frightening, in political, social, and economic affairs; the new states, "Fascist" or "Socialist" in varying degrees, but inevitably Nationalist; the rumors of another and greater war have been treated in countless volumes with scarcely a mention of the one stable and enduring institution which is developing mightily, and promises to stand secure when the storm of impending and actual revolution has swept away a dozen imposing but less stable structures. There is much in the chaotic world around us to which the Church can be indifferent. There are evils in institutions and movements, in doctrines and tendencies, which will in the long run produce a reaction toward sanity and the Church of Christ. But never in human history has the Church been faced with adversaries quite so confident of success, and never has she been quite so ready for the struggle.

Pius X, lamenting the wide-flung "apostasy from God," undertook before the War to "restore all things in Christ," and succeeded beyond human calculation. In Benedict XV there was an apparent reversion to the type of Leo XIII. In a war-torn world he was "the pope of peace." Pius XI, in face of a diseased society verging toward a blasphemous statolatry, is still laboring with titanic energy to re-establish "the peace of Christ in the Kingdom of Christ." All have built further on the foundation left by Leo XIII, as Leo himself built on the foundation left by his predecessors. It would be hard to point out a period in which the pessimist could find more to feed his fears upon in the milling forces of good and evil around him. But there is justification also for a healthy optimism. The mad intellectuals of the French Revolution brought forth a youthful world; the present anti-God appeal to the young has all the symptoms of decrepitude. The persecuted Church came out of the earlier revolution renewed in spirit; she will survive the present tempest, from all indications, in the full vigor of mature strength. Or, if one more historical allusion may be permitted, she will stand amid the ruins of a crumbling world as she did in the fifth century of our era. Again, perhaps, she will preserve the accumulated treasures of a civilization, turn to new barbarians, and become the Mother of a new humanity. She rose in a pagan world in which the "natural" man had a record of great achievements; a bloated neopaganism with its decidedly "unnatural" pretensions and carrying the germ of dissolution from its birth is not nearly so formidable a foe.

In any brief and rapid survey of the twentieth century the names of three great popes must be prominent. Looking forth upon the world about them they have beheld the Liberal-Capitalist-Materialist evolution developing into a Nazi statolatry, the insane Nationalist rivalry of their day preparing a bloodbath for humanity and threatening to wreck the creations of a beneficent science, the host of philanthropic social reformers bridging the gap between a heartless individualism and paternalist governments, the deluge of pseudo-philosophies vitiating much of the popular literature of the time. Papal interest in all these things has depended on the effect they have had in the moral and doctrinal sphere of which the pope is the constituted guardian. When circumstances beyond papal control had eliminated the pope from temporal affairs, the voice that was thus apparently silenced became all the more insistent where souls were concerned. The social atheism of the lay State had banished God and His representative from a secularized society only to find the Vicar of Christ conscious of a duty and a consequent right to pronounce upon almost every political, economic, and social question.

Humanly speaking, the enemies of the Church had grounds for rejoicing when the fine intelligence, the delicate diplomacy, and the political experience of Leo were no longer at the service of the Church. But the simple "parish priest," with no ambition to play the game of statesmen and diplomats, who succeeded him, possessed two qualities most needed in his high office. Pius X knew the soul of the people. All his active life he had been a pastor of souls. More important still, his own soul was delicately attuned to the inspirations of grace. The man of the people was also, and above all, a man of prayer, a man of God. It is in no way injurious to Leo to point out the balance of human learning and the light of faith in his masterly teachings. In him there was a marked co-ordination of reason and revealed truth. But Pius X, like the saints, moved almost exclusively in the realm of faith. His decisions, his determination in enforcing them, even his apparent indiscretion were at times beyond the comprehension of more earthly minded critics. Resolved as Supreme Pastor to bring "all things under the headship of Christ," he was himself filled with the Spirit of Christ.

The codification of Canon Law, the restoration of the Vulgate, the revision of the Breviary, the purification of the Liturgy by the reintroduction of Gregorian chant — these and other purely spiritual achievements of Pius X, including wise provisions for a better trained clergy, are characteristic of this highly spiritual pontificate. The same spiritual note is evident in his early pronouncements on popular action and his correction of Christian Democracy as well as in the firm stand he took against the excesses of the well-meaning, but errant

Pius X

French *Sillon*. A like singleness of purpose marks his conduct of the hopeless situation in France which ended in the separation of Church and State. But the "parish priest," whose parish embraced all nations, will be long remembered as the "Pope of the Eucharist." To restore all things in Christ he revived the practice of frequent Communion for all the faithful, and of early Communion for children. Confessors and educators of the young remarked the almost immediate effect. The origins of a great spiritual revival can be traced further back, but no pope has had a larger share in it than Pius X, and it is hard to see how he could have done more in this regard than he actually did.

But Pius, the shepherd of souls, edifying the Church by the warmth of his kindly personality and the contagion of his own lively faith, promoting piety by his decrees and exhortations, building for the future by his wise reforms, is not the whole man. He could be stern as duty itself in dealing with error. If he had the meekness of Christ among men of good will, he also had the fiery zeal to purify the temple of truth. So much so, that his battle with Modernism has in the minds **Modernism** of many eclipsed his more positive labors. Ruthless, almost cruel in extirpating the poison of a bad philosophy, this naturally mild and unaggressive pontiff finds his justification in his keen sense of danger to the faith. The deluded "intellectuals" who were so pitilessly crushed were so many wolves, one might better say, serpents, within the fold of Christ. They had to be exterminated before Pius could go on with his great constructive program.

Whether the name is appropriate or not, the thing that was called Modernism was a distillation of all or most of the mental and moral poison of the nineteenth century. It was a "synthesis of all heresies." With roots in early humanism and individualism and nurtured by the pseudo-enlightenment of the eighteenth century, it drew from the vagaries of Kant, Hegel, Schleiermacher and their kind a noxious excrescence of Agnosticism, Rationalism, Pantheism, Immanentism, Higher Criticism, Liberalism, and Evolutionism. It was bad history, bad philosophy, bad theology. It distorted the idea of faith, dogma, the Church, Christ and God. Had this concentrate of deadly poisons been permitted to infect the younger clergy, and through them the people, the consequences would have been terrible. But after several individual condemnations, the *Lamentabili,* a syllabus that recalls a similar index to nineteenth-century aberrations under Pius IX, gathered Modernist errors in sixty-five repudiated propositions. In the same summer of 1907 the masterly encyclical, *Pascendi Gregis,* provided a detailed analysis of this insidious attempt to bring the Church "into harmony with the modern mind." But Pius X did not stop with mere diagnosis and exposure of the infection. He applied an antiseptic in his Oath against Modernism, and in a more positive way he assured the health of the whole body ecclesiastic by urging a deeper study of sound philosophy in all seminaries.

One might leave this last brief paragraph as a final comment upon the diseased elements of the nineteenth century. It may, however, be maintained that the World War, including the diplomatic chicanery which thwarted papal efforts to effect an earlier peace, is the best index to the great unbalanced century. But we shall conclude with a mere allusion to the great pope who unites the best qualities of his great predecessors, and who is now dealing so admirably, and we hope not futilely, with the problems, political, economic, social and religious, which are the evil fruitage of a civilization, stupendous in its material aspects, but progressively more and more estranged from God and the supernatural.

APPENDICES

A

TEXT OF THE SYLLABUS

No document reveals the "Liberal" spirit of the nineteenth century better than the Syllabus of 1864. Its eighty propositions were condemned by Pius IX, though a few of them, separated as they are from their context, would seem to have an acceptable meaning. The sense in which they were condemned can be known only from an investigation of the Allocutions, Encyclicals, and other documents from which they were extracted. Adequate references are found in the *Enchiridion Symbolorum* of Denzinger-Bannwart. An excellent study of 100 pages, *The Syllabus of Errors of Pius IX,* by Robert R. Hull, was published in 1926 by *Our Sunday Visitor.* The present translation was prepared by George J. McHugh, S.J., and Clement J. McNaspy, S.J.

I. Pantheism, Naturalism, and Absolute Rationalism

1. There exists no supreme, all wise, most provident divine Being, distinct from the universe; God and nature are one, and God is therefore subject to change; actually, God is produced in man and in the world; God and the world are identical, as are spirit and matter, true and false, good and evil, just and unjust.

2. All action of God upon man and upon the world is to be denied.

3. Human reason, without any regard whatsoever to God, is the sole judge of the true and the false, of good and evil; it is a law unto itself, and suffices by its natural powers to secure the welfare of men and nations.

4. All truths of religion derive from the natural force of human reason; hence reason is the principal rule by which man can and should attain the knowledge of all truths of whatever kind.

5. Divine revelation is imperfect, and therefore subject to continued and indefinite progress, which corresponds to the progress of human reason.

6. Faith in Christ is opposed to human reason; and divine revelation is not only unprofitable, but is even harmful to the perfection of man.

7. Prophecies and miracles, set forth and narrated in Holy Scripture, are poetical fictions; the mysteries of Christian faith are the results of philosophic investigations; in the books of both Testaments are contained mythical inventions; and Jesus Christ Himself is a mythical fiction.

II. Moderate Rationalism

8. Since human reason is on a level with religion itself, it follows that theological studies are to be treated as we treat philosophical studies.

9. Without exception, all the dogmas of the Christian religion are the object of natural science or philosophy; and human reason, developed solely by history, can by its own natural strength and principles arrive at the true knowledge of even the more abstruse dogmas, provided these dogmas be proposed as the object of reason.

10. Since the philosopher is one thing, and philosophy another, the philosopher has the right and duty to submit himself to that authority which he shall recognize as true; but philosophy neither can nor should submit itself to any authority.

11. The Church should never animadvert to philosophy, but ought to tolerate its errors and leave it to correct itself.

12. The decrees of the Apostolic See and the Roman Congregation hinder the free progress of knowledge.

13. The method and principles by which the ancient scholastic Doctors developed Theology are by no means suited to the needs of our age and the progress of the sciences.

14. Philosophy should be treated without any regard for supernatural revelation.

III. Indifferentism, Latitudinarianism

15. Every man is free to embrace and profess that religion which, guided by the light of reason, he shall believe true.

16. Men may, in any religion, find the way of eternal salvation and attain eternal salvation.

17. We may entertain at least a hope for the eternal salvation of all those who are in no way in the true Church of Christ.

18. Protestantism is nothing but another form of the same true Christian religion, in which it is equally possible to please God as in the Catholic Church.

IV. Socialism, Communism, Secret Societies, Biblical Societies, Clerico-Liberal Societies

Plagues of this variety are reprobated in the strongest terms in various Encyclicals.

V. Errors Concerning the Church and Her Rights

19. The Church is not a true, perfect and entirely free society, nor does she enjoy peculiar and perpetual rights conferred upon her by her Divine Founder; it belongs to the civil power to define what are the rights of the Church and the limits within which she can exercise them.

20. The Ecclesiastical power must not exercise its authority without the permission and assent of civil government.

21. The Church has not the power of defining dogmatically that the religion of the Catholic Church is the only true religion.

22. The obligation under which Catholic teachers and writers are bound applies only to those things which are proposed by the infallible judgment of the Church as dogmas of faith.

23. The Roman Pontiffs and the Ecumenical Councils have exceeded the limits of their power, have usurped the rights of rulers, and have erred even in the definition of matters of faith and morals.

24. The Church has no right to employ force, nor any direct or indirect temporal power.

25. Besides the power inherent in the Episcopate, a further temporal power is granted to it either expressly or tacitly by the civil authority, which power is on that account revocable by the civil authority at its pleasure.

26. The Church has no natural and legitimate right to acquire and possess property.

27. The ministers of the Church and the Roman Pontiff ought to be absolutely excluded from all care and dominion over temporal things.

28. It is not right for Bishops without the permission of the government to promulgate even their apostolic letters.

29. Favors granted by the Roman Pontiff must be considered null unless requested by the civil government.

30. The immunity of the Church and of ecclesiastical persons derives its origin from civil law.

31. Ecclesiastical courts for temporal cases of the clergy whether civil or criminal should by all means be abolished, even without the concurrence and despite the protest of the Apostolic See.

32. The personal immunity exempting clerics from military service may be abolished without violation of natural right or equity; civic progress demands its abolition especially in a society constituted upon principles of liberal government.

33. It does not pertain exclusively to ecclesiastical jurisdiction by any proper and inherent right to direct the teaching of theology.

34. The teaching of those who compare the Roman Pontiff to a free sovereign acting in the universal Church is the doctrine that prevailed in the Middle Ages.

35. There is nothing to prevent the sentence of a general council or the act of the assembled nations from transferring the supreme pontificate from the Bishop and city of Rome to some other Bishop or city.

36. The definition of a national council admits of no further discussion, and the civil administration may regard such an affair as settled.

37. National Churches can be established after being withdrawn

and openly separated from the authority of the Roman Pontiff.

38. The arbitrary rulings of the Roman Pontiffs have brought about the separation of the Church into eastern and western divisions.

VI. ERRORS CONCERNING CIVIL SOCIETY CONSIDERED BOTH IN ITSELF AND IN ITS RELATION TO THE CHURCH

39. The commonwealth is the origin and source of all rights, and enjoys rights which are not circumscribed by any limits.

40. The teaching of the Catholic Church is opposed to the well-being and interests of society.

41. The civil power, even when exercised by an unbeliever, possesses an indirect and negative right over religious affairs; therefore it possesses not only the right called *exequatur*, but also that called *appellatio ab abusu*.

42. In the case of conflicting laws of the two powers, civil law prevails.

43. Without the consent of the Holy See and even against its protest, the lay power has the authority to break and to declare and render null the solemn treaties, commonly called concordats, concluded with the Apostolic See concerning the use of rights appertaining to ecclesiastical immunity.

44. The civil authority may interfere in matters pertaining to religion, morality, and spiritual government. Hence it has control over the instructions which the pastors of the Church issue for the guidance of consciences and conformable to their duty. Furthermore, with regard to the administration of the divine sacraments, it possesses the power to decree the dispositions necessary for their reception.

45. The entire direction of public schools in which the youth of any Christian state are educated, except to some extent in the case of episcopal seminaries, may and must belong to the civil power; and this in such a way that no other authority whatsoever shall be recognized as having any right to interfere in the discipline of the schools, the direction of studies, the conferring of degrees, and the choice and approval of teachers.

46. Even in ecclesiastical seminaries the method of studies is subject to civil authority.

47. The best theory of civil authority demands that the public schools which are open to the children of all classes, and in general all public institutions intended for the education of youth in letters and higher learning, shall be free from all ecclesiastical authority, government, and interference, and shall be completely subjected to the civil and political authority according to the desires of the rulers and the opinions of the age.

48. Catholics may approve of that theory of education for youth which separates it from Catholic faith and ecclesiastical power, and

which is confined exclusively, or at least primarily, to the knowledge of natural order alone and the purpose of social life on earth.

49. The Civil authority may prevent Bishops and the faithful from free and mutual communication with the Roman Pontiff.

50. Civil authority has in itself the right of presenting Bishops, and can demand that they take over their dioceses before they have received canonical institution and the apostolic letters from the Holy See.

51. Furthermore, lay government has the right of deposing Bishops from the exercise of their pastoral ministry, and it is not bound to obey the Roman Pontiff in those things which refer to the institution of episcopal sees and Bishops.

52. The government has the right to change the age prescribed by the Church for religious profession of women as well as of men, and it can require all religious orders to admit no one to solemn vows without its permission.

53. The laws which pertain to the protection of religious bodies and of their rights and duties should be abrogated; moreover, the civil government can assist all those who wish to abandon the religious life and to break their solemn vows; likewise the government can suppress religious bodies, collegiate churches, and simple benefices, even those of private patronage, and take over their goods and revenues to be administered and disposed of by the civil power.

54. Kings and princes are not only exempt from ecclesiastical rule but are even superior to the Church in disputed questions of jurisdiction.

55. The Church should be separated from the State, and the State from the Church.

VII. Errors Concerning Natural and Christian Ethics

56. Moral laws do not require a divine sanction, nor is there any need for human laws to be conformable to the law of nature or to receive their binding force from God.

57. The science of philosophy and morals, and likewise of civil laws may and should be withdrawn from divine and ecclesiastical authority.

58. No other forces are to be recognized save those which reside in matter; and all moral teaching and moral excellence ought to consist in the accumulation of riches by every possible means, and in the enjoyment of pleasure.

59. Rights consist in the mere material fact, and all human duties are an empty name, and every human deed has the force of right.

60. Authority is nothing but the result of numerical superiority and material force.

61. An unjust act, when successful, inflicts no injury upon the sanctity of right.

62. The principle of nonintervention, as it is called, ought to be proclaimed and adhered to.

63. It is lawful to refuse obedience to legitimate princes, and even to rebel against them.

64. The violation of a solemn oath and any atrocious crime against the eternal law is not only not reprehensible but lawful and worthy of the highest praise when done for the love of country.

VIII. ERRORS CONCERNING CHRISTIAN MARRIAGE

65. The teaching that Christ elevated marriage to the dignity of a sacrament can in no way be admitted.

66. The sacrament of matrimony is but an accessory of the contract and separable from it, and the sacrament consists in the nuptial blessing alone.

67. The marriage bond is not indissoluble according to the natural law, and in certain cases divorce, properly so called, may be sanctioned by civil authority.

68. The Church has no power to enact the diriment impediments to marriage. That power belongs to the civil authority, which can do away with the existing impediments.

69. The Church began to introduce impediments only in later times, and then not by her own right but a right borrowed from civil power.

70. The canons of the Council of Trent which placed the censure of anathema on those who dare deny the Church the power of enacting diriment impediments either are not dogmatic or should be understood as a delegated power.

71. The Tridentine form does not oblige under penalty of nullity where the civil law prescribes another form or wishes to validate the marriage by means of this new form.

72. Boniface VIII was the first to declare that the vow of chastity pronounced at ordination rendered a marriage null.

73. A civil contract can constitute true marriage among Christians; and it is false to affirm either that the marriage contract was always sacramental or that there is no contract if the sacrament be excluded.

74. Matrimonial cases and espousals belong by their very nature to civil jurisdiction.

IX. ERRORS REGARDING THE CIVIL POWER OF THE ROMAN PONTIFFS

75. Good Catholics dispute among themselves upon the compatibility of the temporal with the spiritual power.

76. The abrogation of the civil power of the Apostolic See conduces in the highest degree to the freedom and happiness of the Church.

X. ERRORS CONCERNING LIBERALISM OF THE DAY

77. In our times it is no longer necessary that the Catholic religion should be the only religion of the State to the exclusion of all others whatsoever.

78. Hence it has been wisely provided by law that in certain regions, Catholic in name, immigrants shall be allowed the public exercise of their own forms of religion.

79. Moreover, it is falsely maintained that civil liberty of every kind of worship and full power granted everybody to manifest openly and publicly any opinions whatever, conduce to corrupt more easily the minds and morals of the people and to the propagation of the plague of indifferentism.

80. The Roman Pontiff can and should reconcile and align himself with progress, liberalism, and modern civilization.

B

CHURCH AND STATE

The Church is a "perfect society." So is the State. Each is sovereign and independent in its own sphere; each has its proper end and purpose; each is equipped with all the means necessary to attain its end; each derives whatever authority it possesses from the source of all authority, God. The State is a natural institution whose origin, prerogatives, and limitations are known from the study of ethics. The Church owes its existence and its mission to a direct divine-positive act at a definite historical moment. Thus, both have the same Author. Both have the same subjects, individual men, whose ultimate end, natural and supernatural, is God. Toward this end both must aid man, directly or indirectly. Hence, the relationship between them should be one of harmony and mutual co-operation.

But neither is charged with the whole care of man. In the temporal order the State supplements man's efforts toward temporal happiness and well-being; in the spiritual order the Church aids and directs man in his earthly task of earning his title to heaven and saving his soul. In purely temporal matters the State is supreme. In the business of eternal salvation, in preaching the Gospel, guarding the moral law, dispensing the sacraments, and providing for public worship the Church has a divine warrant for independent action. In so-called mixed matters each must respect the rights of the other, though in cases of real conflict the spiritual power, which presides over man's highest interests, must prevail. In the abstract, these principles should be clear enough. Friction, which inevitably arises, is due to human weakness, ignorance, or malice.

When we speak of the Church we mean, of course, the Church of Christ, essentially one and unchanging, unique and potentially universal, with its mission to teach, baptize, and rule the spiritual destinies of all nations. When we speak of the State we mean any one of a hundred sovereign political societies, each owing its particular form to human agencies and historical circumstance. In the present discussion anticlerical France will loom large in the reader's mind. The Third Republic differs profoundly from the France of the Old Regime or of St. Louis, as it differs from Norman England, Habsburg Spain, Hohenzollern Germany, and the United States. Yet each of these is *a* State; each may be called for our purposes *the* State.

So far as principles are concerned we may fix our attention, for instance, upon the United States. In the preamble of the American Constitution we have, quite conveniently, an expression of the nature and purpose of the State. Whatever the motives of the Founding Fathers, and whatever their individual theories of government, they have left us a very acceptable statement in their opening paragraph:

We the People of the United States, in Order to form a more perfect Union, establish Justice, insure domestic Tranquillity, provide for the common Defense, promote the general Welfare, and secure the Blessings of Liberty to ourselves and our Posterity, do ordain and establish this Constitution for the United States of America.

In contrast to this, we have an analogous declaration in the *Constitutio dogmatica de Ecclesia Christi* of the Vatican Council:

The Eternal Shepherd and Bishop of our Souls, in order to perpetuate the saving work of the Redemption, determined to establish and build His Holy Church, in which as in the House of the Living God all the Faithful should be bound together by the bond of a common Faith and Charity.

On these premises what should be the normal relations, one may ask, between a unique divine-human society on the one hand and, on the other hand, any one or all of the great natural societies which, though founded and formed by the free determination of human wills to meet a need of the times, are yet the indirect creations of the same omnipotent, all-wise Creator from whom all authority is derived? Certainly, not conflict and mutual enmity. Nor does an attitude of complete aloofness of one from the other seem to accord with the plan of the God of unity and the Common Father of all mankind.

Moreover, there is the universal Kingship of Christ, which knows no limits in this visible universe. He is constituted Lord of mankind. To Him belong, objectively, the ownership of all created things and the allegiance of all rational creatures. Culpably or inculpably, men may not acknowledge this sovereignty; they may not even be aware of it. But it is imperative to grasp this essential fact. Once accepted, at least as a working hypothesis, it clarifies the whole knotty problem of Church and State. Rejected, the objective reality remains unchanged, but the student is doomed to darkness and error. Here, there is question of objective order, of things as they should be. This is the necessary point of departure for any application of principles to concrete conditions. This is the ground on which the Catholic Church and her hierarchy must take their stand. In states of which the citizens are Catholic the position should offer no difficulty. In those of mixed religion, or in states wholly infidel, the ordinary and obvious rules of human prudence must be applied. The Church has a definite doctrine of *union* of Church and State, founded in reason and divine revelation. She also has a doctrine of *separation* for times and circumstances which, however normal and universal in appearance, she regards as abnormal and passing.

In the *Syllabus* of 1864 Pius IX condemned the proposition which reads: *Ecclesia a statu, statusque ab ecclesia sejungendus est*, namely, that the Church must be separated from the State and the State from the Church. This bold and unqualified condemnation of the separation of Church and State was one of the major objects of attack in the storm of indignation stirred up by the courageous Pontiff's "anathema against civilization." It seemed to reprobate, for example, the situation which Catholics still find most conducive to the welfare of the Church and religion in the United States. It was eagerly set upon by the anticlerical and irreligious press. But six weeks after the *Syllabus* appeared, Bishop Dupanloup published a commentary which effectually removed all misunderstandings. His famous distinction between *la thèse* and *l'hypothèse* satisfied all well-meaning objectors and received, moreover, the approbation of Pius IX and of some six hundred and thirty bishops. It had, in fact been anticipated by the ultra-conservative *Civiltà cattolica* in its issue of October 2, 1863. In an anonymous article from the pen of a Jesuit editor there is a lengthy and very sane discussion of the Catholic Congress of Malines and Modern Liberties. The writer insists . . . *che si distingua la* TESI *dall'* IPOTESI, and continues:

> These liberties, stated as a thesis, that is, as principles of universal application to human nature and to the divine plan, should be and have been condemned absolutely by the Roman Pontiffs, particularly by Pius VI, Pius VII and Pius IX [in 1852]. But in the form of hypothesis, that is, as an arrangement suitable to special conditions in this or that nation, they may well be legitimate. As such Catholics may cherish and defend them. . . .

Bishop Dupanloup placed all the anathemas of the *Syllabus*, including the one against separation of Church and State, in their proper context, showing that they held for the Christian society which should exist, but that in the unfortunate conditions then prevalent, in which insistence upon the ideal would be futile, the Church might be content with less.

If the situation in the United States, which again we may take as an example, is unusual, this is scarcely an argument against the Catholic Church and her teaching. In fact, the American experiment would seem to prove that harmony and mutual respect are possible, reasonable, and most desirable. Neither to American theory nor to American practice can the naïve and passion-blinded French anticlerical appeal. His typically French perversion, the "Lay State," a bad product of Rationalism and the Revolution, professes to copy American institutions; in reality it is the instrument of an atheistic Masonic clique in open opposition to natural and revealed religion, to reason, and to common sense. America may be slowly drifting from her moorings, but her "separation of Church and State" bears little resemblance to the Latin revolt against history, reason, and revelation. At least, we still have, however precariously, a union of State and *religion*, which under the circumstances is here the nearest feasible thing to a union of Church and State.

Union of Church and State is often a bewildering and misleading concept. As revealed in the Capitularies of Charlemagne, it worked beneficently. But throughout the feudal period there was always the lurking danger that each service rendered by the civil power must be purchased by the enslavement of the Church. Abuses in the system were, of course, "accidental." But they were altogether too frequent and too widespread. Gallican Regalism, a medley of bullying and protection, is also a sad chapter in ecclesiastical history. Philip the Fair and his *Légistes*, the Bourbon kings and their ministers, and even Napoleon, maintained in theory a union of Church and State, while in practice they worked untold harm to Christian souls. In the nineteenth century numerous concordats were an expedient, often ineffectual, resorted to by the physically helpless Church. But in every age the conscience of those who represented the stronger power determined ultimately how much protection and co-operation the Church was to receive. Historically, the union of Church and State has not been an unmixed blessing.

But in what does the union of Church and State consist. Certainly, it does not mean a unity in which either is absorbed by the other. Each must remain what it is, an independent and, for its own purposes, self-sufficient unit. Positive co-operation there should be. But the essential thing is that each be left to do its own work. Civil authorities have their duties, and consequently their rights. But Caesar has no warrant to control "the things that are God's," nor may he presume to ignore the higher purposes of the Creator. By a like token the Church on her part has no direct interest in markets or road building or other purely civic affairs. But the subjects of the State, and its rulers as well, and society as a whole, are bound to acknowledge and worship the Divine Author of their being. Individuals and groups of individuals are bound to keep the moral law. And the Church in the discharge of her duties not only may, but must insist, whenever she can make her voice heard, on the observance of these obligations, positive and negative. The Church cannot be simply indifferent to what the State does or fails to do; the State that pretends to be passively neutral in matters of fundamental religion and morality, whatever the circumstances that seem to excuse this ostrich policy, is out of harmony with the necessary and natural order of things.

Between a union of the Church with a State upholding Canon Law, openly professing the Faith, and above all not interfering with the prerogatives and privileges which are needed for the proper performance of ecclesiastical functions, and most of the unions which history knows there is a marked difference. This last feature of non-interference would seem to be the most desirable. The essence of union has, however, been sought in the recognition by the State of the autonomy of the Church, but everything depends on whether this recognition is practical or merely theoretical. Incidentally, financial support on the part of the State is in no way essential to a correct relationship. Where it exists it is, too frequently, merely a compensation for confiscated property, and its effects are seldom wholesome.

In the modern world harmony, co-operation and a mutual recognition of each other's rights have been rudely disturbed, when not utterly destroyed. The Liberals of the nineteenth century demanded the exclusion of the Church from public life, its subordination to the State, and in many instances its complete destruction. Cavour, the moderate Liberal, enamoured of freedom for freedom's sake advocated a "free Church in a free State." More rabid anticlericals of the Jacobin tradition, anticipating the militant atheism of the Soviets, would crush the Church and annihilate religion altogether. Between the milder Cavour, with his dangerous and consciously or unconsciously dishonest formula, and the forerunners of militant atheism stood the Liberals of various hues who would emancipate the State and the individual from the "oppression of the clergy," deprive the clergy of every privilege that offended their sense of "equality," and reduce the Church to the status of a private, voluntary organization under the common law of the land.

"Separation of Church and State" was the Liberal slogan. It meant, essentially, that the Church as a purely private corporation should have "no part in the sphere of State action," that is in the organization, functioning, and direction of public affairs. Education, marriage, funerals, holidays were, as a consequence, under the control of the omnicompetent State, which the Liberals exalted progressively as they curbed and robbed the Church. This is Social Atheism. Beginning with the specious plea for liberty of conscience and liberty of worship, it ended logically in outlawing all religion. At least one thing is certain, there is nothing in the United States approaching what in France is called "Separation of the Church and State." And no one who knows the facts can wonder that the popes should condemn it.

For those who would pursue this subject further attention may be called here to *The Historical Bulletin* (St. Louis University) for January, 1936, which is entirely devoted to a symposium on Church and State. The article on "Separation of Church and State," by Wilfrid Parsons is especially enlightening. Father Francis S. Betten has a helpful introduction to this problem in his *Historical Terms and Facts*. The article in *The Catholic Encyclopedia* was written by Father Charles Macksey, with his usual clarity of expression. The best source book is *Quellen zur Geschichte von Staat und Kirche*, compiled by Zaccaria Giacometti.

C

GLOSSARY OF NINETEENTH-CENTURY ISMS

This is largely a catalogue of diseases, or symptoms of disease, in the nineteenth century. The list is not all-inclusive, nor is the diagnosis exhaustive in each case. Reasons of brevity demand condensation. It will be easy for the reader to supplement or, perhaps, amend the definitions or descriptions here offered. For the beginning student this may serve as an introduction to a century, one of whose major faults was muddled thinking and another the misuse of words. Its primary purpose will be attained if it proves helpful as a handy reference in moments of doubt.

Warning should be given, however, that many terms which are widely in use today were not as yet formulated, or at least not popularized, in the nineteenth century. That will account for their absence from this list. As an illustration we may mention "Distributism."

ACTIVISM. A by-product of the tremendous energy displayed after 1870 in trade, industry, finance, and exploitation of the sources of wealth. An exaltation of violence, war, slaughter, cruelty, fostered and strengthened by ethnologists and pseudo-historians.

AGNOSTICISM. The pseudo-philosophy which teaches that the essence of things, and first and final causes are unknowable. "We know not, and we never shall know." The despair of Bible-Christians before advancing Science. Huxley and Spencer were the archagnostics in England; Comte and Littré in France; Ingersoll in America. Reason, repudiated by Rationalists, was defended by the Vatican Council: "God the Beginning and End of all can by the natural light of human reason be known with certainty from the works of creation." The repudiation of metaphysics and theology dates from the "Enlightenment" of the eighteenth century.

AMERICANISM. Theologically, an inchoate heresy condemned by Leo XIII in 1899. The stressing of active as opposed to "Passive" virtues, of the natural as opposed to the supernatural; an accommodation of Catholic truth to the American mind to facilitate conversions. Caused perturbation chiefly in France. Akin to German *Reformkatholizismus* and to Modernism. Term also employed arbitrarily by Europeans to designate typical American qualities: energy, drive, resourcefulness, externalism, superficiality, money-mindedness.

ANARCHISM. Proposes to do away with forms of government, law, authority, and institutions generally. "God is evil; property is theft." Proudhon is its chief exponent. The Russian variety, easily allied to Communism, aims at wholesale destruction. Benevolent Anarchists build their utopias on "natural goodness" and the delusion of voluntary co-operation.

ANTICLERICALISM. Originally, opposition to meddling of clergy in politics: "our religion from Rome, our politics from home." As a contemporary force, chiefly in Latin countries, it is no longer a protest against unwarranted clerical action, but the outcome of two incompatible theories of State, the Catholic and the neutral lay state. It leads to downright persecution, though often a mere political dodge. Gambetta's formula (1877): *Le cléricalisme, voila l'ennemi.*

ANTISEMITISM. A reaction against the Jews, born of Nationalistic contempt, fear, envy, and economic grievances; often intensified to point of racial persecution. Most effective in Nazi Germany. The frequent cause of Jewish pogroms in Czarist Russia.

ATHEISM. Speculative: denial of existence of God; practical: living as if there were no God; militant: aggressive war on God and religion; social: the exclusion of God from politics, business, and social life. Inevitable in reign of Materialism, a logical outcome of Deistic Rationalism. The root of all modern ills, the forerunner of chaos.

BOLSHEVISM. The Bolsheviki were the radical, left-wing, "majority group" of Social Revolutionaries, who separated from the Mensheviki in 1903. Though only a small fraction of the Russian population, the Party rose to power in 1917 and has maintained itself thanks largely to the leadership of Lenin, its ruthless methods, and its definite aims. Bolshevism has come to mean an attack on the institutions of civilization.

CAPITALISM. "The organization of business upon a large scale by an employer or company of employers possessing an accumulated stock of wealth wherewith to acquire raw materials and tools, and hire labor, so as to produce an increased quantity of wealth which shall constitute profit." In its exaggerated form it implies financial tyranny over trade, industry, government, and the lives of individuals. The dictatorship of the banker. A perversion of values which makes profit the primary purpose of all human activity. Duly curbed by a vigilant State and with the capitalistic spirit exorcised, the good elements in the system and its efficiency in production may be preserved.

CHAUVINISM. A hyper-Nationalist mania: "Right or wrong, my country." Analogues in Jingoism and Junkerism. The name is French; the thing is present in Pan-Slav and Pan-German movements.

CLERICALISM. Exaggerated claims to political influence on the part of the clergy. For the most part a convenient bogey of Liberalism and Secularism.

COLLECTIVISM. A system of Industry in which the material agents of production would be owned and managed by the whole community. An inclusive term applicable to all varieties of Socialism; opposed to Individualism.

COMMUNISM. Used generically, in negative and positive sense, for possession in common. More specifically, it is the "Scientific Socialism" of Karl Marx, an atheist, materialist, determinist philosophy. It is the label of a party, striving especially in the U.S.S.R. toward a utopian goal: the dictatorship of the proletariat in a classless society, the "withering away of the State," the workers' paradise in which each shall "work according to his ability and receive according to his need."

DARWINISM. The theory of transformation or evolution, based on natural selection and the survival of the fittest in the struggle for existence. Popularly, but inaccurately, the theory of evolution in general. Its vogue was both cause and effect of the so-called "scientific, materialist, progressive" spirit of the second half of the nineteenth century.

DEISM. Denial of Providence and revelation. The Lord of the Universe winds up the machine, hurls it off into space, and thereafter neglects it. Synonymous with "natural religion." Herbert of Cherbury was among its earliest exponents in seventeenth-century England. Voltaire made it fashionable in France. Logically it leads to later atheism.

DETERMINISM. The denial of free will, and of any free agency in the universe. More specifically, Economic Determinism makes the production, exchange, and consumption of material goods the determining factor in history. Religious, moral, philosophical, and political concepts are determined by economic conditions.

DUALISM. A philosophic and religious system according to which the universe is the work of two co-eternal and mutually opposed principles, the one good, the other bad. Also, very properly, the common-sense Realism which holds the existence of both spirit and matter, and is opposed to Materialism and Idealism. Descartes, however, introduced a "dualism" of soul and body which makes them two separate entities.

EMPIRICISM. The assumption that all our mental processes are the products exclusively of purely sensuous experiences. John Locke fathered this fallacy in its modern form.

ERASTIANISM. A doctrine advocating State control of the Church. The Established Church in England is an example of the Erastian system. The name is derived from the Swiss writer, Thomas Lieber (1524–1583), otherwise known as Erastus.

EVOLUTIONISM. Strictly, the transformation of species only. But Evolution is applied more generally by Herbert Spencer to the physical world, to ethics, to man and society.

FABIANISM. Fabian Socialism, a reaction from Marxian methods and principles, calls for the emancipation of land and industrial capital from individual and class ownership, for the nationalization of land and of such industries as can be conveniently managed socially. Rent and interest must be added to the reward of labor. The Fabian Society, organized in 1884, influences wide circles through able writers, the Webbs, Shaw, H. G. Wells.

FATALISM. Denial of free will. All effects are produced by a blind necessity determining the activities of men and things. The modern variety is remotely connected with sixteenth-century Predestination. Spinoza's Pantheism contains elements of fatalistic philosophy.

FEBRONIANISM. A German variety of episcopal Gallicanism. System formulated by Nicholas von Hontheim: the pope not superior to bishops in council; power of Holy See in Germany limited. An eighteenth-century product, but lingering effects present in nineteenth.

FIDEISM. Faith is the foundation of philosophy. Revelation is the criterion of truth. This was a reaction against Rationalism.

FUNDAMENTALISM. A reaction to Modernist tendencies among Protestants. Higher Criticism and theories of Evolution had destroyed the old faith of many Bible Christians. Others became more intense in their adhesion to literal interpretation of the Scriptures.

GALLICANISM. Royal, episcopal, and parliamentary. In each case a degree of independence regarding the Holy See. Formulated by Bossuet in the Declaration of the Four Articles of 1682; infallibility is vested in the whole episcopate; the king is entirely free in the temporal sphere; the pope is subordinate to a general council and bound by the customs and canons of the Church. Effectually killed in the Vatican Council.

HIGHER CRITICISM. The subjecting of the sources of Christian revelation to rigorous and generally hostile criticism. Its methods were largely *a priori* starting with the Rationalist assumption that miracles and revelation were impossible. It showed a fondness for so-called internal criticism.

HUMANISM. In the Renaissance period Humanism meant devotion to the "Humanities," to classical literature. Progressively it came to mean thought or action centering in distinctly human interests, without reference to God or divine things: a belief in the self-sufficiency of the natural man and of human values. At present it is a halfway station between materialist Naturalism and the more complete view which includes man's supernatural destiny. Once a reaction to the supernatural, it is now a reaction to animal nature.

HUMANITARIANISM. A broad philanthropy based on "scientific" study, and evolving into a worship of humanity. Its best features were manifested in agitation for factory legislation, prison reform, and the abolition of slavery. It frequently degenerated into a gushy thing, becoming a sentimental substitute for religion.

IMPERIALISM. A logical outgrowth of Nationalism. Strong nations reach out for conquests. "Manifest destiny"; "the white man's burden"; "sacred duty to civilize backward peoples." Motivated by greed, national pride, humanitarian zeal and, toward the end of the nineteenth century, chiefly by industrial and financial interests.

INDIFFERENTISM. Lack of interest in religion or religious questions. Ignoring the existence of God and the duty to worship Him. "One religion is as good, or bad, as another." "The only useful function of religion is to keep the lower classes in ignorance and subjection." The parent of nineteenth-century tolerance.

INDIVIDUALISM. A legacy of the Renaissance. An assertion of exaggerated individual rights and liberties to the exclusion of the rights of society and the family. "I against the world"; "Captain of my soul." Economic Individualism, closely allied to Bourgeois Capitalism, was the philosophy of which *Laissez faire* was the dogmatic slogan. "Everybody for himself, and the devil take the hindmost!" The era of free competition gave way to the era of combination, mass production, mass amusements and standardization.

INDUSTRIALISM. The glorification of the machine and mechanical processes. An absorption in the production of comforts and conveniences. Generally accompanied by an atrophying of the religious sense.

IRREDENTISM. An extension of Nationalism. Reaches out for territories partially inhabited by nationals, e.g., *Italia irredenta* was largely peopled by Austrians. Alsace-Lorraine, partly German, partly French, is another example.

JACOBINISM. Radicalism in political and social organization, advocating extreme democracy and absolute equality. A legacy of the French Revolution, and still strong under the Third Republic.

JANSENISM. A seventeenth-century heresy, persisting into the nineteenth: rigorist in discipline; determinist in its doctrine of free will and grace. A Catholic semi-Calvinism or Puritanism. Appealed to middle classes. In the eighteenth century it was chiefly anti-Jesuitism.

JOSEPHISM. The Imperial Austrian analogue of Royal Gallicanism. Joseph II asserted a complete control over the Church, and meddled in the details of worship, discipline, and doctrine: *Mon frère, le sacristain!* The Church in Germany suffered from this feature of the *Aufklärung* in the nineteenth century.

LAICISM. Practically, the exclusion of the clergy from public life. Closely akin to anticlericalism in France; most felt in the laicizing of education by suppressing religious instruction and the teaching orders. Synonymous with Secularism in Latin countries.

LATITUDINARIANISM. "Broadness" in religious matters. False tolerance; indifference. A Bourgeois attitude.

LIBERALISM. A many-sided system or doctrine advocating the emancipation of man from the supernatural, moral, and divine-positive order. Essentially negative, it must be defined by reference to the thing from which the Liberal would be free. It may be political, economic, intellectual, moral, religious, or all of them combined. Integral Liberalism asserts the absolute freedom of the individual in thought, worship, conscience, speech, writing, and action, thus denying all authority derived from God. An all-pervading virus, impossible to isolate. In English-speaking lands a moribund and vague attitude of mind, but still virulent among Latin anticlericals.

MALTHUSIANISM. The theory that population, increasing geometrically, tends to outrun the means of subsistence, which increase arithmetically, and should be controlled. Formulated by Thomas Malthus, who advocated self-restraint as the proper means of limiting population. Neo-Malthusians have none of his moral scruples. The theories of Malthus were eagerly accepted by pessimistic economists who preached the "dismal science."

MATERIALISM. A perennial pseudo-philosophy, which teaches that we know nothing but matter, and that there is no ground for supposing thought and the human mind to be anything beyond a function of organized material substance. Materialism is latent in most of the "isms" of the century. In a less philosophical sense, but scarcely less important, Materialism stands for an immersion in material things, in money-making, pleasure, comfort, and power. Living as if there were no soul, no God, no future life. A characteristic of the era of prosperity and expansion after 1870.

MECHANISM. A theory which conceives the world as a vast machine, self-moving and self-existent from all eternity, devoid of freedom and intelligent purpose, perpetually changing. Creator and creation are unnecessary. Man is a cog in this automatic system. Prevalent in "scientific" evolutionary thought of the century.

MILITARISM. The primacy of the army within the State, and the tendency to subordinate all other national interests to military preparedness. Popular pride in the armed strength of the nation, and the willing submission to exorbitant taxation to support ever-increasing armaments.

MODERNISM. A rationalization of Christianity: the Church should accommodate doctrines and discipline to the modern mind! "A synthesis of all heresies," finding a welcome among Protestants, but effectually crushed within the Church by Pius X. *Pascendi*

Gregis condemns the Modernist as believer, philosopher, historian, theologian, and reformer.

NATIONALISM. The dominant characteristic of the nineteenth century, to which Liberalism and Democracy succumb when in conflict with it. A ruthless force making for international anarchy and imperialism. A phenomenon of social psychology: it is aggressive, combative, utterly selfish. Beginning in patriotic love of country, it evolves into hatred of rival countries. It becomes a religion, with the nation as the supreme value in life.

NATURALISM. In conduct Naturalism means following nature and natural inclinations, an abdication of human dignity and a sinking to the animal level. As a pseudo-philosophy it rejects revelation and the supernatural, or with the Pantheists confounds God with nature. It is closely allied to Rationalism and Materialism.

NEO-MERCANTILISM. A revival of the older Mercantilism, which consisted in government regulation of trade and industry in the interests of national wealth. The more aggressive industrial nations adopted a system of economic Nationalism, treating industry, trade, labor, and agriculture as "national interests."

NIHILISM. A reaction to Czarist absolutism. A ferment of negation. A frantic attempt to destroy all civilization. In the second half of the century a group of half-educated "intellectuals" launched a wholesale attack on history, traditions, beliefs, customs, marriage, the family, society, property, the State, liberty, responsibility, and the distinction between good and evil. Hence the name.

OPTIMISM. A cheerful frame of mind among prosperous and successful Bourgeois devotees of Progress. A belief that "this is the best of all possible worlds," in which the upward march of humanity toward indefinite perfection will be uninterrupted.

PACIFISM. An exaggerated antiwar spirit; the advocacy of "peace at any price." A theory that war can have no useful function nor justification. Compounded of half truths and emotion.

PANTHEISM. A monistic belief in the identity of God and the universe: the denial of a personal Creator, and deification of material substance. "We are all parts of one stupendous whole, whose body nature is, and God the soul." Merely a hangover from earlier centuries.

PIETISM. A seventeenth-century Protestant movement toward a purer and more devout life; strongly pseudomystical. Excesses caused the name to be employed contemptuously, implying exaggeration or affectation.

POSITIVISM. Auguste Comte's (1798–1857) philosophy which rejected all metaphysics, and recognized only "positive facts." Fact-finding, the assembling and counting of facts, was to be the function and purpose of sociology. Comte attempted to clothe his materialism in a religious garb, and to found a Humanitarian religion.

PRAGMATISM. An unphilosophical system which proved the truth in physics, metaphysics, or religion by its practical results. A proposition or a system is true "if it works," if it satisfies a human need. A typically American "ism."

PREDESTINARIANISM. A still lingering Calvinist heresy, according to which salvation depends on the wholly arbitrary election of God, irrespective of the free will of the saved or damned, or of their merits or demerits.

RATIONALISM. The unreasonable doctrine that the human reason is the sole source and the final test of truth, denying the supernatural character of revelation and affirming that all religious knowledge is derived from man's unaided reason. Rampant in the eighteenth-century "Enlightenment," but in its nineteenth-century manifestations largely indebted to Kant.

REALISM. Various meanings. Opposed to Idealism, to imagination, and dreaming. After 1850, a preoccupation with "facts"; in art, literature, politics, and life; Naturalism; "seeing things as they are." Bismarck's "Blood and iron"; Darwin's "struggle for existence"; "Nature red in tooth and claw" are expressions of Realism.

RELATIVISM. A denial of the existence of absolute values. Truth, goodness, right are relative terms. Standards are subjective and change with changing circumstances.

ROMANTICISM. In literature, art, and all phases of life Romanticism was a revolt against the worship of "Classical" models and rules. Individualism. Naturalism. A return to the primitive and medieval. Emotion and sentiment were guides to the "true"; beauty was sought in freedom of treatment as opposed to restraint.

SECULARISM. The exclusion of God and religion from life. A this-worldly attitude which sought the foundations of morality and religion in Nature alone. Associated with Industrialism, Liberalism, Materialism, Nationalism, Science, and the vogue of Evolution. The secularization of Church property and the Lay school in France are manifestations of the spirit of Secularism.

SKEPTICISM. The system, more or less positive, of doubt, more or less universal. Prevalent in an age of untenable and ephemeral philosophies. The dogmatic certainties of "Science" were paralleled by a "flight from reason" in things metaphysical, and followed by an inevitable sense of disillusionment. The breakdown of "Religion" under the attack of Higher Criticism also made for Skepticism.

SOCIALISM. An accepted definition is: common ownership of the means of production, distribution, and exchange. An amorphous and floating concept, varying from earlier social-mindedness and zeal for social betterment to the present dictatorship of Stalin. Robert Owen, Fourier, Saint Simon, Kingsley, Marx, Henry George, and even Adolf Hitler are "Socialists." The U.S.S.R. is a Socialist State. Pius XI has declared that Socialism as a doctrine, historical fact, or movement "cannot be brought into harmony with the dogmas of the Catholic Church . . . because it conceives human society in a way utterly alien to Christian truth." Socialists are now moving toward the right (Nationalism and Capitalism) and the left (Communism).

SPIRITISM. The doctrine formulated by Allan Kardec, of which reincarnation is the central article of belief. Frequently the term is applied as synonymous with Spiritualism.

SPIRITUALISM. The theory that the living can communicate with the souls of the departed. An outgrowth of pseudo-religion, and a reaction to Materialism. The word was in use by practitioners of this cult as early as 1852. Frequently referred to as Spiritism, particularly in the United States.

SUBJECTIVISM. As a philosophy Subjectivism denies objective truth and an objective moral order, and reduces all knowledge to the subject knowing, which projects his sensations and ideas externally. Kant is largely responsible for this modern aberration. As an uncritical attitude Subjectivism makes every individual a law unto himself, with conscience, good or bad, as his only norm of action. Modern education cultivates "viewpoints" and attitudes at the expense of reality.

SYNDICALISM. The grouping of all workers in each of the major industries for purposes of revolutionary attack on the present political and social system, by means of "direct action" and the general strike. The end aimed at is the ownership of the means of production within each industry by the workers in that industry. The American form is known as the I.W.W.

THEISM. Belief in a Higher Power. In best sense, equivalent to Monotheism, or the belief in One God; and opposed to Deism.

TRADITIONALISM. An early nineteenth-century reaction against the Rationalism of the Enlightenment. By reason alone, it was held, man could not arrive at the truths of religion. Hence the need to recur to the past for knowledge and the criterion of truth.

ULTRAMONTANISM. The centralizing tendency within the Catholic Church; "looking beyond the mountains"; a reaction to French Gallicanism, and German Febronianism and Josephism. Also opposed to Liberalism. Ultramontanes were vigorous supporters of Papal infallibility, the exercise of the primacy and increased papal prestige.

UNIVERSALISM. The doctrine holding the ultimate salvation of all men, commonly expressed in the statement: "I don't believe in Hell." There is a sect of American Unitarians known as the Universalists.

UTILITARIANISM. A political and social philosophy formulated by

Jeremy Bentham in 1812. "Utility" is taken as the norm of morality. In complete disregard for nobler aspirations, it ignores the spiritual side of man's nature and his hopes for a future life, and teaches that the last end of man is found in this world. It is essentially selfish, but has an altruistic ring in the principle of "the greatest happiness of the greatest number."

UTOPIANISM. A mood prevalent in the early nineteenth century, characterized by exuberance of imagination in every field: poetry, philosophy, political and social theorizing, and history. Idealist, enthusiastic, impractical. Karl Marx sneered at the "Utopian Socialists." Utopians generally rejected religion, substituting Rousseau's "natural goodness" for original sin.

ZIONISM. A Jewish Nationalist movement, political and cultural rather than religious; a defense reaction against Antisemitism, and an imitation of Nationalism. Zionists aspire to independent statehood in Palestine.

D

CHRONOLOGICAL TABLE

RULERS AND GOVERNMENTS

Popes

Pius VI	1775–1799
Pius VII	1800–1823
Leo XII	1823–1829
Pius VIII	1829–1830
Gregory XVI	1830–1846
Pius IX	1846–1878
Leo XIII	1878–1903
Pius X	1903–1914
Benedict XV	1914–1922
Pius XI	1922–x

England

George III	1760–1820
George IV	1820–1830
William IV	1830–1837
Victoria	1837–1902
Edward VII	1902–1910
George V	1910–1936

Austria

Francis I	1806–1835
Ferdinand I	1835–1848
Francis Joseph I	1848–1916

France

Louis XVIII	1814–1824
Charles X	1824–1830
Louis Philip	1830–1848
2nd Republic	1848–1852
Napoleon III	1852–1870
3rd Republic	1870–x

Prussia

Frederick Wm. III	1797–1840
Frederick Wm. IV	1840–1861
William I	1861–1888
German Empire	1871–1918
Frederick I	1888–
William II	1888–1918

CHRONOLOGICAL SURVEY, 1789–1914

1789	Outbreak of the FRENCH REVOLUTION. John Carroll, First Bishop of Baltimore. Constitution of the United States adopted.
1790	The Civil Constitution of the Clergy.
1792	The September Massacres in Paris.
1793	Execution of Louis XVI. The "Terror." War in la Vendée.
1795	The "Directory." Last Partition of Poland. The Theophilanthropists.
1798	The Roman Republic. Exile and Captivity of Pius VI.
1799	Death of Pius VI at Valence. Napoleon Bonaparte First Consul.
1802	The French Concordat. *La Génie du Christianisme.*
1803	The "Secularizations" in Germany.
1804	Napoleon Emperor.

1806   End of "Holy Roman Empire."
1808   ⸰Spanish Colonies revolt.
              University Monopoly in France.
1809   Incorporation of the Papal States in the Empire of
              Napoleon. Exile and Captivity of Pius VII, 1809–1814.
              Excommunication of Napoleon.
1812   War with Russia. Spanish "Liberal" Constitution.
1813   The Great War of Liberation.
1814   (1815) The Fall of Napoleon. May 24, Return of Pius
              VII to Rome. August 7, Restoration of the Society
              of Jesus.
1814–1815   The CONGRESS OF VIENNA. Holy Alliance.
1817–   Concordats with the German States.
1822   Founding of the Society for the Propagation of the Faith.
1829   CATHOLIC EMANCIPATION in Great Britain and
              Ireland.
1830   The JULY REVOLUTION in Belgium, France, Italy, etc.
              BELGIUM independent of Holland.
1832   *L'Avenir* and Catholic Liberalism. Fall of the Lamennais.
              Mirari vos.
1833–1845   The OXFORD MOVEMENT.
              Society of St. Vincent de Paul.
1835   Founding of the Catholic University of Louvain.
              Lacordaire at Notre Dame.
1837–1840   The Cologne Controversy.
1845   The Conversion of NEWMAN.
1848   The FEBRUARY REVOLUTION in France, Hungary,
              Italy, etc. The SECOND REPUBLIC IN FRANCE.
              The Flight of Pius IX to Gaeta.
              Communist Manifesto.
1850   ESTABLISHMENT OF THE CATHOLIC HIER-
              ARCHY IN ENGLAND.
1852   The SECOND FRENCH EMPIRE; NAPOLEON III.
              Founding of the Catholic Universities, Laval and Dublin.
              The First Plenary Council of Baltimore.
1853   Establishment of the Catholic Hierarchy in Holland.
1854   Dogma of the IMMACULATE CONCEPTION. (Appari-
              tions at Lourdes, 1858.)
1859   Darwin's *Origin of Species.*
1860   Gradual occupation of the Papal States by the Pied-
              montese.
1863   Renan's *Viè de Jèsus.*
1864   The SYLLABUS of Pope Pius IX.
              First International.
1866   The Second Plenary Council of Baltimore.
1867   First volume of *Das Kapital.*

1869	Disestablishment of the Anglican Church in Ireland.
1869–1870	The VATICAN COUNCIL. The "Old Catholics." Döllinger's Fall († 1890).
1870–1871	The Franco-German War. The New German Empire, 1871–1918. The Third Republic in France.
1871–	The KULTURKAMPF. The Roman Question.
1879	Newman made a Cardinal.
1883–	Opening of the Vatican Archives.
1884	The Third Plenary Council of Baltimore.
1889	Founding of the Catholic Universities at Washington, D. C., and at Freiburg, Switzerland.
	Plenary Council of Latin-America held at Rome.
1903	Suppression and expulsion of teaching orders in France.
1905	Separation of Church and State in France. Abrogation of the Concordat.
1907	The *Syllabus* of Pope Pius X, against Modernist errors. The Encyclical *Pascendi*.

E

BIBLIOGRAPHICAL NOTE

Anything like a complete list of authorities would seem out of proportion with the popular contents of this book. Such a list could be compiled with relative ease, and there would be some justification for it in the remote influence of works consulted over a long period. A short working bibliography, however, will suffice. Monumental sources such as Johannes D. Mansi, *Sacrorum Conciliorum nova et amplissima collectio* (53 vol.) and the *Acta et decreta s. conciliorum recentiorum* (1870–1886, 7 vol., Freiburg), better known as the *Collectio Lacensis* are, of course, needed for occasional reference. The same is true of the *Acta Sanctae Sedis* (Rome, 1865–1909), now continued by the *Acta Apostolicae Sedis,* and Angelo Mercati, *Raccolta di concordati* (Rome, 1919). But for practical purposes the indispensable handbook is the Denzinger-Bannwart-Umberg, *Enchiridion Symbolorum,* which is rich in dogmatic and near-dogmatic material. To this may be added the antipapal Carl Mirbt, *Quellen zur Geschichte des Papsttums und des römischen Katholizismus* (Tübingen, 1924) and Zaccaria Giacometti, *Quellen zur Geschichte der Trennung von Staat und Kirche* (Tübingen, 1926). For papal pronouncements the London *Tablet* is the most satisfactory source. The best single volume in English for the period covered is *The Great Encyclicals of Pope Leo XIII* (New York, 1903). There are, however, more complete collections of Leo's pronouncements in Latin, French, and German.

The most recent survey of the Church in the nineteenth century is that of Joseph Schmidlin, *Papstgeschichte der neuesten Zeit,* I, II (München, 1933–1934). Schmidlin continues unofficially the work of Ludwig von Pastor with like erudition and in the same scholarly spirit, though he seems to slight America unduly. Among the general Church histories, James MacCaffrey's *History of the Church in the Nineteenth Century* (2 vols., Dublin, 1909) still ranks with the best works of its kind in any language. The second volume, devoted to the English-speaking world, is especially detailed in its treatment of Ireland. Fernand Mourret, *Histoire générale de l'Eglise,* VIII, IX (Paris, 1924–1925), gives, despite the French author's predelection for France, the most readable account. Joseph Hergenröther, *Kirchen-*

geschichte, IV (Freiburg, 1925), remains the standard text in German. For the problems peculiar to the nineteenth century and for a fuller treatment of the typical character of the century. Andreas Veit, *Die Kirche im Zeitalter des Individualismus* (Freiburg, 1933), is thoughtful and thought-provoking, in spite of his anti-Jesuit bias. Individual preferences will differ, and some may even find similar works by Funk-Bihlmeyer, Marion, Marx, and others more satisfactory.

The personal element enters largely into any assessment of relative values in the broad field of historical monographs. It would still be possible to check the greater number of those which have influenced the present writing by way of lecture notes prepared for courses in several phases of nineteenth-century history. Among the books at the writer's elbow are a dozen and more volumes by Georges Goyau, the best of which have to do with the Church in Germany. Before and since his entry into the French Academy in 1908, Goyau has been a prolific producer of historical studies at once scholarly and popular. German scholars admit that this Frenchman has shown a wonderful insight into their history. The present writer is deeply indebted to him. A recent work by Franz Schnabel, *Deutsche Geschichte im neunzehnten Jahrhundert,* IV: *die religiöse Kräfte* (Freiburg, 1937), is the best single volume of its kind. For the Church in France the panegyrical and typically French *Un siècle de l'Eglise de France* (Paris, 1900) by Msgr. Baunard is full of contagious enthusiasm; but the most useful study has been by Parker T. Moon, *The Labor Problem and the Social Catholic Movement in France* (New York, 1921). An inspirational study of the Italian scene is H. L. Hughes' *The Catholic Revival in Italy, 1815–1915* (London, 1935). With attention centered chiefly on the Continental or main body of the Church, the present writer has, at least in recent years, been less interested in the steadily expanding literature on the Church in English-speaking countries. However, besides standard biographies of the great cardinals, Wiseman, Manning, and Newman, Wilfrid Ward's *William George Ward and the Catholic Revival* (London, 1893), has been of immediate utility. Cuthbert Butler's *The Vatican Council* (2 vols., London, 1930), is all but indispensable. The importance of Constantin Kempf's *The Holiness of the Church in the Nineteenth Century* (St. Louis, 1919), will be readily apparent. To these secondary works may be added a long shelf of selected writings: memoirs, letters, addresses, historical and philosophical studies, of Balmes, Brownson, Chateaubriand, Donoso Cortes, Döllinger, Dupanloup, Gibbons, Görres, Hergenröther, Ketteler, Lacordaire, Lamennais, de Maistre, Manning, Montalembert, Newman, O'Connell, Schlegel, Veuillot, and Wiseman. At least a dozen Catholic periodicals have served as contemporary sources for the latter half of the century. They have also provided scholarly articles on the whole century. Obviously, the encyclopedias in various languages, especially the sometimes unappreciated *Catholic Encyclopedia,* were drawn upon for data not otherwise available.

For the nonecclesiastical features of the century C. J. H. Hayes has given us in his *Political and Cultural History of Modern Europe,* II (New York, 1936) an admirable synthesis. The same author has written the best introduction to the all-pervading topic of Nationalism. For the equally important Liberalism at least a score of monographs are at hand. The most exhaustive, though frequently exasperating, is Guido Ruggiero's *History of European Liberalism* (New York, 1927). A very useful manual is the collection of lengthy extracts, *Social Reformers* (New York, 1934), by Donald O. Wagner. Biographies, of course, exist by the hundred. To read them all would have been impossible, and not at all necessary. For the forty and more "isms" which sum up the character, good and bad, of the century the most available and the most satisfactory source of information must be the encyclopedias: *Americana, Britannica, Catholic Encyclopedia, Dictionaire de la foi apologétique, Dictionaire de la théologie catholique, Encyclopedia of the Social Sciences, Enciclopedia Universal (Espasa), Kirchenlexikon, Italiana, Larousse, Staatslexikon,* and *Lexikon für Theologie und Kirche.* A more impressive array of authorities could be given. Merely accidental circumstances must be the explanation for the writer's dependence upon the sources here listed.

INDEX

INDEX